Learning Azure DevOps

Second Edition

Master Azure DevOps, GitHub Copilot, Terraform, and Bicep to Ship Faster, Secure Every Stage, and Scale with Confidence

Myra Kelnor

Published by: GitforGits

www.gitforgits.com

Printed in India

First Printing: April 2026

ISBN: 978-93-49174-83-2

Cover Design by: Kitten Publishing

Disclaimer:

This book, including all its text, diagrams, and illustrations, is an original work developed for educational and informational purposes. The content is not affiliated with, endorsed by, or sponsored by or any other company, brand, or entity referenced within. All brand names, product names, and trademarks mentioned are the property of their respective owners and are used in a descriptive, educational context only. Every effort has been made to ensure that no copyrighted or trademarked material has been copied or misused in this book. All diagrams and illustrations that are not original have been used with proper attribution and credit to their respective sources.

If you believe that any content in this book infringes upon your copyright or trademark, please contact us immediately at support@gitforgits.com. Upon notification, corrective action will be taken promptly.

Prologue

There is a moment every engineer remembers. The moment a deployment that once took three days and a conference room full of tense people was reduced to a pull request, a green checkmark, and a coffee. That moment is not magic. It is the result of discipline, automation, and a set of practices that the industry has come to call DevOps. When I first wrote about Azure DevOps, the conversation was largely about moving fast without breaking things. It was about replacing manual release gates with automated pipelines, replacing tribal knowledge with YAML, and replacing blame culture with observability. Those goals still matter deeply. But the world has moved on, and this second edition moves with it.

We are living through one of the most consequential shifts in the history of information technology. Artificial intelligence is no longer a research curiosity or a feature toggle on an experimental product page. It is rewriting the economics of software delivery. The foundation models are being embedded into development environments, CI pipelines, security scanners, and cloud provisioning tools at a pace that would have seemed implausible just three years ago. The GitHub Copilot suggests your next line of code. Azure's AI services spin up in seconds behind a Bicep template. Intelligent agents now read your work items, propose infrastructure changes, and open pull requests on your behalf.

Speed without safety is recklessness. Safety without speed is irrelevance. DevOps is the discipline that earns you both at the same time.

This matters to every practitioner because AI-driven systems demand more from the pipelines that deliver them, not less. Training runs, inference endpoints, model registries, vector databases, and responsible AI governance layers all need to be provisioned, versioned, tested, secured, and deployed with the same rigour we apply to any other production workload. The organisations that will win the next decade are not simply the ones that adopt AI. They are the ones whose engineering culture is disciplined enough to ship AI reliably, repeatedly, and safely. The DevOps sits at the exact intersection where that discipline is built. This book is not a survey of features. It is a guided construction project. By the time you finish the final chapter, you will have built a production-grade system with a multi-stage pipeline that compiles, tests, scans, provisions infrastructure with Terraform and Bicep, deploys with zero downtime, validates with Newman, manages packages through Azure Artifacts, and instruments every stage with the security controls that modern AI-era applications require.

Whether you are new to Azure DevOps or returning to it after time away, I wrote this second edition with one ambition of handing you not just the knowledge of how these tools work, but the confidence to wield them on the systems that matter most. The pipeline that changed everything is waiting to be built. Let us build it together.

— Matthew Rosch

Content

Preface

Build once. Ship it always.

The whole point of Azure is that every team should be able to ship code confidently, automatically secure it and scale up without any hassle. And this hands-on second edition on Learning Azure DevOps shows you how to build a production-grade multi-stage pipeline from scratch using a single evolving Spring Boot REST API.

Each chapter adds a new capability, like YAML pipeline authoring, infrastructure provisioning with Bicep and Terraform, zero-downtime blue-green deployments, package management with Azure Artifacts, automated API contract testing with Newman, shift-left security with GitHub Advanced Security, and AI-assisted development with GitHub Copilot Agent Mode. It's all very practical. Every concept is shown using tried-and-tested code, real pipeline stages and real Azure resources.

Whether you're an Azure developer looking to automate your first pipeline, or a DevOps engineer modernising a legacy release process, or a team lead building a security-conscious delivery culture, this book has got you covered. It's got DORA metrics, DevSecOps lifecycle controls, Azure DevOps MCP Server integration, and responsible AI governance, which are the things that modern cloud teams need the most.

In this book you will learn how to:

- Build multi-stage Azure Pipelines YAML with reusable templates and approval gates.
- Provision Azure infrastructure idempotently using Bicep and Terraform in CI pipelines.
- Execute zero-downtime production deployments using App Service blue-green slot swaps.
- Manage Maven, npm, and PyPI packages through private Azure Artifacts upstream feeds.
- Shift security left using SonarLint, detect-secrets, CodeQL, and dependency scanning.
- Automate API contract validation using Postman collections and Newman in pipelines.
- Measure and improve engineering performance using the four DORA delivery metrics.
- Control feature rollout safely without redeployment using Azure App Configuration flags.
- Orchestrate AI-assisted DevOps tasks using GitHub Copilot Agent Mode and MCP Server.
- Apply DevSecOps across all seven lifecycle stages from planning through runtime monitoring.

GitforGits

Prerequisites

If you're an Azure developer, DevOps engineer or team lead and you're looking to get your first pipeline automated, build security-conscious delivery and modernise a legacy release process, then this book is for you. It meets you where you're at and takes you further.

Codes Usage

Are you in need of some helpful code examples to assist you in your programming and documentation? Look no further! Our book offers a wealth of supplemental material, including code examples and exercises.

Not only is this book here to aid you in getting your job done, but you have our permission to use the example code in your programs and documentation. However, please note that if you are reproducing a significant portion of the code, we do require you to contact us for permission.

But don't worry, using several chunks of code from this book in your program or answering a question by citing our book and quoting example code does not require permission. But if you do choose to give credit, an attribution typically includes the title, author, publisher, and ISBN. For example, "Learning Azure DevOps, Second Edition by Myra Kelnor".

If you are unsure whether your intended use of the code examples falls under fair use or the permissions outlined above, please do not hesitate to reach out to us at support@gitforgits.com.

We are happy to assist and clarify any concerns.

Acknowledgement

I owe a tremendous debt of gratitude to GitforGits, for their unflagging enthusiasm and wise counsel throughout the entire process of writing this book. Their knowledge and careful editing helped make sure the piece was useful for people of all reading levels and comprehension skills. In addition, I'd like to thank everyone involved in the publishing process for their efforts in making this book a reality. Their efforts, from copyediting to advertising, made the project what it is today.

Finally, I'd like to express my gratitude to everyone who has shown me unconditional love and encouragement throughout my life. Their support was crucial to the completion of this book. I appreciate your help with this endeavour and your continued interest in my career.

CHAPTER 1
GETTING STARTED WITH AZURE DEVOPS

Overview

Before we write a single line of pipeline code or push a single commit, we need a clear and working foundation. This chapter is meant for it. It is going to build that foundation step by step, in a way that mirrors exactly what a DevOps practitioner does on the first day of a new project. We will be setting up our Azure DevOps account, establish our organization and project, understand each core service that the platform provides, configure the Azure CLI and the Azure Developer CLI (azd), and get our Visual Studio Code environment production-ready, including our first encounter with GitHub Copilot for Azure.

Later, we will also position Azure DevOps clearly in relation to GitHub, because in 2025 these two platforms are converging in ways that every practitioner must understand. Throughout this chapter we will clone and configure the Spring Boot REST API sample application that we will carry forward throughout every subsequent chapter. Every pipeline we write, every security scan we run, and every infrastructure template we create in later chapters will point back to this same application, so the time we invest here pays dividends across the entire book.

So, let us begin then!

What is Azure DevOps?

As a cloud-hosted platform from Microsoft, the Azure DevOps is a suite of DevOps solutions that aims to bring together every tool a software team needs to plan, build, test, and deliver software. It truly unifies version control, CI/CD pipelines, package management, test management, and project tracking under a single portal accessible at ***https://dev.azure.com***. Rather than assembling a disconnected stack of third-party tools, teams can use Azure DevOps as the single pane of glass through which the entire software delivery lifecycle flows, from a developer's first commit all the way to a production deployment.

One of the defining characteristics of it, is its **flexibility**. The teams are not required to adopt every service at once. A team that is already using GitHub for version control can plug Azure Pipelines in as their CI/CD engine while keeping all other tooling unchanged. Conversely, a team starting from scratch can adopt the full suite and benefit from native cross-service traceability, where a work item in Azure Boards links directly to the pipeline run that deployed the fix and the commit in Azure Repos that introduced the change. Now, such a level of end-to-end auditability is difficult to achieve with loosely coupled external tools.

Another core strength is **scalability**. The platform is architected to serve a solo developer working on a personal project as comfortably as it serves a global enterprise running thousands of pipeline jobs per day. As we move through each chapter and build progressively more advanced capabilities on top of our Spring Boot application, we will see how Azure DevOps grows with us rather than becoming a bottleneck.

Azure DevOps Services Overview

There are five integrated services, that are built into Azure DevOps. And ,each one addresses a distinct phase of the software delivery lifecycle, and each one is fully usable on its own. So, when we wire them together, we get a workflow where a change in one service automatically propagates context to every other service. We will work with all five services throughout this book, so it is worth spending a moment on each one before we start configuring anything.

We will now start with ***Azure Repos.*** It is the version control service within the platform. It supports full Git repositories as well as the legacy Team Foundation Version Control system. For all practical purposes, we will work exclusively with Git. It extends standard Git with pull request workflows, branch policies, and required reviewer rules that enforce code quality gates before any code reaches a protected branch. The deep integration with Azure Pipelines means that a completed pull request can automatically trigger a build, run tests, and gate the merge on a passing pipeline, all without any external webhook configuration.

The next is, ***Azure Pipelines.*** This is the CI/CD engine of the platform. It can build, test, and deploy code written in virtually any language or framework, targeting virtually any environment, from an Azure App Service to a Kubernetes cluster to an on-premises virtual machine. The pipelines are defined as YAML files that live inside the repository, which means pipeline definitions are version-controlled, reviewed as part of pull requests, and as reproducible as the application code itself. We will spend two full chapters on Pipelines, covering both continuous integration in Chapter 3 and continuous delivery in Chapter 4.

Then, there is ***Azure Boards.*** It is the project management and work tracking service. It supports Scrum, Kanban, and custom Agile processes, giving teams a flexible space to plan sprints, track user stories, log bugs, and visualize workflow. The boards integrate bidirectionally with Repos and Pipelines, so we can link a work item to a commit, a pull request, or a pipeline run. Such a cross-service linking creates a traceable thread from a stakeholder requirement all the way through to the deployed artifact, which is exactly the kind of audit trail regulated industries demand.

There is ***Azure Test Plans*** as well. It is the manual and exploratory testing service. It provides a structured space for creating test cases, organizing them into test suites and plans, executing them against a specific build, and recording outcomes. Beyond manual testing, the Test Plans integrates with automated test frameworks, allowing pipeline-executed test results to flow back into Test Plans dashboards. In Chapter 6 we will configure Test Plans in conjunction with our CI pipeline so that every automated test run is traceable to a formal test case.

And finally, ***Azure Artifacts*** which is the package management service. It hosts private feeds for NuGet, **npm**, Maven, Python, and Universal Packages. The teams use Artifacts to publish internally built libraries and to proxy external package registries, giving them a single trusted source for all dependencies. We will work through Artifacts in depth in Chapter 5, where we publish packages from our App pipeline and consume them across projects.

Azure DevOps vs GitHub

Since Microsoft acquired GitHub in 2018, practitioners have regularly asked which platform to use. The honest answer in 2025 is that the two platforms are converging rather than competing. In my opinion, the GitHub has truly became the Microsoft's primary developer platform, with GitHub Actions as its CI/CD backbone and GitHub Copilot as its AI layer. The Azure DevOps, meanwhile, remains the preferred choice for enterprises that need its advanced pipeline capabilities, Azure Boards' deep project management features, and native integration with Azure services.

As a DevOps practitioner, the practical picture looks like the following:

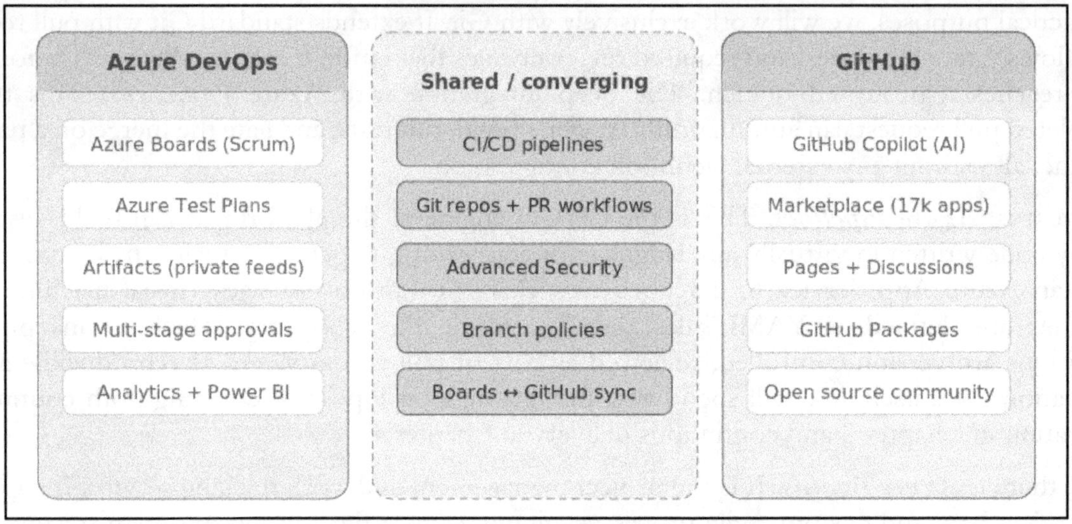

Fig 1.1: Convergence of Azure DevOps with GitHub

Many teams today use Azure Repos and Azure Pipelines for their core workflow while also connecting GitHub repositories to Azure Pipelines for open-source components. Others use GitHub as the source repository while routing all CI/CD through Azure Pipelines because of its richer multi-stage gating features. In Chapter 8, I am going to configure this hybrid setup explicitly for you to practice it. For now, what matters most is that we understand Azure DevOps as the operations and delivery platform, and GitHub as the developer and community platform, with GitHub Copilot for Azure bridging the two by bringing AI assistance directly into our DevOps workflows.

One concrete illustration of this convergence is GitHub Advanced Security for Azure DevOps, which we will enable in Chapter 3 and explore in depth in Chapter 9. It actually brings GitHub's code scanning, secret scanning, and dependency scanning engines directly into Azure Pipelines, so teams do not need to leave the Azure DevOps portal to manage application security alerts.

Azure DevOps as Unified Platform

The five services described below, are each useful in isolation. Their real power actually emerges when we connect them with each other. For example, a developer creates a user story in Azure Boards, branches the repository in Azure Repos, and opens a pull request. Now here, the pull request automatically triggers an Azure Pipeline that compiles the application, runs unit tests, executes ***SonarCloud*** static analysis, and reports results back to the pull request. If all checks pass, the pipeline publishes a versioned artifact to Azure Artifacts and promotes it through staging to production with approval gates. Every step in the following chain is linked to the original work item. It really creates an unbroken audit trail.

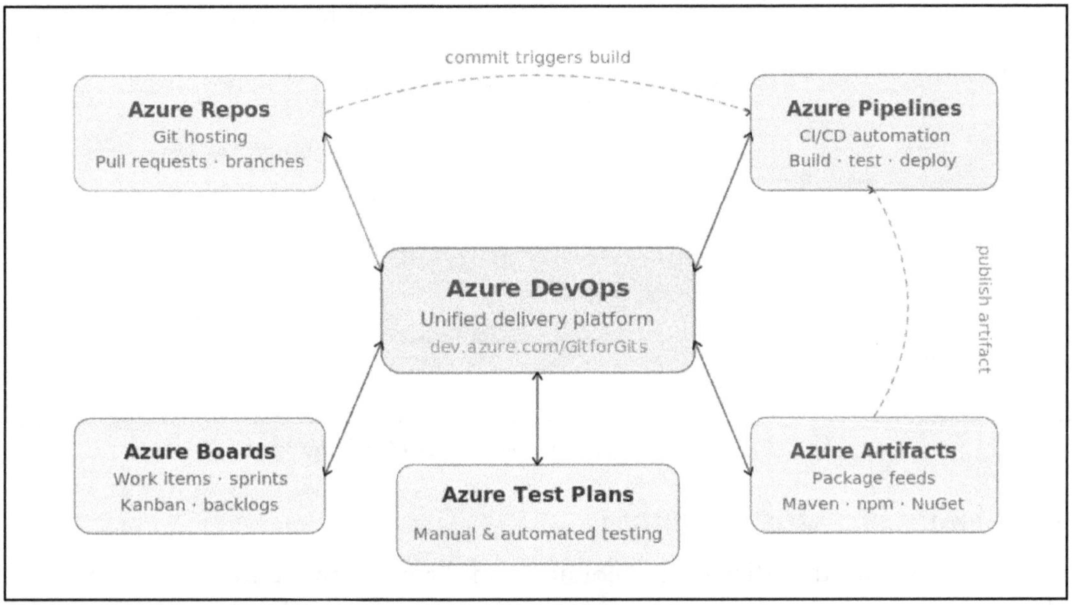

Fig 1.2: Azure DevOps Architecture (Simplified)

Now, such type of end-to-end traceability is what makes Azure DevOps more than a collection of individual tools. When a production incident occurs and we need to answer the question "which requirement led to this change, who approved it, and which pipeline version deployed it?", the answer is always one click away inside the Azure DevOps portal. As we build our setup in the sections that follow, we will keep this integrated picture in mind so that each configuration decision reinforces the whole rather than optimizing in isolation.

Setting up Projects and Organization

Everything in Azure DevOps lives inside an organization. An organization is the top-level container that holds all our projects, users, billing settings, and global policies. We will create an organization named GitforGits as our only home base throughout this book. Inside it, we will create a project named ***SpringBootAPI*** that will house our application repository, our pipelines, our boards, and our test plans.

In the below illustration, we will see how the projects and the organization is housed together:

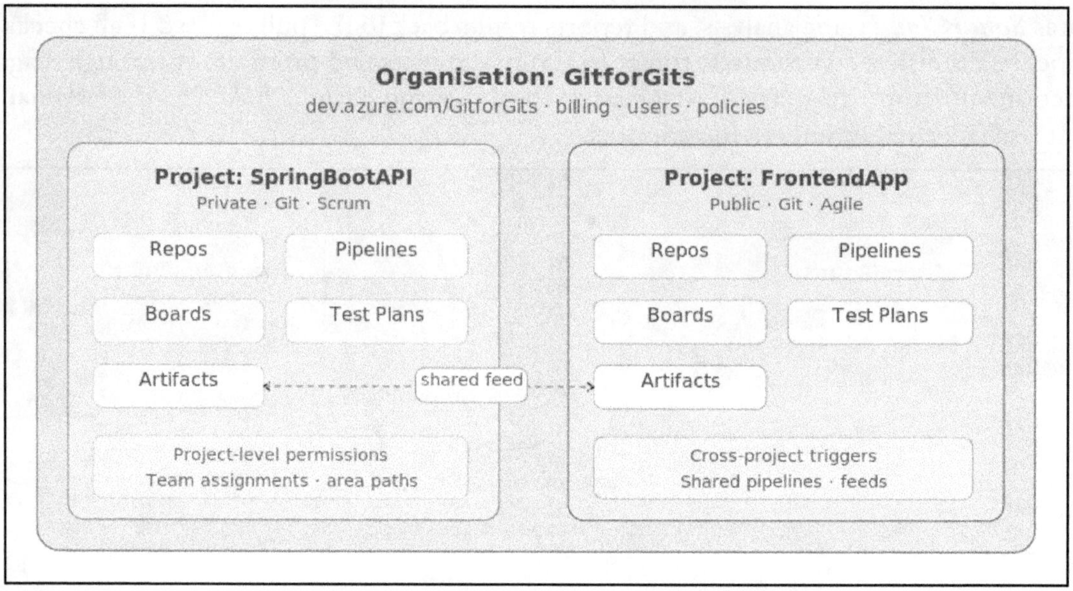

Fig 1.3: Organisation and Project Hierarchy

Creating Azure DevOps Account

At the very first, we need a Microsoft account or an Azure Active Directory identity to access Azure DevOps successfully. Once we have it, we then sign in immediately, navigate to the below URL, and click **Start Free**.

https://azure.microsoft.com/en-us/products/devops/

After signing in, we land on Azure DevOps portal at ***https://dev.azure.com.*** This portal presents a list of any existing organizations associated with our identity. Since this is a fresh start, the list will be empty and the portal will prompt us to create a new organization immediately. If we are signing in with an existing Microsoft account that already has Azure DevOps organizations, we will see them listed here and can choose to create a new one alongside them.

Setting up Organization

On the portal's welcome screen. The portal will ask us to confirm the organization name and select a hosting region. We will name our organization as **GitforGits** and choose the region closest to where our team is located. The reason behind choosing nearby region is to minimize the latency for all pipeline runs and repository operations. After this, we click continue, the organization is provisioned in seconds and we are redirected to the GitforGits organization home page.

Now, the organization home page is where we manage users, billing, security policies, and projects. For now, the first thing we need to do is create our working project.

Creating SpringBootAPI Project

From the GitforGits organization home page, we will click upon **New Project**. The project creation dialog asks for a project name, an optional description, the visibility setting, and the version control type, which we then fill in as below.

```
Project name   : SpringBootAPI
Visibility     : Private
Version control: Git
Work item process: Scrum
```

We choose **Scrum** as our work item process because it maps most naturally to the sprint-based delivery model we will be using in Chapter 8. After clicking **Create**, it provisions the project and lands us on the project's summary page. From here, we can navigate to any of the five services using the left-hand navigation pane.

Configuring Repository

When the project is provisioned, the Azure DevOps automatically creates an empty Git repository named **SpringBootAPI**. We can see this by clicking **Repos** in the left-hand navigation.

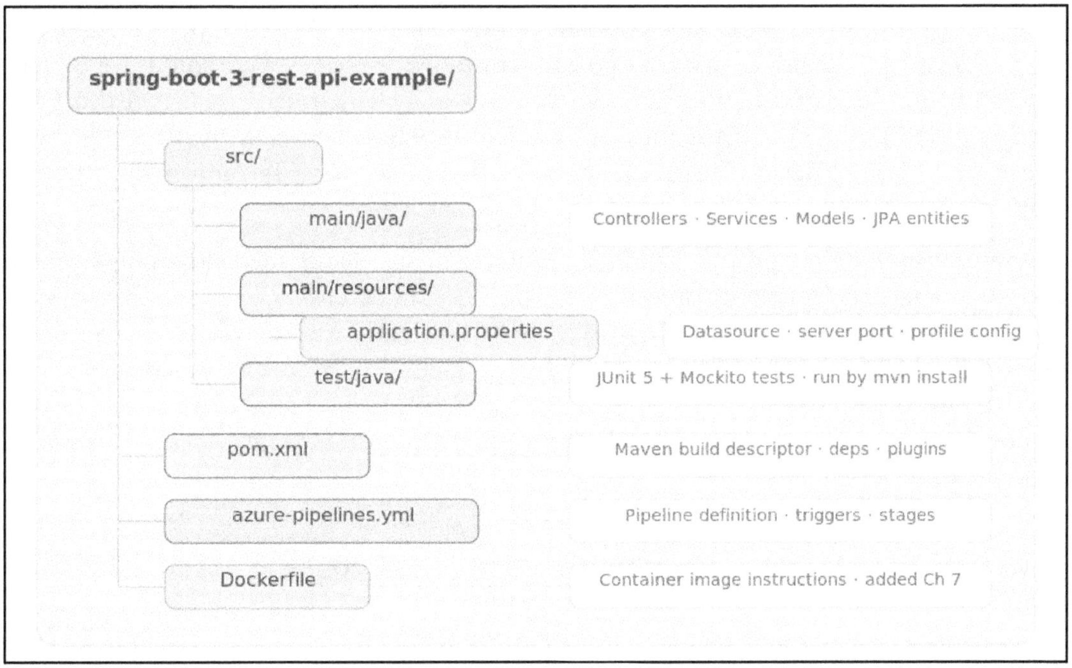

Fig 1.4: Spring Boot Repository Structure

The page shows an empty repository with instructions for pushing an existing repository or cloning the empty one. We will be coming back to push our application code in the final section of this chapter. For now, we will note the following URL:

https://dev.azure.com/GitforGits/SpringBootAPI/_git/SpringBootAPI

Before we move on, it is useful to enable the branch policy on the main branch to protect it from direct pushes. To do this, we click on **Repos**, then **Branches**, then hover over the main branch row and click the ellipsis menu. After this, we then select **Branch policies**. Next, we then enable the 'Require a minimum number of reviewers policy' and set the minimum to **1**. This means all changes to main must arrive through a pull request with at least one approval, which is a foundational governance control we will rely on when we configure our CI pipeline in Chapter 3.

Preparing Pipeline Entry Point

We will define our first pipeline in Chapter 2, but it is useful to navigate to **Pipelines** now to understand how the portal is structured. For this, we will click **Pipelines** in the left navigation. The page will be empty and it will invite to create our first pipeline. We will return here in Chapter 2 after we have learned how to author YAML pipeline definitions. For this chapter, you just have to simply know, that the Pipelines hub exists and is connected to our SpringBootAPI repository, which is sufficient enough for now.

Setting up Testing Environment

In the left navigation, we click **Test Plans** and then click **New Test Plan**. We will name it as **Sprint 1 Tests** and set the iteration to the current sprint. This creates a container for all test cases associated with our first sprint. We will populate this plan with formal test cases in Chapter 6 when we integrate Azure Test Plans into our CI/CD pipeline. For now, just having the plan in place means we already have a home for test results when our first automated pipeline run completes.

As our work grows, we may need to manage several projects under the GitforGits organization, for example a separate front-end project alongside our back-end SpringBootAPI. The Azure DevOps handles this cleanly. From the GitforGits organization home page, we can click **New Project** at any time to add a second project, and each project gets its own isolated set of repositories, pipelines, boards, and test plans. The permissions can be managed both at the organization level (granting a user access to all projects) and at the project level (restricting a user to a single project).

Installing and Configuring Azure CLI and Azure Developer CLI

The Azure portal is excellent for visual exploration, but for real DevOps work we need command-line tools. There are two tools, that are essential for us throughout this book. The first is the Azure CLI (**az**), which is Microsoft's general-purpose command-line tool for managing Azure resources. The second is the Azure Developer CLI (**azd**), which is a newer, higher-level tool designed specifically for the inner loop of cloud-native application development.

Installing Azure CLI

I am assuming you all are quite compfortable with Ubuntu. So, to begin with, we will first install Azure CLI using the official Microsoft package repository. For this, we will open the terminal and run following commands in sequence.

```
curl -sL https://aka.ms/InstallAzureCLIDeb | sudo bash
```

The first command fetches the Microsoft signing key, the second adds the repository, and the third installs the package.

Once the installation completes, we can verify it by checking the version.

```
az --version
```

The terminal displays the installed Azure CLI version, confirming that the installation was successful.

```
azure-cli                         2.61.0
core                              2.61.0
telemetry                          1.1.0
Dependencies:
msal                              1.28.0
azure-mgmt-resource               23.1.1
...
```

Logging into Azure CLI

With Azure CLI installed, the next step is to authenticate against our Azure subscription. For this, we will run the following login command.

```
az login
```

After this, the browser window will open automatically and prompt for our Azure credentials. Once we complete the sign-in, the terminal prints a JSON list of subscriptions associated with our account.

```
[
  {
    "cloudName": "AzureCloud",
    "id": "xxxxxxxx-xxxx-xxxx-xxxx-xxxxxxxxxxxx",
    "isDefault": true,
```

```
    "name": "Pay-As-You-Go",
    "state": "Enabled",
    "tenantId": "yyyyyyyy-yyyy-yyyy-yyyy-yyyyyyyyyyyy"
  }
]
```

If we have multiple subscriptions, we can set the active one with the command below, in which we are replacing the placeholder with the id value from the output above.

```
az account set --subscription "xxxxxxxx-xxxx-xxxx-xxxx-xxxxxxxxxxxx"
```

Configuring Azure CLI Defaults

We can save ourselves from typing repeated flags by setting default values for the most frequently used parameters. The two most useful defaults for our work are the output format and the default resource group. We will also add the Azure DevOps extension, which enables the az devops family of commands that we will use in later chapters to interact with pipelines and repositories from the terminal.

```
az config set defaults.output=table
az extension add --name azure-devops
```

We can confirm that our configuration saved correctly by running the following command, which prints all active CLI defaults.

```
az config get
```

The terminal displays the current Azure CLI configuration, grouped by setting name and value.

```
Group    Name    Value
-------  ------  -----
defaults output  table
```

Commonly Used Azure CLI Commands

Before we get into the Azure Developer CLI, we will take a look at some of the Azure CLI commands that we will be using very frequently later throughout the book. I have grouped them by resource type below so that we can have a handy reference as we proceed.

Resource groups

The ***resource groups*** form the fundamental organizational unit in Azure. All resources we provision must belong to a resource group. The commands below create, list, and delete resource groups.

```
# Create a resource group
az group create --name SpringBootRG --location eastus
# List all resource groups
az group list
# Delete a resource group and all its resources
az group delete --name SpringBootRG --yes --no-wait
```

Virtual Machines

The ***virtual machines*** will be used in Chapter 7 as self-hosted pipeline agents and as deployment targets.

Following is a quick example of using it:

```
# Create an Ubuntu VM
az vm create --resource-group SpringBootRG --name SpringBootVM \
  --image Ubuntu2204 --admin-username azureuser --generate-ssh-keys
# List VMs in the resource group
az vm list --resource-group SpringBootRG
# Stop and deallocate a VM
az vm deallocate --resource-group SpringBootRG --name SpringBootVM
```

Azure DevOps Pipeline

The ***Azure DevOps pipeline commands*** let us trigger and monitor pipelines without opening a browser. In the following, we will configure our organization URL once for the CLI session.

```
# Set organization and project defaults
az devops configure --defaults \
  organization=https://dev.azure.com/GitforGits \
  project=SpringBootAPI
# List all pipelines
az pipelines list
# Run a pipeline by name
```

```
az pipelines run --name "SpringBootAPI-CI"
```

The terminal displays the pipeline run details, including the pipeline ID, name, current status, and queue time.

```
ID    Name               Status    Queue Time
----  -----------------  --------  ----------
1     SpringBootAPI-CI   enabled   -
```

AKS Cluster

The ***AKS cluster commands*** will become relevant in Chapter 7 when we deploy our containerized application to Azure Kubernetes Service.

```
# Create an AKS cluster
az aks create --resource-group SpringBootRG --name SpringBootAKS \
  --node-count 2 --enable-addons monitoring --generate-ssh-keys
# Fetch credentials for kubectl
az aks get-credentials --resource-group SpringBootRG --name SpringBootAKS
# List clusters
az aks list
```

Storage Accounts

The ***storage accounts*** are used as backends for Terraform state files. You can find them put into use in Chapter 7.

```
# Create a storage account
az storage account create --name springboottfstate \
  --resource-group SpringBootRG --location eastus --sku Standard_LRS
# List storage accounts
az storage account list
```

Installing Azure Developer CLI (azd)

The Azure Developer CLI is a higher-level companion to the Azure CLI. Where **az** operates on individual Azure resources, **azd** operates on complete application environments. It understands application templates, can scaffold infrastructure as Bicep files, and can deploy an entire application stack with a single command. We will use **azd** in Chapter 10 when we explore AI-assisted infrastructure authoring with GitHub Copilot for Azure.

For now, we will install it:

```
curl -fsSL https://aka.ms/install-azd.sh | bash
azd version
```

The terminal then confirms the installed version of Azure Developer CLI.

```
azd version 1.10.1 (commit xxxxxxx)
```

After this, we can authenticate azd against our Azure subscription with the following command. It opens a browser window in the same way **az** login does, and after authentication **azd** stores credentials independently of the Azure CLI.

```
azd auth login
```

Introduction to Visual Studio Code for DevOps Tasks

Throughout this book, we use Visual Studio Code (VS Code) as our primary editor, since it has an extension ecosystem that covers every tool in our DevOps stack. Here, I will walk you through the installation, the key built-in features we rely on most, the extensions we need to install today, and then finish with a section dedicated to GitHub Copilot for Azure, which transforms VS Code into an AI-powered DevOps cockpit.

Installing VS Code

The cleanest way to install VS Code is through the official **Snap** package, which keeps the editor up to date automatically.

```
sudo snap install code --classic
```

Once the installation finishes, we can launch VS Code from the terminal with the code command or from the application menu. In case if you want to work on Windows, then you can download the installer from ***https://code.visualstudio.com/Download,*** run the **.exe** and ensure the option to add VS Code to the system PATH is selected during installation. That PATH option is what allows us to type code in any terminal to open the current directory in VS Code.

VS Code for DevOps

There are several built-in features of VS Code, which will be in constant use as we progress through the book. The integrated terminal, Git integration, and the Command Palette are the three we want to become fluent with before we do anything else.

The ***Integrated Terminal*** opens with the keyboard shortcut Ctrl + ` (backtick). We can open multiple terminal instances and give each one a name, which makes it easy to have one terminal for **az** commands, another for Git, and a third for running the application locally. All CLI commands shown in this book are intended to be typed inside the VS Code integrated terminal so that we never need to switch between windows. The ***Git Integration*** is accessible through the Source Control icon in the left activity bar (the branching icon). From here we can stage files, write commit messages, and push and pull from remote repositories without ever leaving the editor. The status bar at the bottom of VS Code always shows the currently active branch, and clicking it opens a branch picker that lets us create and switch branches in one step. And, the ***Command Palette*** opens with Ctrl + Shift + P. It gives us instant access to every VS Code command, extension command, and setting by name. As we install extensions in the next subsection, we will use the Command Palette to invoke extension-specific commands without memorizing keyboard shortcuts.

Extensions for Azure and DevOps

Once we install the right extensions, the VS Code's value multiplies dramatically. We can open the Extensions pane with Ctrl + Shift + X and install each of the following extensions by searching for its name.

Azure Account

This extension manages authentication between VS Code and our Azure subscription. Once installed, we just have to run the command **`Azure: Sign In`** from the Command Palette. After authenticating, every other Azure extension can access our subscription without requiring separate credentials.

Azure CLI Tools

This adds IntelliSense, syntax highlighting, and autocompletion for Azure CLI commands inside VS Code terminal and .azcli script files. This is particularly useful when we write automation scripts in Chapter 7.

Azure Pipelines

This one provides schema validation and IntelliSense for **`azure-pipelines.yml`** files. When we hover over a YAML key, this extension shows us the allowed values and links to official documentation. We will rely on this extension heavily starting in our next chapter 2.

Docker

This one gives us a visual panel for managing running containers, images, and registries directly inside VS Code. It becomes useful in Chapter 7 when we containerize our App and push the image to Azure Container Registry.

Java Extension Pack

This one is a collection of Java-specific extensions including the Language Server, Maven support, and a debugger. Since our sample application is a Spring Boot project built with Maven, this pack is essential for building and running the application locally.

GitHub Copilot in VS Code

Since mid-2025, GitHub Copilot for Azure is considered to be one of the most powerful productivity tools in DevOps toolkit. It integrates with GitHub Copilot to provide two interaction modes inside VS Code. One is the Ask mode, where we ask natural-language questions about our Azure environment and receive answers grounded in our real resource context, and the other is Agent mode, where Copilot autonomously orchestrates multi-step DevOps tasks on our behalf.

To install it, search for GitHub Copilot for Azure in the Extensions pane and click Install. This extension requires an active GitHub Copilot subscription, which is available as a free trial or as part of GitHub Enterprise. Once installed and authenticated, we can open the Copilot Chat panel with Ctrl + Shift + I and begin interacting with it using the **`@azure participant`**.

We are going to use Copilot for Azure extensively in Chapter 10, but we want to introduce it here because it changes how we design infrastructure and pipelines from the very first chapter. As a preview, you can also try typing the following in the Copilot Chat panel after installation.

```
@azure What resources do I currently have in my subscription?
```

The response will be a fully contextualized explanation of our current Azure subscription, including resource groups, active services, and any cost anomalies Copilot can detect from our resource metadata.

```
Agent mode in GitHub Copilot for Azure can execute multi-step tasks such
as generating Bicep templates, running az commands, and validating
deployments, all from a single natural language prompt. We will explore
Agent mode hands-on in Chapter 10.
```

Setting up Spring Boot REST API

Throughout this book we will work with a single sample application that grows in complexity as we progress. The application is a Spring Boot 3 REST API that exposes CRUD endpoints for a simple tutorial data model. We chose Spring Boot because it is a realistic enterprise Java application with Maven as its build tool, making it an excellent subject for demonstrating CI pipelines, artifact management, containerization, and infrastructure provisioning. Every pipeline we configure, every test suite we run, and every deployment strategy we implement will use this application as its target.

Cloning Repository

At first, we will open the VS Code integrated terminal and navigate to the directory where we want to store our work.

```
mkdir -p ~/azure-devops-workspace && cd ~/azure-devops-workspace
```

```
git clone https://github.com/bezkoder/spring-boot-3-rest-api-example.git
cd spring-boot-3-rest-api-example
```

In the above, we are creating a dedicated workspace directory so as to have things clean.

After the clone completes, we will open the project in VS Code. The dot at the end of the code command tells VS Code to open the current directory as the workspace root.

```
code .
```

After we open the project, the VS Code detects, that it is a Java Maven project and may prompt us to open the Java Projects view. We can accept that prompt, and the Explorer pane on the left will show the full project structure. The directories and files we care about most at this stage are the following.

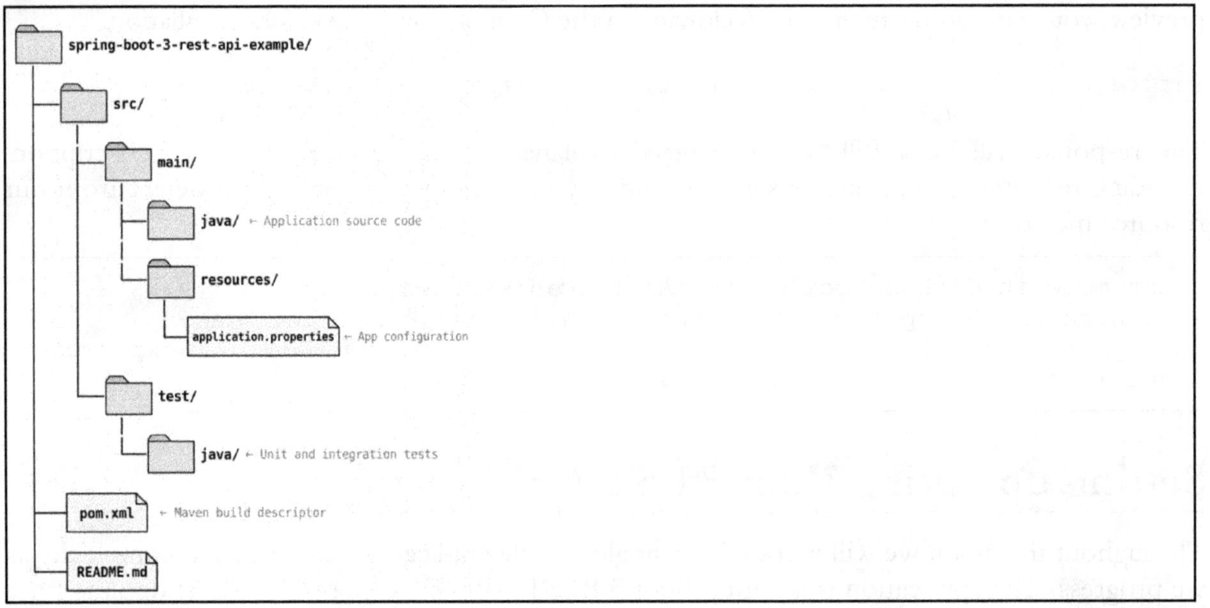

Building Application Locally

Before we connect this application to Azure DevOps, we will confirm if it builds cleanly on local machine. This is the same validation our CI pipeline will perform automatically in Chapter 3, so running it once locally gives us confidence that the baseline is solid.

Next, we also need Java 17+ and Maven 3.8+ on our system. We can easily verify both of them with the following commands.

```
java -version
mvn -version
```

The terminal confirms the installed versions of OpenJDK and Maven on the system.

```
openjdk version "17.0.11" 2024-04-16
OpenJDK Runtime Environment ...
Apache Maven 3.9.6
Java version: 17.0.11, vendor: Eclipse Adoptium
```

Once our prerequisites confirmed, we can then run the Maven build. The clean phase removes any previous build output, and the install phase compiles the source, runs all tests, and packages the application as a JAR file in the target directory.

```
mvn clean install
```

The final lines of the build output confirm that all tests pass and the application JAR is packaged successfully.

```
[INFO] Tests run: 1, Failures: 0, Errors: 0, Skipped: 0
[INFO] ------------------------------------------------------------------------
[INFO] BUILD SUCCESS
[INFO] ------------------------------------------------------------------------
[INFO] Total time:  18.432 s
[INFO] Finished at: 2025-07-01T10:23:45Z
[INFO] ------------------------------------------------------------------------
```

Running Application Locally

After a successful build we run the application using the Spring Boot Maven plugin. This starts the embedded Tomcat server on port 8080.

```
mvn spring-boot:run
```

The startup lines confirm that Spring Boot has initialised and the embedded Tomcat server is listening on port 8080.

```
...
2025-07-01T10:24:10.123Z  INFO --- Tomcat started on port(s): 8080
2025-07-01T10:24:10.456Z  INFO --- Started SpringBoot3RestApiApplication
in 3.2s
```

We can also verify if the application is responding, by opening a second terminal panel and running a quick **`curl`** test.

```
curl -s http://localhost:8080/api/tutorials | head -c 200
```

After this, the terminal returns an empty JSON array, and confirms that the API is live and responding correctly with no data yet seeded.

```
[]
```

The above empty JSON array is the correct response for a freshly started application with no data. The API is live and responsive. We can stop the running server with Ctrl + C in the first terminal before we proceed.

Pushing Application to Azure Repos

Now we connect our local application to the SpringBootAPI repository we created in Azure DevOps earlier in this chapter. Here, we will add the Azure Repos remote URL and push the code. The application currently has its original GitHub remote as origin. So now, we will add the Azure Repos URL as a new remote named azure so that both remotes coexist cleanly and we can reference the upstream GitHub project if needed in the future.

```
git remote add azure \
  https://dev.azure.com/GitforGits/SpringBootAPI/_git/SpringBootAPI
git push azure main
```

The terminal confirms that Git has transferred all objects to the Azure Repos remote successfully as shown below:

```
Enumerating objects: 87, done.
Counting objects: 100% (87/87), done.
Delta compression using up to 8 threads
Compressing objects: 100% (54/54), done.
Writing objects: 100% (87/87), 42.31 KiB | 8.46 MiB/s, done.
Total 87 (delta 18), reused 0 (delta 0), pack-reused 0
To https://dev.azure.com/GitforGits/SpringBootAPI/_git/SpringBootAPI
 * [new branch]      main -> main
```

After this, we can confirm the push was successful by returning to the Azure DevOps portal, clicking **Repos** in the left navigation, and seeing all the Spring Boot source files listed in the repository. From this point forward, every chapter will treat this repository as the source of truth for our application and every pipeline we write will reference it.

As a final preparation step, we will also add an **azure-pipelines.yml** file to the root of the repository. We will fill this file with a proper pipeline definition in Chapter 2, but creating the file now means it will be present in Azure Repos and visible to the Pipelines service when we return to configure our first CI pipeline.

```
cat > azure-pipelines.yml << 'EOF'
# Azure Pipelines configuration
# Full pipeline definition added in Chapter 2
trigger:
  - main
pool:
  vmImage: 'ubuntu-latest'
steps:
  - script: echo "Pipeline placeholder"
    displayName: 'Placeholder step'
EOF
git add azure-pipelines.yml
git commit -m "Add pipeline placeholder for Chapter 2"
git push azure main
```

In the above, we create the file with a minimal placeholder so that VS Code registers it as a YAML pipeline file and the Azure Pipelines extension begins providing schema assistance immediately.

Summary

To quickly summarize, we have truly covered a lot of ground in this chapter. We started by understanding what Azure DevOps is and how its five services, Azure Repos, Pipelines, Boards, Test Plans, and Artifacts, combine into a unified delivery platform. We positioned Azure DevOps clearly within the broader Microsoft ecosystem, particularly its converging relationship with GitHub and the significance of GitHub Copilot for Azure as a bridge between the two. We created our GitforGits organization and our SpringBootAPI project, configured a branch policy on the main branch, and sketched out a test plan for the sprint ahead. We installed and authenticated both the Azure CLI and the Azure Developer CLI, set up our default configuration, added the Azure DevOps CLI extension, and walked through the most important command families we will use throughout the book.

We also set up VS Code with all the extensions we need, including a first introduction to GitHub Copilot for Azure. We finished by cloning the Spring Boot REST API application, building it locally to confirm the baseline, running it to verify it responds correctly, and pushing it to Azure Repos where it is now protected by version control and branch policies.

CHAPTER 2
PIPELINE AS CODE WITH YAML

Overview

At the end of Chapter 1, we pushed our Spring Boot REST API to Azure Repos and added a placeholder **`azure-pipelines.yml`** file to the repository root. In this chapter we will replace that placeholder with a real, fully working pipeline definition. We do this progressively, starting from the smallest valid YAML that Azure Pipelines will accept and growing it, section by section, into a complete multi-stage pipeline that builds the application, runs unit tests, publishes test results, and packages the compiled artifact.

Later, we will spend time on the tooling that makes working with YAML comfortable inside VS Code. That includes the YAML extension from Red Hat, the Azure Pipelines extension from Microsoft, IntelliSense, linting, custom snippets, and pipeline template reuse. At the close of this chapter, our **`azure-pipelines.yml`** file will be structured, validated, version-controlled, and ready to be extended in every chapter that follows.

Introduction to Pipeline as Code

Traditionally, the CI/CD pipelines were configured through graphical user interfaces where a team member would click through a wizard, fill in form fields, and save settings into a proprietary database that no one else could easily read or review. Such approach produced pipelines that were fragile, opaque, and impossible to audit. If the person who built the pipeline left the team, the configuration became a mystery. And, that's where, the concept of Pipeline as Code solves all of this by moving the pipeline definition into a plain text file that lives inside the application repository, versioned alongside the source code it builds.

With the pipeline definition stored in Git, every change to the pipeline goes through the same pull request review process as a change to the application code. A reviewer can read the diff, ask questions, request changes, and approve or reject the modification before it reaches the main branch. If a pipeline change introduces a regression, we can roll it back with a single **`git revert`** command. We can branch the pipeline alongside feature branches, test a new deployment strategy in isolation, and merge it only when we are confident. None of that was possible with GUI-based pipeline configuration.

The other major advantage is **portability**. Because the pipeline is a file in the repository, anyone who clones the repository gets a complete, runnable description of how the software is built and deployed. Hence, if we onboard a new team member, it is simply handing them a clone URL, not a walkthrough of a configuration portal. It also means that the pipeline definition can be linted, tested, and reviewed with the same automated tools we apply to application code. This is the philosophy we will apply throughout this book.

YAML in Pipeline as Code

The YAML is a human-readable, indentation-based format that strikes a useful balance between machine parseability and human legibility. Unlike JSON, which requires braces and quotes around every value, the YAML reads almost like structured prose. Unlike XML, it does not demand opening and closing tags. For pipeline work, where we need to express hierarchical structures like stages containing jobs containing steps, the YAML's indentation-driven hierarchy is a natural fit.

The core YAML concepts we need to understand for Azure Pipelines are scalars, mappings, and sequences. A scalar is a plain value such as a string, number, or boolean. A mapping is a key-value pair separated by a colon and a space, and it is how we set configuration properties. A sequence is an ordered list of items, each prefixed by a dash and a space. In Azure Pipelines, the sequences appear everywhere, like the list of trigger branches, the list of steps within a job, and the list of stages within a pipeline are all expressed as YAML sequences.

One aspect of YAML that trips up newcomers more than any other is **indentation**. Unlike most programming languages, the YAML uses whitespace as syntax. The mixing of tabs and spaces, or using inconsistent indentation levels, produces parse errors that can be frustratingly opaque. The convention we follow throughout this book, and the one Azure Pipelines itself prefers, is two spaces per indentation level, no tabs anywhere. Our VS Code extensions will enforce this automatically, and we will set that up in a later section of this chapter.

Benefits of YAML

Human readability is the most immediate benefit. A well-structured **`azure-pipelines.yml`** file reads like a specification, in which it tells us what the pipeline does, in what order, under what conditions, and with what inputs. Any engineer on the team can open the file and understand the delivery process without needing access to the Azure DevOps portal. That transparency reduces the knowledge silos that typically form around CI/CD infrastructure and makes on-call incident response faster, because the engineer investigating a failed deployment can read the pipeline definition without needing special permissions.

The second major benefit is **modularity**. The Azure Pipelines supports YAML templates, which allow us to extract reusable blocks of pipeline logic into separate files and reference them from multiple pipelines. If our organization runs twenty microservices that all follow the same Maven build pattern, we write the build steps once in a shared template and reference it from each service's pipeline file. When the build pattern needs to change, for example to add a new code-coverage report, we update the template once and every consuming pipeline gets the change automatically on its next run.

The third major benefit is **automation and repeatability**. A YAML pipeline runs identically every time it is triggered. The same steps, the same environment, the same inputs. There is no risk that a human forgot to run a step or ran it in the wrong order. In combination with trigger rules that fire on every push to a protected branch, the YAML pipelines give us a guarantee that, if the pipeline passes, the application meets every quality gate we have defined. Such a guarantee is the foundation on which continuous delivery is built, and it is why we invest the time to author pipelines carefully.

YAML for Azure Pipelines

In this section, we will now move from concepts to practice. We will open the **azure-pipelines.yml** file, wipe the placeholder content, and build the pipeline definition from the ground up. We do this section by section so that each YAML keyword we introduce has context and a clear reason for being there. All the commands in this section are run from the VS Code integrated terminal at the root of the **spring-boot-3-rest-api-example** directory.

Understanding Pipeline File Structure

Every Azure Pipelines YAML file follows a predictable top-level structure. At the outermost level we have four major keys, i.e. **trigger**, **pool**, **variables**, and either **steps** or **stages**. For simple single-job pipelines, we use **steps** directly. And, for multi-stage pipelines, we make use of **stages**, which nests jobs inside stages and steps inside jobs.

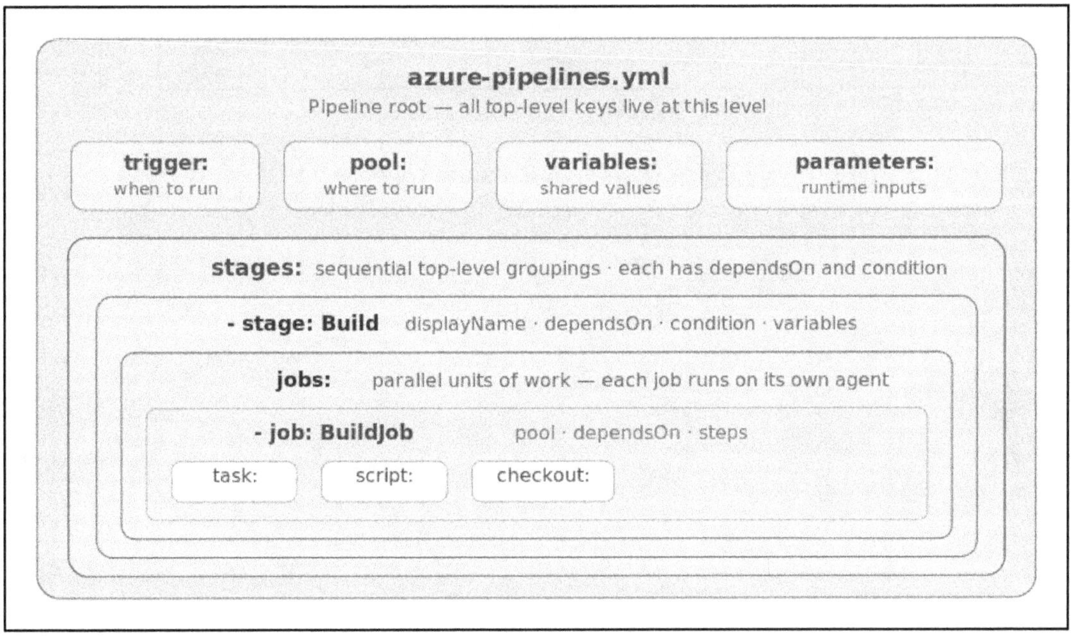

Fig 2.1: YAML Pipeline Structure Hierarchy

The complete anatomy of an Azure Pipelines YAML file can be represented as a hierarchy. If you understand this hierarchy very well, it surely prevents the confusion that comes from trying to learn structure and syntax.

For a single-stage pipeline, the **stages** and **jobs** layers can be omitted and **steps** can be placed directly under the root. This form keeps the file short and allows us to focus on the step definitions, which is where most of the meaningful pipeline logic lives.

Defining Triggers

A trigger tells Azure Pipelines which branch or tag events should cause the pipeline to run automatically. Without a trigger, the pipeline only runs when we click Run manually in the portal.

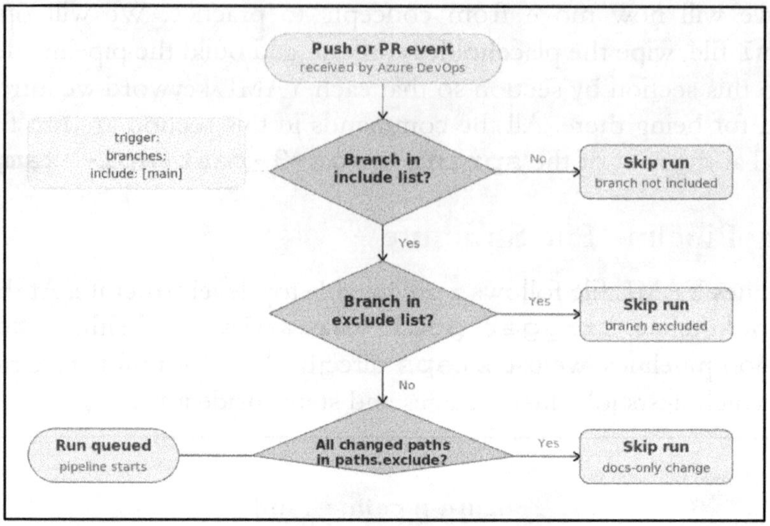

Fig 2.2: Trigger Decision Flowchart

For continuous integration, we always want an automatic trigger so that every push to a protected branch is validated. We can write the trigger section as shown below:

```
trigger:
  branches:
    include:
      - main
  paths:
    exclude:
      - '**/*.md'
      - 'docs/**'
```

This trigger runs the pipeline on every push to **main** but skips runs that only touch Markdown files or the **docs/** directory. That exclusion prevents a documentation edit from consuming a pipeline agent. The **paths.exclude** key accepts glob patterns, so we can tune this list as the repository grows.

Specifying Pipeline Agent

The **pool** key tells Azure Pipelines which agent to use for running jobs. Now here, an agent is a virtual machine that Azure provisions on demand and discards after the job finishes. The Microsoft-hosted agents come pre-installed with common runtimes and tools. For our App, we will need a Linux agent with Java and Maven available. So here, we will add the pool definition directly below the trigger.

```
pool:
  vmImage: 'ubuntu-latest'
```

The **ubuntu-latest** image includes Java 17, Maven 3.9, Docker, and the Azure CLI pre-installed, which means our pipeline does not need to install any of those tools before using them.

Defining Pipeline Variables

Well, the variables assist us to define values once and reference them throughout the pipeline file. The Azure Pipelines also provides a set of predefined variables such as **$(Build.ArtifactStagingDirectory)** and **$(Build.BuildId)** that we can use without declaring them.

For our application here, we will define one custom variable to pin the Maven goals so that we can change them in one place if needed.

```
variables:
  mavenGoals: 'clean install'
  artifactName: 'springboot-api'
```

We later reference these variables in task inputs using the **$(variableName)** syntax. The variables defined at the top of the file are accessible to every step in the pipeline. The variables can also be defined at the stage or job level, in which case they are scoped to that stage or job only. We will use job-scoped variables when we introduce the multi-stage structure later in this chapter.

Defining Build Step with Maven

The **steps** section is where the real work happens. Each entry under **steps** is either a **task**, a **script**, or a **checkout**. A **task** invokes a named, versioned action from the Azure Pipelines task library. A **script** runs a shell command directly. A **checkout** controls how source code is fetched onto the agent. As a default behavior, the Azure Pipelines adds an implicit **checkout: self** step before all others, so our repository is already present on the agent when our first task runs.

We will now add the Maven build task. The **Maven@3** task wraps the Maven command-line tool and provides structured inputs for the **pom.xml** path, the goals to execute, and optional settings for code coverage and authentication.

```
steps:
- task: Maven@3
```

```
  displayName: 'Build and unit-test with Maven'
  inputs:
    mavenPomFile: 'pom.xml'
    goals: '$(mavenGoals)'
    publishJUnitResults: true
    testResultsFiles: '**/surefire-reports/TEST-*.xml'
    javaHomeOption: 'JDKVersion'
    jdkVersionOption: '1.17'
    mavenVersionOption: 'Default'
```

In the above, the **displayName** key gives the step a human-readable label that appears in the Azure DevOps pipeline run view. Every step should have a **displayName** that reads like a sentence describing its intent. The **publishJUnitResults** input tells the task to hand test result XML files to the pipeline engine, which then makes them available in the Tests tab of the run summary.

Copying JAR to Staging Directory

After Maven produces the **.jar** file inside the **target/** directory, we need to copy it to the pipeline's staging directory before we can publish it as an artifact. The staging directory is a well-known, agent-managed location referenced by the predefined variable **$(Build.ArtifactStagingDirectory)**.

```
- task: CopyFiles@2
  displayName: 'Copy JAR to staging directory'
  inputs:
    sourceFolder: '$(System.DefaultWorkingDirectory)/target'
    contents: '*.jar'
    targetFolder: '$(Build.ArtifactStagingDirectory)'
```

In the above, the **contents** input accepts glob patterns, so ***.jar** copies every JAR file produced by Maven.

Publishing Build Artifacts

With the **.jar** in the staging directory, we publish it as a named pipeline artifact. The published artifacts are stored by Azure DevOps and made available to downstream stages and jobs. Every deployment stage we write in Chapter 4 will download this artifact rather than rebuilding the application from source, which is the correct pattern of build once, deploy many times.

```
- task: PublishBuildArtifacts@1
  displayName: 'Publish JAR as pipeline artifact'
  inputs:
    PathtoPublish: '$(Build.ArtifactStagingDirectory)'
    ArtifactName: '$(artifactName)'
    publishLocation: 'Container'
```

From the above script, the **`ArtifactName`** input uses the **`$(artifactName)`** variable we defined at the top of the file. This means all our steps refer to the artifact by the same name, and if we need to rename it we change it in one place. The **`publishLocation: 'Container'`** value tells Azure DevOps to store the artifact in its own managed storage.

Pushing Pipeline and Running First Build

Finally, we will now commit the completed **`azure-pipelines.yml`** file to **`main`** and push it to Azure Repos. The Azure Pipelines will detect the change and trigger the pipeline automatically because of the branch trigger we defined.

```
git add azure-pipelines.yml
git commit -m "Add complete single-stage CI pipeline"
git push azure main
```

After the push completes, the Azure DevOps detects the change to **`main`** and queues a new run. We then navigate to Pipelines in the left-hand menu of the SpringBootAPI project and watch the run appear with the status ***Queued***. Within a few seconds, an agent is provisioned and the status changes to ***Running***.

A successful first run produces the output below in the pipeline console log when the Maven step completes. The logs confirm that the source was checked out, dependencies were resolved, all tests passed, and the artifact was published.

```
##[section]Starting: Build and unit-test with Maven
Executing Maven with goals: clean install
...
[INFO] Tests run: 1, Failures: 0, Errors: 0, Skipped: 0
[INFO] BUILD SUCCESS
...
##[section]Finishing: Build and unit-test with Maven
##[section]Starting: Publish JAR as pipeline artifact
```

```
Uploading 1 files
Artifact springboot-api published.
##[section]Finishing: Publish JAR as pipeline artifact
```

After the run finishes, the Artifacts tab in the run detail page shows the **springboot-api** artifact containing our compiled **.jar** file. This artifact is stored by Azure DevOps and persists until it is automatically cleaned up according to the retention policy, which is 30 days by default for the free tier. In Chapter 4, the deployment stage will download this exact artifact rather than triggering a new build.

Structuring Multi-Stage YAML Pipelines

The single-stage pipeline we just created is perfectly adequate for continuous integration, but real delivery workflows have more structure. The code must pass through a build stage before it can be deployed to a staging environment, and it must pass validation in staging before it can go to production. Each of those phases is a distinct stage in a multi-stage pipeline as shown below:

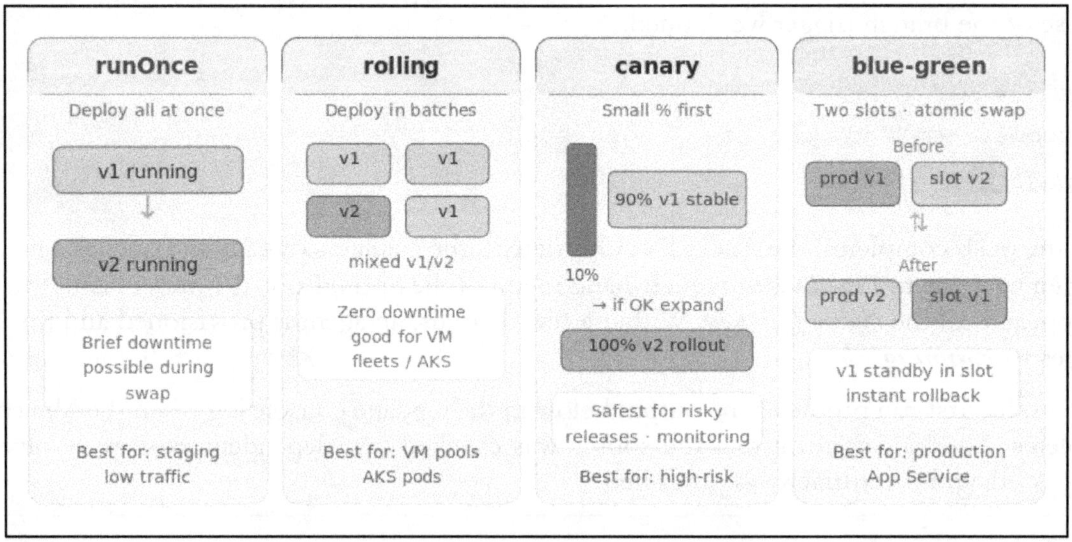

Fig 2.3: Comparison of Deployment Strategy

In a multi-stage YAML pipeline, the **stages** key replaces the top-level **steps** key. Each stage contains one or more **jobs**, and each job contains **steps**. The stages can declare dependencies on other stages using the **dependsOn** key, and they can express conditions that must be true before the stage runs. This is how we enforce the rule that staging never deploys unless the build succeeded, and production never deploys unless staging succeeded.

Defining Build Stage

We will now refactor our **azure-pipelines.yml** to introduce the **stages** structure. The first stage, **Build**, contains exactly the steps we wrote in the previous section, wrapped inside the required stage and job hierarchy as follows.

```
trigger:
  branches:
    include:
      - main
  paths:
    exclude:
      - '**/*.md'
      - 'docs/**'
variables:
  mavenGoals: 'clean install'
  artifactName: 'springboot-api'
stages:
- stage: Build
  displayName: 'Build and Test'
  jobs:
  - job: BuildJob
    displayName: 'Compile, test, and package'
    pool:
      vmImage: 'ubuntu-latest'
    steps:
    - task: Maven@3
      displayName: 'Build and unit-test with Maven'
      inputs:
        mavenPomFile: 'pom.xml'
        goals: '$(mavenGoals)'
        publishJUnitResults: true
        testResultsFiles: '**/surefire-reports/TEST-*.xml'
        javaHomeOption: 'JDKVersion'
        jdkVersionOption: '1.17'
        mavenVersionOption: 'Default'
```

```
    - task: CopyFiles@2
      displayName: 'Copy JAR to staging directory'
      inputs:
        sourceFolder: '$(System.DefaultWorkingDirectory)/target'
        contents: '*.jar'
        targetFolder: '$(Build.ArtifactStagingDirectory)'
    - task: PublishBuildArtifacts@1
      displayName: 'Publish JAR as pipeline artifact'
      inputs:
        PathtoPublish: '$(Build.ArtifactStagingDirectory)'
        ArtifactName: '$(artifactName)'
        publishLocation: 'Container'
```

Here, in the above script, you can notice that the **pool** has moved from the top level into the **job** definition. In a multi-stage pipeline each job can independently specify its pool, which means different stages can run on different agent types if needed.

Defining Staging Deployment Stage

The second stage deploys the application to a staging environment. It depends on the **Build** stage and only runs when that stage succeeds. The deployment target in Chapter 4 will be Azure App Service, but here we use a placeholder script so that the multi-stage structure is in place and can be committed and tested before we configure the full deployment pipeline.

```
- stage: Staging
  displayName: 'Deploy to Staging'
  dependsOn: Build
  condition: succeeded()
  jobs:
  - deployment: DeployStaging
    displayName: 'Deploy Spring Boot to staging'
    pool:
      vmImage: 'ubuntu-latest'
    environment: 'staging'
    strategy:
      runOnce:
```

```
        deploy:
          steps:
          - download: current
            artifact: $(artifactName)
          - script: |
              echo "Artifact downloaded. Staging deployment placeholder."
              ls $(Pipeline.Workspace)/$(artifactName)/
            displayName: 'Verify artifact and prepare staging deployment'
```

In the above, the **`deployment`** job type, rather than **`job`**, is what Azure DevOps requires for jobs that target a named environment. The **`environment: 'staging'`** line connects this job to the staging environment we will configure in the Azure DevOps portal in Chapter 4.

The **`strategy.runOnce.deploy`** block is one of three deployment strategies Azure Pipelines supports. The **`runOnce`** is the simplest, as it runs the deploy steps once against the target. The other two strategies, **`rolling`** and **`canary`**, are covered in Chapter 4 when we implement blue-green and canary deployments.

Defining Production Stage

The third stage mirrors the staging stage structure but targets the production environment. It depends on **`Staging`** and will, in Chapter 4, include an approval gate that requires a human sign-off before execution. For now, we will add the structural definition so that our **`azure-pipelines.yml`** reflects the full three-stage delivery pipeline from the outset.

```
- stage: Production
  displayName: 'Deploy to Production'
  dependsOn: Staging
  condition: succeeded()
  jobs:
  - deployment: DeployProduction
    displayName: 'Deploy Spring Boot to production'
    pool:
      vmImage: 'ubuntu-latest'
    environment: 'production'
    strategy:
      runOnce:
        deploy:
```

```
        steps:
        - download: current
          artifact: $(artifactName)
        - script: |
            echo "Artifact downloaded. Production deployment
placeholder."
            ls $(Pipeline.Workspace)/$(artifactName)/
          displayName: 'Verify artifact and prepare production
deployment'
```

Using Pipeline Parameters for Flexibility

While variables are set at file-definition time and can be overridden via the portal, the parameters are explicitly declared with types and default values, and they appear as input fields in the manual run dialog. They are the right tool for values that differ between environments but should not be hardcoded into the YAML file.

So here, we will now add a parameter to our pipeline that controls whether the staging and production stages run. It will give us a way to trigger a build-only run without touching either environment, which is going to be very useful during pipeline development and for validating hotfix branches that are not ready for deployment.

```
parameters:
- name: runDeployment
  displayName: 'Deploy after build?'
  type: boolean
  default: true
```

After this, we then update the **Staging** and **Production** stage conditions to respect this parameter. For this, we will replace **condition: succeeded()** with a compound condition that checks both the parameter value and the upstream stage result.

```
condition: and(succeeded(), eq('${{ parameters.runDeployment }}', true))
```

In the above, the **${{ parameters.runDeployment }}** syntax uses the compile-time expression format with double braces. The parameters are resolved before the pipeline runs, which is why they use **${{ }}** rather than the **$()** runtime variable syntax.

Running Multi-Stage Pipeline

With all three stages defined and the parameter added, we will now commit the updated file and push it to Azure Repos through the following command:

```
git add azure-pipelines.yml
git commit -m "Refactor to multi-stage pipeline with Build, Staging, Production"
git push azure main
```

After this, the Azure DevOps queues a new run immediately. We will now navigate to Pipelines and open the run detail page. The pipeline view now shows three stage tiles arranged left to right, viz, ***Build***, ***Staging***, and ***Production***. And here, each tile shows a spinner while it is running and a green tick when it succeeds. At this point the Staging and Production stages will succeed because they only run an **echo** command, but the stage structure is established and ready for the real deployment steps we add in Chapter 4.

Once the run finishes, the pipeline run summary shows the complete output below, confirming that all three stages executed in sequence.

```
Stage: Build              ✓ Succeeded    1m 42s
Stage: Staging            ✓ Succeeded      18s
Stage: Production         ✓ Succeeded      17s
Tests: 1 passed, 0 failed
Artifacts: springboot-api published (1 file)
```

Using Pipeline Templates for Reusability

In future, we will be running similar pipelines for multiple microservices, however copying the same Maven build steps into each service's **azure-pipelines.yml** will be creating a maintenance burden. The Azure Pipelines resolves this with templates, which is a separate YAML file that defines reusable steps, jobs, or stages.

In the following, we will create a templates directory in our repository and extract the Maven build steps into a reusable file.

```
mkdir -p templates
touch templates/maven-build-steps.yml
```

Next, we then open **templates/maven-build-steps.yml** and write the following:

```
parameters:
- name: mavenGoals
  type: string
```

```
  default: 'clean install'
- name: artifactName
  type: string
  default: 'springboot-api'
steps:
- task: Maven@3
  displayName: 'Build and unit-test with Maven'
  inputs:
    mavenPomFile: 'pom.xml'
    goals: '${{ parameters.mavenGoals }}'
    publishJUnitResults: true
    testResultsFiles: '**/surefire-reports/TEST-*.xml'
    javaHomeOption: 'JDKVersion'
    jdkVersionOption: '1.17'
    mavenVersionOption: 'Default'
- task: CopyFiles@2
  displayName: 'Copy JAR to staging directory'
  inputs:
    sourceFolder: '$(System.DefaultWorkingDirectory)/target'
    contents: '*.jar'
    targetFolder: '$(Build.ArtifactStagingDirectory)'
- task: PublishBuildArtifacts@1
  displayName: 'Publish JAR as pipeline artifact'
  inputs:
    PathtoPublish: '$(Build.ArtifactStagingDirectory)'
    ArtifactName: '${{ parameters.artifactName }}'
    publishLocation: 'Container'
```

With the template file saved, we then proceed to update **BuildJob** to reference it instead of inlining the steps.

```
  - job: BuildJob
    displayName: 'Compile, test, and package'
    pool:
```

```
      vmImage: 'ubuntu-latest'
    steps:
    - template: templates/maven-build-steps.yml
      parameters:
        mavenGoals: '$(mavenGoals)'
        artifactName: '$(artifactName)'
```

At runtime, the Azure Pipelines fetches the template file, substitutes the parameter values, and inlines the resulting steps exactly as if they had been written directly in the main file. The pipeline behaviour is identical, but the **`azure-pipelines.yml`** file is now shorter and any future change to the build steps needs to be made only in **`templates/maven-build-steps.yml`**.

Using VS Code Extensions for YAML

Most of the developers have frequently experienced that the hand-written YAML are very prone to errors. Even a single misplaced space tends to invalidate the entire file. The Azure Pipelines task library has hundreds of tasks, each with its own set of required and optional inputs, and memorising all of them is neither practical nor necessary. So here, the VS Code extensions is going to fill this gap by providing real-time validation, autocompletion, schema enforcement, and formatting.

In the following, we will install and configure the extensions to make our YAML authoring experience significantly more productive for the rest of the book.

Installing YAML Extension

We can now open the Extensions pane in VS Code with **`Ctrl + Shift + X`** and search for **YAML**. We then install the extension published by ***Red Hat***. This extension provides syntax highlighting and structure validation for all YAML files in our workspace, not just pipeline files. After installation, any YAML file we open benefits from colour-coded key-value pairs, indentation guides, and real-time error highlighting that catches structural problems before we ever push the file to the repository.

The YAML extension reads a **`.yamllint`** configuration file if one exists in the workspace root. So now, we will create one to enforce the two-space indentation convention:

```
cat > .yamllint << 'EOF'
extends: default
rules:
  indentation:
```

```
    spaces: 2
    indent-sequences: consistent
  line-length:
    max: 120
  truthy:
    allowed-values: ['true', 'false']
EOF
```

With this above file in place, the YAML extension will flag any line that exceeds 120 characters, any indentation that uses a value other than 2 spaces, and any boolean value that uses a non-standard representation such as **yes**.

Installing Azure Pipelines Extension

The second extension we install is ***Azure Pipelines***, published by ***Microsoft***. We find it in the Extensions pane by searching for **Azure Pipelines**. After installation, this extension registers the Azure Pipelines YAML schema against all files named **azure-pipelines.yml** and any file that contains the comment **# Azure Pipelines** at the top.

The practical effect is that when we open **azure-pipelines.yml** and start typing a task name, the VS Code presents a dropdown of every task in the Azure Pipelines task library, filtered by what we have typed so far. Once we select a task, the extension automatically scaffolds all the required **inputs** keys for that task, preventing the "missing required field" errors that cause pipeline runs to fail at startup. The optional inputs are shown as comments that we can uncomment if needed.

Leveraging IntelliSense

In VS Code, IntelliSense refers to the combined experience of autocompletion, parameter hints, and hover documentation. With both the YAML and Azure Pipelines extensions active, IntelliSense operates at two levels inside our pipeline file.

At the structural level, when we press **Ctrl + Space** at any point in the file, VS Code suggests the valid YAML keys for the current indentation context. At the top level of the file it suggests **trigger**, **pool**, **variables**, **parameters**, and **stages**. Inside a **job** block it suggests **steps**, **pool**, **dependsOn**, **condition**, and others. This means we never need to remember the full schema of navigating it interactively as we write.

At the task level, after we type **-task:** and press **Ctrl + Space**, the VS Code presents a scrollable list of all available built-in tasks. We then select **Maven@3** from the list and then press **Ctrl + Space** inside the **inputs** block, which then shows every input that task accepts, with required inputs marked distinctly. It eliminates the need to consult the Azure DevOps documentation for every task input, which substantially speeds up pipeline authoring.

Enabling Formatting with Prettier

The formatting prevents the indentation drift that accumulates when multiple team members edit the same YAML file using different editors. For this, we will add Prettier, which we can install by searching for ***Prettier - Code Formatter***.

After installation, we then configure VS Code to use Prettier as default formatter for YAML files. And then, we open VS Code settings, type **`Preferences: Open Settings (JSON)`**, and add the following entries:

```
{
  "[yaml]": {
    "editor.defaultFormatter": "esbenp.prettier-vscode",
    "editor.formatOnSave": true
  },
  "prettier.tabWidth": 2,
  "prettier.useTabs": false
}
```

With **`editor.formatOnSave`** set to **`true`**, now every time we save **`azure-pipelines.yml`**, the Prettier automatically normalises the indentation, removes trailing whitespace, and enforces consistent quoting style.

Custom Snippets for YAML Editing

The snippets are used to define short trigger words that expand into larger blocks of frequently used YAML. The VS Code ships with a built-in snippet system that works across all languages including YAML.

To use it, we first open the User Snippets editor, type **`Preferences: Configure User Snippets`**, and select **`yaml.json`**. And then, we add the following snippets to the file.

```
{
  "Azure Pipelines stage": {
    "prefix": "azstage",
    "body": [
      "- stage: ${1:StageName}",
      "  displayName: '${2:Stage display name}'",
      "  dependsOn: ${3:PreviousStage}",
      "  condition: succeeded()",
```

```
      "  jobs:",
      "  - job: ${4:JobName}",
      "    pool:",
      "      vmImage: 'ubuntu-latest'",
      "    steps:",
      "    - script: echo \"${5:placeholder}\"",
      "      displayName: '${6:Step display name}'"
    ],
    "description": "Scaffold a new Azure Pipelines stage"
  },
  "Maven build task": {
    "prefix": "mvntask",
    "body": [
      "- task: Maven@3",
      "  displayName: '${1:Build with Maven}'",
      "  inputs:",
      "    mavenPomFile: 'pom.xml'",
      "    goals: '${2:clean install}'",
      "    publishJUnitResults: true",
      "    testResultsFiles: '**/surefire-reports/TEST-*.xml'",
      "    javaHomeOption: 'JDKVersion'",
      "    jdkVersionOption: '1.17'"
    ],
    "description": "Scaffold a Maven@3 build task"
  }
}
```

With these snippets saved, we can type **`azstage`** anywhere inside a YAML file and press **`Tab`** to expand it into a fully scaffolded stage block. The **`${1:StageName}`** placeholders are tab stops, in which pressing **`Tab`** again moves the cursor to the next placeholder to fill in all required values rapidly without touching the mouse.

Validating and Testing YAML Files

Even with IntelliSense and live validation active, my always preferred practice is to run a local YAML lint pass before pushing a pipeline change.

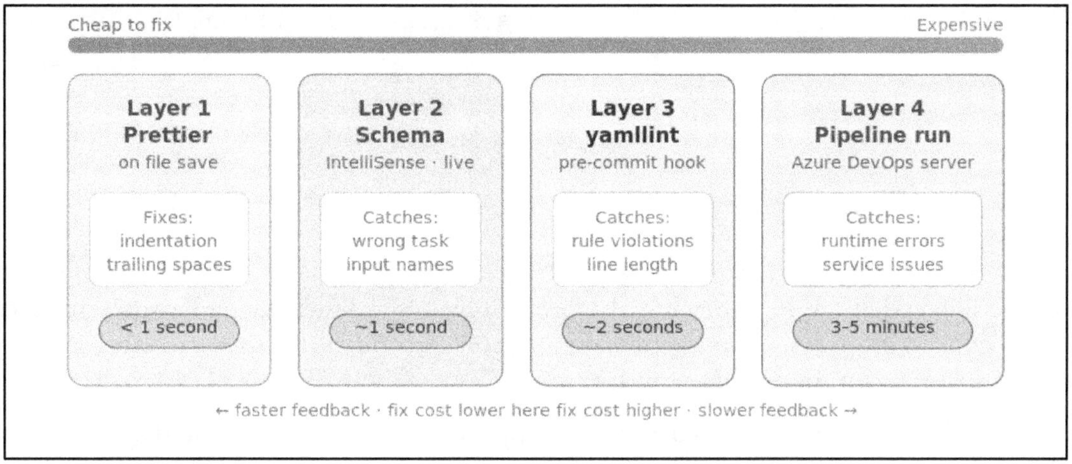

Fig 2.4: YAML Validation Shift-Left Feedback Loop

The **yamllint** command-line tool enforces the **.yamllint** rules against the file and exits with a non-zero code if any rule is violated.

So now, we will install it for once:

```
pip install yamllint --break-system-packages
```

Next, we then validate our pipeline file before every commit.

```
yamllint azure-pipelines.yml
```

After running this, if our file is clean, then it will produce no output and exits with code 0. If there is any rule violation, then it will produce a line like the following, showing the file, line number, column, severity, and message.

```
azure-pipelines.yml
  42:3    error    wrong indentation: expected 4 but found 2  (indentation)
  67:81   warning  line too long (132 > 120 characters)  (line-length)
```

Next, we can also automate this validation step by adding a Git pre-commit hook that runs **yamllint** before any commit is finalised.

We can create the hook file as follows:

```
cat > .git/hooks/pre-commit << 'EOF'
#!/bin/bash
yamllint azure-pipelines.yml
if [ $? -ne 0 ]; then
```

```
  echo "YAML lint failed. Fix the errors before committing."
  exit 1
fi
EOF
chmod +x .git/hooks/pre-commit
```

With the pre-commit hook in place, any attempt to commit a YAML file that violates our linting rules will be blocked at the local machine before the change reaches Azure Repos. This creates a fast, free feedback loop that catches formatting errors seconds after they are introduced rather than minutes later when the pipeline run fails.

In addition, the Azure Pipelines extension also supports a "Validate" command accessible via the Command Palette. It sends the current YAML file to the Azure DevOps API for schema validation and returns any errors that the local extension might miss, such as references to service connections or variable groups that do not exist in the project.

Summary

To sum up, we started by understanding Pipeline as Code and why YAML is the right language for expressing that code. We then built the pipeline incrementally, introducing the trigger, pool, variables, and steps keys one at a time. After the single-stage pipeline was running and verified, we then refactored it into a three-stage multi-stage pipeline with **`Build`**, **`Staging`**, and **`Production`** stages. We also introduced pipeline parameters for runtime flexibility, and we extracted the Maven build steps into a reusable YAML template that any other service pipeline in our organization can reference.

Later, we configured VS Code YAML tooling environment, including the Red Hat YAML extension, the Microsoft Azure Pipelines extension, Prettier for auto-formatting, a **`.yamllint`** configuration file, and a **`yamllint`** pre-commit hook. After all this, we can ensure that every **`azure-pipelines.yml`** change we push to Azure Repos is structurally valid, consistently formatted, and schema-compliant before it reaches the pipeline engine.

Chapter 3
Continuous Integration with Azure Pipelines

Overview

In the previous chapter, we had a working three-stage pipeline with a proper **`Build`** stage, a **`Staging`** stage, and a **`Production`** stage, all wired together with **`dependsOn`** and **`condition`** guards. In this chapter, we will learn to transform that foundation into a real Continuous Integration pipeline by adding everything that separates a build script from a professional CI gate. We will configure pull request triggers so that every proposed change to **`main`** is automatically validated before merging. We will add JUnit 5 and Mockito tests to our App and wire them into the pipeline correctly. We will integrate SonarCloud for static analysis and quality gate enforcement.

In addition, we will add GitHub Advanced Security for Azure DevOps to activate code scanning, secret scanning, and dependency scanning directly inside our pipeline. Finally, we will cover pipeline resource authorization and the security controls that protect our service connections and agent pools from misuse. Overall, we will have our CI pipeline to be a production-grade in every meaningful sense of the word.

Getting Started with Continuous Integration

As a practice, the process of Continuous Integration (CI) requires merging every developer's working copy back to the shared mainline branch as frequently as possible, with an automated build and test cycle validating each integration. The shorter the integration interval, the smaller each change, and the smaller each change, the easier it is to identify which specific commit introduced a regression. This feedback loop is the foundation of everything else in the DevOps delivery pipeline, and it only works if it is fully automated, fast, and trusted by the team.

For our Spring Boot REST API, CI means, every push to **`main`** and every pull request targeting **`main`** triggers our Azure Pipeline automatically. The pipeline checks out the code, compiles it, runs the full test suite, performs static analysis, scans for secrets and vulnerable dependencies, and either passes or fails with a clear summary. If it passes, the developer has high confidence that their change does not break the application. If it fails, they receive a precise report within minutes identifying exactly what went wrong and where. No manual steps, no guesswork, no delay.

The branch policy we configured on **`main`** in Chapter 1 is what gives CI its teeth. Without a policy, a developer could push directly to **`main`** and bypass the pipeline entirely. With the policy in place, every change to **`main`** must arrive via a pull request, every pull request must have at least one reviewer approval, and the pipeline must pass before the merge button becomes available. The combination of a passing pipeline and a human review is what we mean when we say a change has been validated.

Understanding Build Triggers

In chapter 2, we defined a **trigger** that fires on every push to **main**. That trigger is the continuous integration trigger. It ensures the pipeline runs on every direct commit to the protected branch.

The second trigger type is the pull request trigger, declared with the **pr** key. This trigger fires whenever a pull request is opened, updated with a new commit, or synchronised. The pull request trigger is the most important CI trigger in day-to-day development because it validates proposed changes before they merge, rather than after.

We will add both trigger types to our pipeline file in the next section.

Configuring Pull Request and Path-Filter Triggers

So now, we open **azure-pipelines.yml** and update the trigger block to include both the CI trigger and the pull request trigger. We also add path filters so that documentation-only changes do not consume a pipeline agent. The trigger block we wrote in Chapter 2 already includes **paths.exclude** for the CI trigger, and we replicate that logic for the PR trigger as well in the following:

```
trigger:
  branches:
    include:
      - main
  paths:
    exclude:
      - '**/*.md'
      - 'docs/**'
pr:
  branches:
    include:
      - main
  paths:
    exclude:
      - '**/*.md'
      - 'docs/**'
```

Here, the **pr** trigger block mirrors the structure of the **trigger** block. With **main** under **pr.branches.include**, we tell Azure Pipelines to validate any pull request whose target branch is **main**. This means that when a developer opens a pull request from **feature/add-**

tutorial-endpoint into **main**, the pipeline runs immediately against the merged state of the two branches, not just against the feature branch alone. The Azure Pipelines calls this a merge validation run, and it is more reliable than testing the feature branch in isolation because it catches integration conflicts early.

We can also configure branch exclusions under **pr.branches.exclude** for branches we never want to validate via pull request, such as long-running release branches that have their own dedicated pipeline. For our project, the configuration above is sufficient. We will test the pull request trigger later in this chapter after we have added the test suite and static analysis steps.

Testing Pull Request Trigger

To confirm that the trigger works, we create a feature branch, make a small change, push it, and open a pull request against **main**:

```
git checkout -b feature/ci-trigger-test
echo '# CI trigger test' >> README.md
git add README.md
git commit -m "Trigger test: add comment to README"
git push azure feature/ci-trigger-test
```

After the push, we navigate to Azure Repos in the Azure DevOps portal and open a new pull request from **feature/ci-trigger-test** to **main**. Within seconds of submitting the pull request, the pipeline is queued automatically. The pull request page displays a status check section showing the pipeline run name and its current state. The terminal output when the run completes confirms the trigger fired correctly.

```
##[section]Starting: Checkout feature/ci-trigger-test@merge
Syncing repository: SpringBootAPI (Azure Repos Git)
...
##[section]Starting: Build and unit-test with Maven
[INFO] BUILD SUCCESS
##[section]Finishing: Build and unit-test with Maven
```

In the above output, the **@merge** suffix in the checkout log confirms that Azure Pipelines checked out the merged state of the feature branch and **main**, which is exactly the behaviour we want.

After confirming the trigger works correctly, we close the pull request without merging.

Automating Tests with JUnit and Mockito

Our app already has one test that ships with the project scaffold. That test is a basic context-load check that simply verifies the Spring application context starts without errors. It is useful as a smoke test but gives us no confidence that the business logic works correctly.

So here, in this section, we will now write meaningful unit tests for two components of our application using JUnit 5 and Mockito, integrate them correctly into the Maven build, and confirm that the CI pipeline reports test results in the Azure DevOps Tests tab.

Understanding JUnit 5 and Mockito

JUnit 5 is the current generation of the JUnit testing framework for Java. It is composed of three modules, one is JUnit Platform, which provides the test execution engine, the other is JUnit Jupiter, which provides the **`@Test`**, **`@BeforeEach`**, **`@AfterEach`**, and assertion annotations we write in test classes; and the last one is JUnit Vintage, which provides backward compatibility with JUnit 4 tests.

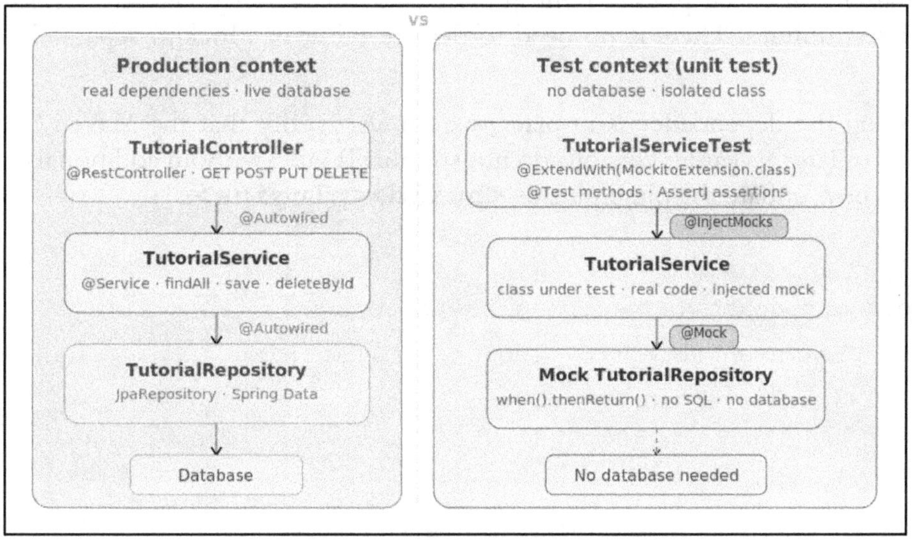

Fig 3.1: JUnit 5 and Mockito Component Relationship

For new projects, we generally prefer to work with JUnit Jupiter. The Spring Boot's test starter pulls in JUnit 5 by default through its **`spring-boot-starter-test`** dependency, so no additional Maven configuration is needed for JUnit itself.

As the most widely used mocking framework for Java, the Mockito allows us to replace real dependencies with controlled fakes during a test. It allows us to replace real dependencies with controlled fakes during a test, so that we can test one class in complete isolation without requiring a database, a network, or any other external service to be available. In an app like our one, the service classes depend on repository interfaces, which in turn communicate with the database. During unit testing we do not want to spin up a database. Instead, we tell Mockito to create a mock object that implements the repository interface, specify what it should return when called with particular arguments, and inject that mock into the service under test.

Verifying Dependencies

Since our application uses **spring-boot-starter-test**, both JUnit 5 and Mockito are already on the classpath in test scope. So here, we now open **pom.xml** and confirm if the dependency is present.

If it is not already there, then we run the following entry inside **<dependencies>** block.

```
<dependency>
    <groupId>org.springframework.boot</groupId>
    <artifactId>spring-boot-starter-test</artifactId>
    <scope>test</scope>
</dependency>
```

This single starter transitively pulls in JUnit Jupiter, Mockito, AssertJ, Hamcrest, JSONassert, and several other test utilities. There is no need to declare JUnit or Mockito separately for a Spring Boot project.

After confirming the dependency is in place, we do also verify that the Maven Surefire plugin version is 3.0.0 or later, as earlier versions do not support JUnit 5 without additional configuration. So for this, we now update the plugin inside **<build><plugins>**.

```
<plugin>
    <groupId>org.apache.maven.plugins</groupId>
    <artifactId>maven-surefire-plugin</artifactId>
    <version>3.2.5</version>
</plugin>
```

Writing Unit Test for Tutorial Service

Our App exposes CRUD operations for a **Tutorial** entity through a **TutorialController** that delegates to a **TutorialRepository**. For this, we will write a unit test for a service layer class that wraps the repository. We will first create the service class, then write the test at **TutorialService.java**:

```
package com.bezkoder.spring.jpa.h2.service;
import com.bezkoder.spring.jpa.h2.model.Tutorial;
import com.bezkoder.spring.jpa.h2.repository.TutorialRepository;
import org.springframework.beans.factory.annotation.Autowired;
import org.springframework.stereotype.Service;
```

```java
import java.util.List;
import java.util.Optional;
@Service
public class TutorialService {
    @Autowired
    private TutorialRepository tutorialRepository;
    public List<Tutorial> findAll() {
        return tutorialRepository.findAll();
    }
    public Optional<Tutorial> findById(long id) {
        return tutorialRepository.findById(id);
    }
    public Tutorial save(Tutorial tutorial) {
        return tutorialRepository.save(tutorial);
    }
    public void deleteById(long id) {
        tutorialRepository.deleteById(id);
    }
}
```

Here, the **`TutorialService`** wraps the four most common repository operations behind a service interface. Each method delegates directly to the **`TutorialRepository`**, which extends Spring Data's **`JpaRepository`**.

Next, we create the test file at **`TutorialServiceTest.java`**:

```java
package com.bezkoder.spring.jpa.h2.service;
import com.bezkoder.spring.jpa.h2.model.Tutorial;
import com.bezkoder.spring.jpa.h2.repository.TutorialRepository;
import org.junit.jupiter.api.BeforeEach;
import org.junit.jupiter.api.Test;
import org.junit.jupiter.api.extension.ExtendWith;
import org.mockito.InjectMocks;
import org.mockito.Mock;
import org.mockito.junit.jupiter.MockitoExtension;
```

```
import java.util.List;
import java.util.Optional;
import static org.assertj.core.api.Assertions.assertThat;
import static org.mockito.Mockito.*;
@ExtendWith(MockitoExtension.class)
class TutorialServiceTest {
    @Mock
    private TutorialRepository tutorialRepository;
    @InjectMocks
    private TutorialService tutorialService;
    private Tutorial sampleTutorial;
    @BeforeEach
    void setUp() {
        sampleTutorial = new Tutorial("Spring Boot CI",
                                  "CI with Azure Pipelines", true);
        sampleTutorial.setId(1L);
    }
    @Test
    void findAll_returnsTutorialList() {
        when(tutorialRepository.findAll())
            .thenReturn(List.of(sampleTutorial));
        List<Tutorial> result = tutorialService.findAll();
        assertThat(result).hasSize(1);
        assertThat(result.get(0).getTitle()).isEqualTo("Spring Boot CI");
        verify(tutorialRepository, times(1)).findAll();
    }
    @Test
    void findById_existingId_returnsTutorial() {
        when(tutorialRepository.findById(1L))
            .thenReturn(Optional.of(sampleTutorial));
        Optional<Tutorial> result = tutorialService.findById(1L);
        assertThat(result).isPresent();
        assertThat(result.get().getTitle()).isEqualTo("Spring Boot CI");
```

```java
        verify(tutorialRepository, times(1)).findById(1L);
    }
    @Test
    void findById_missingId_returnsEmpty() {
        when(tutorialRepository.findById(99L))
            .thenReturn(Optional.empty());
        Optional<Tutorial> result = tutorialService.findById(99L);
        assertThat(result).isEmpty();
        verify(tutorialRepository, times(1)).findById(99L);
    }
    @Test
    void save_persistsTutorialAndReturnsIt() {
        when(tutorialRepository.save(sampleTutorial))
            .thenReturn(sampleTutorial);
        Tutorial result = tutorialService.save(sampleTutorial);
        assertThat(result.getTitle()).isEqualTo("Spring Boot CI");
        verify(tutorialRepository, times(1)).save(sampleTutorial);
    }
    @Test
    void deleteById_callsRepositoryDelete() {
        doNothing().when(tutorialRepository).deleteById(1L);
        tutorialService.deleteById(1L);
        verify(tutorialRepository, times(1)).deleteById(1L);
    }
}
```

In the above test class, there are several important patterns:

- The **@ExtendWith(MockitoExtension.class)** annotation at the class level activates the Mockito JUnit 5 extension, which processes **@Mock** and **@InjectMocks** annotations automatically.
- The **@Mock** annotation on **tutorialRepository** instructs Mockito to create a mock implementation of **TutorialRepository** before each test.

- The **@InjectMocks** annotation on **tutorialService** tells Mockito to instantiate **TutorialService** and inject the mock repository into it via constructor injection or field injection.

Each of the above test method follows the Arrange-Act-Assert pattern. In the **findAll_returnsTutorialList** test, the Arrange phase uses **when(tutorialRepository.findAll()).thenReturn(...)** to program the mock with a predetermined response. The Act phase calls **tutorialService.findAll()**, and the Assert phase uses AssertJ's fluent API to verify the returned list has exactly one element with the correct title. The **verify** call at the end confirms that the service actually delegated to the repository rather than, for example, returning a cached value. This combination of stubbing, acting, asserting, and verifying gives us comprehensive confidence in each code path.

Running Tests Locally

Now, before pushing to Azure Repos, we need to validate the tests locally. So to do this, we run the following:

```
mvn clean test
```

Here, the Maven compiles the test classes, runs all tests annotated with **@Test**, and prints a summary as below:

```
[INFO] -------------------------------------------------------
[INFO]  T E S T S
[INFO] -------------------------------------------------------
[INFO] Running com.bezkoder.spring.jpa.h2.service.TutorialServiceTest
[INFO] Tests run: 5, Failures: 0, Errors: 0, Skipped: 0
[INFO]
[INFO] Running com.bezkoder.spring.jpa.h2.SpringBootJpaH2ApplicationTests
[INFO] Tests run: 1, Failures: 0, Errors: 0, Skipped: 0
[INFO] -------------------------------------------------------
[INFO] Results:
[INFO] Tests run: 6, Failures: 0, Errors: 0, Skipped: 0
[INFO] BUILD SUCCESS
```

In the above output, it says six tests pass, wherein five are from our new **TutorialServiceTest** class and one from the pre-existing context-load test. After this, we commit and push these new files to Azure Repos so that the CI pipeline exercises them on the next run.

```
git add src/
git commit -m "Add TutorialService with JUnit 5 and Mockito unit tests"
git push azure main
```

The push triggers a pipeline run automatically. At this point, we navigate to the Pipelines section and open the run. After the Maven build step completes, the Tests tab on the run summary page shows all six tests passing, their individual durations, and a breakdown by class. From this point forward, any change that causes a test to fail will also cause the pipeline to fail, and thereby it blocks any downstream stages from running.

Code Quality using SonarCloud

There are tools that can examine source code without executing it and identify issues that automated tests alone cannot catch. Some of the examples are like, overly complex methods, code duplication, inconsistent null handling, hard-coded credentials, and security vulnerabilities that arise from common coding mistakes. In our app, I am thinking to use SonarCloud. It is worth using, as it integrates directly with Azure DevOps through a marketplace extension, publishes analysis results to a web dashboard, and can fail the pipeline if the project does not meet a configurable quality gate.

Setting up SonarCloud

To get it set, we go to ***https://sonarcloud.io*** and sign in using our Azure DevOps account. The SonarCloud supports OAuth sign-in with GitHub, Bitbucket, and Azure DevOps identities. After signing in, we click ***Import an organization*** and select our Azure DevOps organization **`GitforGits`**. The SonarCloud reads the list of projects from our organization and presents them for selection. We then select **`SpringBootAPI`** and click ***Set Up***. The SonarCloud creates a project and generates a project key that we will reference in our pipeline file. The project key follows the format **`GitforGits_SpringBootAPI`** unless we customise it during setup.

With the project created, we generate an authentication token. So, we click our account avatar in the top right corner of the SonarCloud portal, select ***My Account***, then ***Security***, and click ***Generate Tokens***. We give the token a descriptive name such as **`azure-devops-pipeline`** and click ***Generate***. The portal displays the token value once. We copy it immediately because it will not be shown again. We store this token as a secret variable in our Azure DevOps pipeline in the next step.

Storing Token as a Pipeline Secret

The pipeline secrets are sensitive values that should never appear in the YAML file or in build logs. The Azure Pipelines stores them as secret variables in a variable group or directly on the pipeline definition. So here, we will now navigate to our pipeline in the Azure DevOps portal, click ***Edit***, then click ***Variables*** in the top right corner. With this ready, we click ***New variable***, set the name to **SONAR_TOKEN**, paste the token value we copied from SonarCloud, and tick ***Keep this value secret***. We then click ***OK*** and ***Save***. After this, the variable is now available to all pipeline steps as **$(SONAR_TOKEN)**, and its value will be masked in all log output.

Installing SonarCloud Extension

To do this, we at first, navigate to the Azure DevOps Marketplace by clicking the shopping bag icon in the top right of the Azure DevOps portal and searching for ***SonarCloud***. We proceed to install the extension published by ***SonarSource*** to our **GitforGits** organization. This extension adds three pipeline tasks to our task library. They are **SonarCloudPrepare@1**, **SonarCloudAnalyze@1**, and **SonarCloudPublish@1**, and each plays a distinct role in the analysis workflow and must appear in the correct position within the pipeline steps.

Adding SonarCloud Tasks to Pipeline

The SonarCloud analysis must wrap the Maven build step rather than appearing before or after it in isolation. The correct sequence is Prepare, then Maven build, then Analyze, and finally Publish. The Prepare task instruments the build process so that the Maven compiler emits the metadata SonarCloud needs.

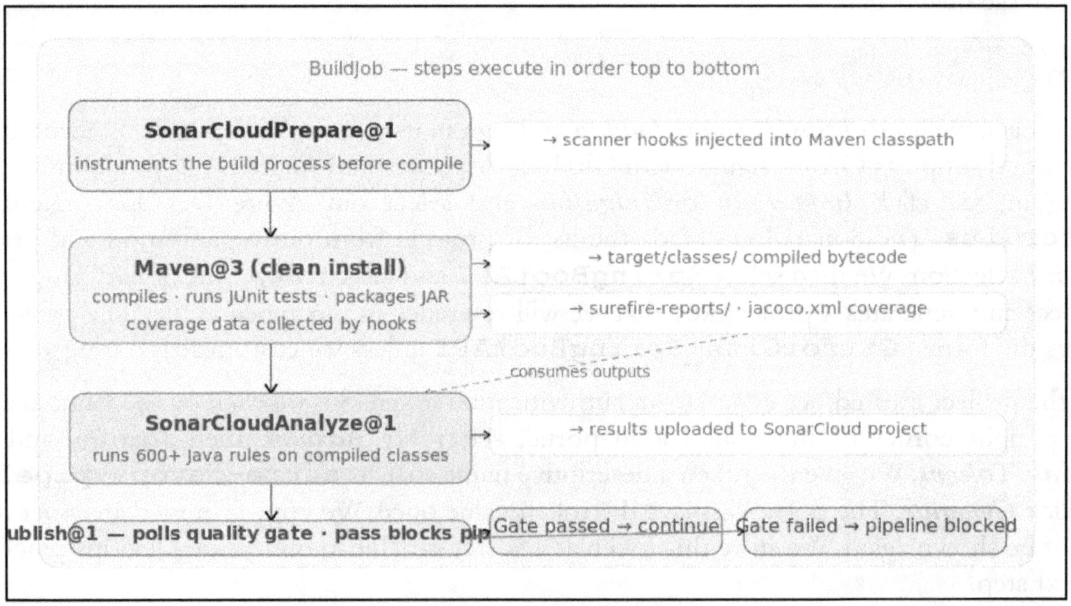

Fig 3.2: SonarCloud Pipeline Task Sequence

If we run Maven before Prepare, the analysis will be incomplete. So here, we will update the **BuildJob** steps inside our **azure-pipelines.yml** file to incorporate all four tasks in the correct order.

```
  steps:
  - task: SonarCloudPrepare@1
    displayName: 'Prepare SonarCloud analysis'
    inputs:
      SonarCloud: 'SonarCloud'
      organization: 'gitforgits'
      scannerMode: 'Other'
      extraProperties: |
        sonar.projectKey=GitforGits_SpringBootAPI
        sonar.projectName=SpringBootAPI
        sonar.java.binaries=target/classes
sonar.coverage.jacoco.xmlReportPaths=target/site/jacoco/jacoco.xml
  - task: Maven@3
    displayName: 'Build, test, and instrument for SonarCloud'
    inputs:
      mavenPomFile: 'pom.xml'
      goals: '$(mavenGoals)'
      publishJUnitResults: true
      testResultsFiles: '**/surefire-reports/TEST-*.xml'
      javaHomeOption: 'JDKVersion'
      jdkVersionOption: '1.17'
      mavenVersionOption: 'Default'
      sonarQubeRunAnalysis: false
  - task: SonarCloudAnalyze@1
    displayName: 'Run SonarCloud analysis'
  - task: SonarCloudPublish@1
    displayName: 'Publish SonarCloud quality gate result'
    inputs:
      pollingTimeoutSec: '300'
  - task: CopyFiles@2
    displayName: 'Copy JAR to staging directory'
    inputs:
```

```
        sourceFolder: '$(System.DefaultWorkingDirectory)/target'
        contents: '*.jar'
        targetFolder: '$(Build.ArtifactStagingDirectory)'
    - task: PublishBuildArtifacts@1
      displayName: 'Publish JAR as pipeline artifact'
      inputs:
        PathtoPublish: '$(Build.ArtifactStagingDirectory)'
        ArtifactName: '$(artifactName)'
        publishLocation: 'Container'
```

In the above, the **SonarCloud** value under the **SonarCloud** input key refers to the name of a service connection we must create in Azure DevOps before the pipeline will run successfully. So here, we will navigate to ***Project Settings*** at the bottom of the left navigation, then ***Service connections***, then ***New service connection***, and select ***SonarCloud*** from the list. We paste our **SONAR_TOKEN** value into the token field and name the connection **SonarCloud**. This name must match the value in the YAML file exactly, including capitalisation.

Also, the **scannerMode: 'Other'** value tells the preparation task to instrument the build without running the scanner itself during the Maven step. The **SonarCloudAnalyze@1** task runs the scanner separately after Maven completes. This two-step approach gives much better control over which Maven goals run before the analysis and is the recommended mode for Maven projects where we want coverage data included in the analysis.

Committing SonarCloud Configuration

After this, we then commit the updated pipeline file and push it to Azure Repos to trigger a fresh pipeline run.

```
git add azure-pipelines.yml
git commit -m "Integrate SonarCloud static analysis into CI pipeline"
git push azure main
```

With this, the pipeline run now includes four additional steps between checkout and the Maven build. After the run completes, we navigate to our project dashboard on ***https://sonarcloud.io***. The dashboard shows the analysis results organised under four categories. ***Bugs*** are issues likely to cause a functional failure, such as a null dereference or an unclosed resource. The ***vulnerabilities*** are security weaknesses such as hard-coded passwords or insecure deserialization patterns.

At the top of the dashboard, the SonarCloud also displays the Quality Gate status as either ***Passed*** or ***Failed***. The default quality gate fails the analysis if any new bugs, vulnerabilities, or security hotspots are introduced by the code changes in the current analysis period. If the quality gate fails, the **SonarCloudPublish@1** task will cause the pipeline step to fail as well, which in turn fails the entire **Build** stage and prevents the **Staging** and **Production** stages from running. And, this is precisely the enforcement model we want, where no code reaches staging unless it passes both automated tests and static analysis.

Integrating GitHub Advanced Security for Azure DevOps

GitHub Advanced Security for Azure DevOps, is very often abbreviated as GHAzDO. It brings three of GitHub's most powerful security capabilities, like code scanning, secret scanning, and dependency scanning, directly into Azure Pipelines. Unlike SonarCloud, which focuses on code quality and maintainability, the GHAzDO is specifically designed to find security vulnerabilities. The code scanning uses the CodeQL analysis engine to detect vulnerabilities such as SQL injection, cross-site scripting, and insecure deserialization in the application source. The secret scanning monitors every commit for credential patterns such as API keys, passwords, and connection strings.

Enabling GitHub Advanced Security on Repository

The GHAzDO is enabled at the repository level in Azure DevOps. We will now navigate to our **SpringBootAPI** project, click ***Repos***, then ***Repositories*** under the project settings. We find the **SpringBootAPI** repository in the list, click the three-dot menu, and select ***Advanced Security***. On the Advanced Security settings page, we toggle on all three scanning features of ***Code scanning***, ***Secret scanning***, and ***Dependency scanning***. The secret scanning activates immediately for all existing commits in the repository and begins scanning push events in real time from the moment it is enabled. The code scanning and dependency scanning require pipeline tasks to be added, which we do in the following subsections.

Adding Advanced Security Dependency Scanning Task

The dependency scanning in GHAzDO works by reading the **pom.xml** file and comparing every declared dependency against the GitHub Advisory Database, which is the same vulnerability database that powers GitHub Dependabot. Any dependency with a known CVE, regardless of whether it is a direct dependency or a transitive one, is flagged with its severity and a suggested remediation.

We then add the dependency scanning task to the **BuildJob** steps. It should run after the Maven build so that the resolved dependency tree is available in the **target/** directory. We can now add the following task immediately after the **Maven@3** task in **azure-pipelines.yml**.

```
- task: AdvancedSecurity-Dependency-Scanning@1
  displayName: 'Scan dependencies for known vulnerabilities'
```

The **AdvancedSecurity-Dependency-Scanning@1** task requires no additional inputs for a standard Maven project. It automatically locates the **pom.xml** file, resolves the dependency tree, and submits the results to the GHAzDO alert system. The alerts will appear under ***Repos*** > ***Advanced Security*** in the Azure DevOps portal, where we can triage, dismiss, or link them to work items for tracking.

Adding CodeQL Code Scanning Task

The code scanning uses the CodeQL engine to build a semantic model of our Java source code and then queries that model for known vulnerability patterns. For Java applications, the CodeQL requires a compilation step during analysis so that it can trace data flows through the compiled classes. The **AdvancedSecurity-CodeQL-Init@1** task initialises the CodeQL database before the build, and the **AdvancedSecurity-CodeQL-Analyze@1** task finalises the analysis and uploads results after the build. Now here, both tasks must wrap the Maven compilation step in the same way that the SonarCloud preparation task wraps it.

WNext, we then update the **BuildJob** steps to include the CodeQL init task before **SonarCloudPrepare@1** and the CodeQL analyze task after **SonarCloudPublish@1**. The complete ordered sequence of steps in the build job is now as follows.

```
steps:
- task: AdvancedSecurity-CodeQL-Init@1
  displayName: 'Initialise CodeQL database'
  inputs:
    languages: 'java'
- task: SonarCloudPrepare@1
  displayName: 'Prepare SonarCloud analysis'
  inputs:
    SonarCloud: 'SonarCloud'
    organization: 'gitforgits'
    scannerMode: 'Other'
    extraProperties: |
      sonar.projectKey=GitforGits_SpringBootAPI
      sonar.projectName=SpringBootAPI
      sonar.java.binaries=target/classes
- task: Maven@3
  displayName: 'Build, test, and instrument for analysis'
  inputs:
```

```
      mavenPomFile: 'pom.xml'
      goals: '$(mavenGoals)'
      publishJUnitResults: true
      testResultsFiles: '**/surefire-reports/TEST-*.xml'
      javaHomeOption: 'JDKVersion'
      jdkVersionOption: '1.17'
      mavenVersionOption: 'Default'
      sonarQubeRunAnalysis: false
  - task: AdvancedSecurity-Dependency-Scanning@1
    displayName: 'Scan dependencies for known vulnerabilities'
  - task: SonarCloudAnalyze@1
    displayName: 'Run SonarCloud analysis'
  - task: SonarCloudPublish@1
    displayName: 'Publish SonarCloud quality gate result'
    inputs:
      pollingTimeoutSec: '300'
  - task: AdvancedSecurity-CodeQL-Analyze@1
    displayName: 'Finalise CodeQL analysis and upload results'
  - task: CopyFiles@2
    displayName: 'Copy JAR to staging directory'
    inputs:
      sourceFolder: '$(System.DefaultWorkingDirectory)/target'
      contents: '*.jar'
      targetFolder: '$(Build.ArtifactStagingDirectory)'
  - task: PublishBuildArtifacts@1
    displayName: 'Publish JAR as pipeline artifact'
    inputs:
      PathtoPublish: '$(Build.ArtifactStagingDirectory)'
      ArtifactName: '$(artifactName)'
      publishLocation: 'Container'
```

The ordering here is deliberately done. The **AdvancedSecurity-CodeQL-Init@1** runs first so that CodeQL begins observing the compilation before any code is compiled. **SonarCloudPrepare@1** runs second for the same reason. Now here, both tools require presence during compilation to produce accurate results. The **Maven@3** task runs third and performs the actual compilation. The dependency scanning runs fourth because it needs the resolved **pom.xml** artefacts. And, the SonarCloud analysis and publication run fifth and sixth. Finally, the **AdvancedSecurity-CodeQL-Analyze@1** runs seventh after everything else, since it finalises the CodeQL database that was being built throughout the entire compilation. Artifact copy and publish run last.

Viewing Advanced Security Alerts

After we commit and push the updated pipeline file and the run completes, all GHAzDO alerts become visible in the Azure DevOps portal under ***Repos*** > ***Advanced Security***. The Alerts page organises findings by type into three tabs, like ***Dependencies***, ***Code scanning***, and ***Secret scanning***. Each alert shows the rule that triggered it, the file and line number where it was detected, the severity level (Critical, High, Medium, or Low), and the date it was introduced.

```
git add azure-pipelines.yml
git commit -m "Add GHAzDO code scanning and dependency scanning to CI pipeline"
git push azure main
```

The dependency scanning tab may show alerts if any of the Spring Boot dependencies pulled in by the parent POM have known CVEs. Each alert includes a ***Fix*** suggestion that links to the recommended version upgrade. We can also link any alert to an Azure Boards work item by clicking the alert row and selecting ***Link work item***. It creates a bidirectional connection between the security finding and our sprint backlog, which is the correct way to track remediation work without losing the security context.

Pipeline Security and Resource Authorization

Every time our pipeline needs to access a protected resource for the first time, such as a service connection to SonarCloud, an agent pool, a variable group, or a secure file, the Azure Pipelines requires explicit authorization before the run can proceed. This authorization model exists to prevent a malicious or accidental pipeline modification from accessing resources it was never intended to use. Knowing how authorization works and how to manage it correctly is essential for maintaining a secure CI environment, especially as the number of pipelines and shared resources in our organization grows.

Understanding Resource Authorization in Azure Pipelines

When a pipeline run encounters a protected resource for the first time, it pauses and displays an authorization prompt in the portal. An administrator must review the request and explicitly grant permission for that specific pipeline to use that specific resource. Once granted, the authorization persists for future runs without requiring repeated approvals. If the authorization is not granted within the timeout window, which as of 2025 is 7 days, the run is automatically cancelled.

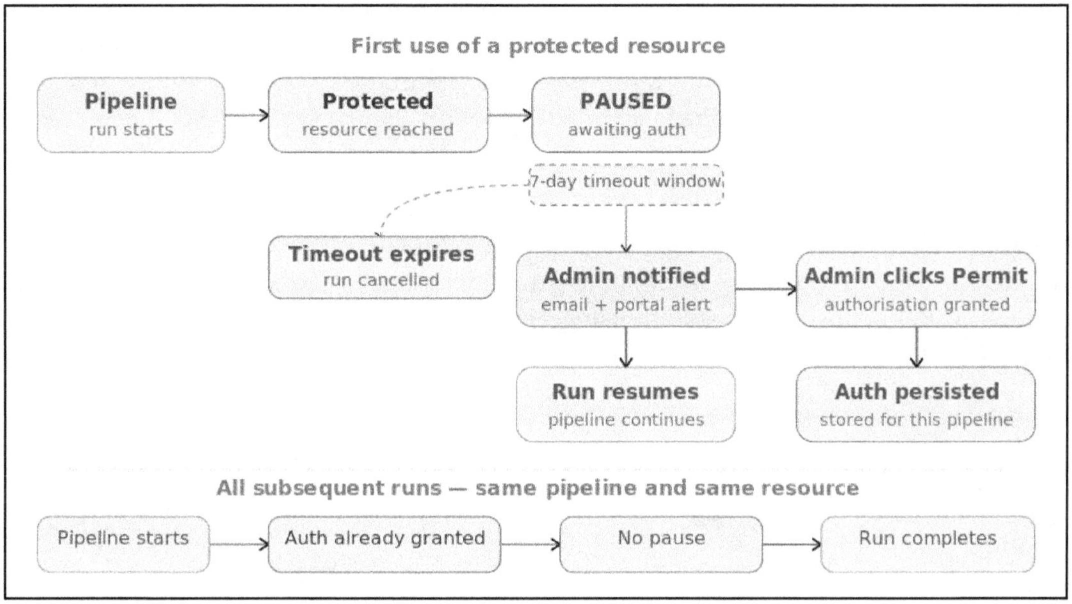

Fig 3.3: Pipeline Resource Authorization Flow

The resources that require authorization in Azure Pipelines are agent pools, service connections, variable groups, secure files, and environments. For our pipeline, the **`SonarCloud`** service connection we created earlier is a protected resource, as is the **`ubuntu-latest`** agent pool. The first time our updated pipeline runs after we added the SonarCloud tasks, we may see the pipeline pause at the **`SonarCloudPrepare@1`** step with a message like the following one:

```
This pipeline needs permission to access a resource before this run
can continue.
Resource: SonarCloud (Service Connection)
Pipeline: SpringBootAPI > Build stage
[ View ] [ Permit ]
```

At this point, we then click ***Permit*** to grant the authorization. The run resumes immediately. And, the subsequent runs will not be paused for the same resource unless the authorization is explicitly revoked.

So, to manage existing authorizations, we navigate to ***Project Settings*** > ***Service connections***, select the **`SonarCloud`** service connection, and click ***Security*** in the top right. The security panel shows every pipeline that has been granted access and allows us to revoke access for any of them.

Protecting Pipelines from Injection Attacks

The Pipeline YAML files present a security risk if we allow untrusted input to influence pipeline behavior. The most common attack vector is an expression injection, where an attacker crafts a branch name, commit message, or pull request title that contains pipeline expression syntax such as **cat /etc/passwd** or **$(cat ~/.ssh/id_rsa)**. If our pipeline passes these values directly into a **script** task using runtime expression syntax like **$(Build.SourceBranchName)**, then the pipeline agent executes the injected command with the agent's privileges.

The mitigation here is straightforward. It always pass untrusted values through environment variables rather than inlining them into **script** blocks. The correct pattern uses the **env** key on a script task to map a pipeline variable to an environment variable, and then references the environment variable inside the script using the shell's **$ENV_VAR** syntax rather than the pipeline's **$(variable)** syntax.

```
- script: |
    echo "Branch: $BRANCH_NAME"
    echo "Commit: $BUILD_ID"
  displayName: 'Print build context safely'
  env:
    BRANCH_NAME: $(Build.SourceBranchName)
    BUILD_ID: $(Build.BuildId)
```

With this above pattern, the pipeline expression **$(Build.SourceBranchName)** is resolved by the Azure Pipelines engine before the script runs and is passed to the shell as a plain string environment variable. The shell cannot interpret it as a command, regardless of what characters it contains. This pattern should be used for any **script** task that references pipeline variables derived from user-controlled inputs, including branch names, pull request titles, commit messages, and any variable whose value comes from an external system.

Monitoring Build Logs

The Azure DevOps provides detailed, step-level logs for every pipeline run. Each step in the run has its own expandable log section accessible from the run detail page. With this ready, we navigate to ***Pipelines*** > our most recent run > ***Build stage*** > ***BuildJob***, and we see every step listed vertically. If we click here any step, it then expands its log stream.

The Tests tab on the run summary page shows a visual breakdown of test results, with passed, failed, and skipped counts and a duration histogram. Clicking any failed test opens the full stack trace. The Artifacts tab shows the **springboot-api** artifact and allows us to browse and download the files it contains. The Analytics tab, available for pipelines that have run at least several times, shows pass rate trends, average duration trends, and individual step duration breakdowns over time.

If the Maven build step fails, the log shows the Maven output verbatim, including the specific test class and method that failed, the assertion message, and the full stack trace. There is no need to reproduce the failure locally first. We can read the pipeline log, identify the issue, push a fix, and confirm the fix via the next pipeline run, all without leaving the Azure DevOps portal.

Validating CI Pipeline

With every component now in place, we perform a final end-to-end validation of the complete CI pipeline. To understand better, we will create a new feature branch, make a meaningful code change that exercises our new test, push the branch, and open a pull request against **`main`**.

The pull request trigger fires automatically, the pipeline runs through all steps, and we observe the results before approving the merge.

```
git checkout -b feature/add-search-by-title
```

Next, we will open:

`src/main/java/com/bezkoder/spring/jpa/h2/service/TutorialService.java`

And, we then add a new method that searches for tutorials by title.

```
    public List<Tutorial> findByTitleContaining(String title) {
        return tutorialRepository.findByTitleContaining(title);
    }
```

We will also add a corresponding test method to **`TutorialServiceTest.java`** that verifies the new method delegates correctly to the repository.

```
    @Test
    void findByTitleContaining_returnsMatchingTutorials() {
        when(tutorialRepository.findByTitleContaining("Spring"))
            .thenReturn(List.of(sampleTutorial));
        List<Tutorial> result =
            tutorialService.findByTitleContaining("Spring");
        assertThat(result).hasSize(1);
        assertThat(result.get(0).getTitle()).contains("Spring");
        verify(tutorialRepository, times(1))
            .findByTitleContaining("Spring");
```

```
    }
```

After this, we commit both changes and push the feature branch to Azure Repos.

```
git add src/
git commit -m "Add findByTitleContaining to TutorialService with test"
git push azure feature/add-search-by-title
```

Later, we then open a pull request from **`feature/add-search-by-title`** to **`main`** in the Azure DevOps portal. The PR trigger fires within seconds. On the pull request page, the status check section shows the pipeline run name and its progress. After approximately two to three minutes, the full suite of steps completes and the run summary shows the following results:

```
Stage: Build                SUCCEEDED    3m 14s
  Step: Initialise CodeQL database             OK     12s
  Step: Prepare SonarCloud analysis            OK      8s
  Step: Build, test, and instrument            OK  1m 43s
  Step: Scan dependencies                      OK     22s
  Step: Run SonarCloud analysis                OK     18s
  Step: Publish SonarCloud quality gate        OK      6s
  Step: Finalise CodeQL analysis               OK     19s
  Step: Copy JAR to staging directory          OK      2s
  Step: Publish JAR as pipeline artifact       OK      4s
Tests: 6 passed, 0 failed
Quality Gate: Passed
Artifacts: springboot-api published (1 file)
Stage: Staging              SUCCEEDED     18s
Stage: Production           SUCCEEDED     17s
```

As you can sdee in the above, every step passes. The Tests tab shows seven tests passing (the original six plus the new search test). The SonarCloud quality gate passes. The CodeQL and dependency scans complete without critical alerts. The pull request status check turns green, and combined with the required reviewer approval from our branch policy, the merge button becomes available. This is exactly the CI enforcement model we set out to build. The code cannot reach **`main`** unless it compiles cleanly, all tests pass, static analysis is satisfied, and a human reviewer has approved the change.

Summary

Throughout this chapter we converted the structural multi-stage pipeline from Chapter 2 into a fully operational CI gate. We began by adding both the push trigger and the pull request trigger to **azure-pipelines.yml**, with path filters that prevent documentation changes from consuming pipeline agents unnecessarily. We then wrote five meaningful JUnit 5 unit tests for our **TutorialService** class using Mockito to isolate the repository layer, confirmed they ran cleanly with **mvn clean test**, and pushed them to Azure Repos where the CI pipeline picked them up automatically.

Next, we integrated SonarCloud for static code quality analysis by creating a SonarCloud service connection, storing the authentication token as a pipeline secret, and wrapping the Maven build step with the **SonarCloudPrepare@1**, **SonarCloudAnalyze@1**, and **SonarCloudPublish@1** tasks in the correct order. We then added GitHub Advanced Security for Azure DevOps. The security alerts also now appear in the Advanced Security portal and can be linked directly to Azure Boards work items for remediation tracking. Finally, we covered pipeline resource authorization, explaining how Azure Pipelines protects service connections and agent pools from unauthorised access, how to pre-authorize resources to avoid pipeline pauses, and how to prevent expression injection attacks by passing pipeline variables through environment variables rather than inlining them in script blocks.

Chapter 4
Continuous Delivery with Azure Pipelines

Overview

So far, our CI pipeline compiled the App, ran a growing suite of JUnit and Mockito tests, enforced a SonarCloud quality gate, and scanned for secrets and vulnerable dependencies using GitHub Advanced Security. The **`Staging`** and **`Production`** stages in our **`azure-pipelines.yml`** file still ran placeholder **`echo`** commands. In this chapter, we replace those placeholders with real deployments. We provision Azure App Service instances for staging and production using Bicep, our chosen Infrastructure as Code language, wire the **`AzureWebApp@1`** deployment task into each stage, configure approval gates and business-hours checks on the production environment, implement a blue-green deployment strategy using App Service deployment slots, and finish by introducing feature flags with Azure App Configuration for safe progressive delivery.

Every step in this chapter builds directly on the pipeline file, the application code, and the Azure DevOps organization we have been working with since Chapter 1. We also address ARM templates briefly as a legacy reference topic, explaining what they are, why Bicep supersedes them for new projects, and how to migrate an existing ARM template to Bicep when that need arises.

Continuous Delivery and Deployment Strategies

Continuous Delivery (CD) is the practice of keeping the main branch in a state that can be deployed to production at any moment, and of automating every step of the journey from a merged commit to a running deployment. The CD carries that validated artifact forward into one or more target environments in a controlled, repeatable, and auditable way. The Azure Pipelines bridges the two by using same **`azure-pipelines.yml`** file to express both the build and the deployment workflow.

The deployment strategies available in Azure Pipelines determines how a new version of the application is introduced to users. The choice of strategy reflects the team's tolerance for risk, the availability requirements of the service, and the capability of the infrastructure to support traffic splitting or parallel instances. There are three strategies available natively in Azure Pipelines YAML deployment jobs, such as **`runOnce`**, **`rolling`**, and **`canary`**. A fourth common pattern, blue-green, is implemented at the infrastructure level using Azure App Service deployment slots, and we will configure it in detail later in this chapter.

Deployment Strategies in Azure Pipelines

The simplest strategy is ***runOnce***. It deploys the new version to every target in the environment in a single operation. This is the strategy we used in the placeholder stages in Chapter 2. It is appropriate when we have a single target instance and can tolerate a brief window of downtime or when the App Service deployment mechanism handles the hot-swap internally. For staging environments with no real user traffic, **`runOnce`** is always the right choice. For production, it is acceptable only when combined with blue-green slot swapping, which eliminates the downtime window entirely.

Then there is ***rolling,*** which deploys the new version to a fraction of the target instances at a time. It allows the system to serve a mix of old and new versions during the rollout. It is most relevant when deploying to a group of virtual machines or container instances where gradual replacement is possible. For our App Service deployment, we do not use the rolling strategy directly, but the concept is important to understand as the application scales horizontally in Chapter 7.

And finally, there is ***canary***, which deploys the new version to a small percentage of the environment's capacity first, observes behaviour for a defined period, and then proceeds to full rollout if no errors are detected. The Azure Pipelines supports canary deployments natively in the YAML deployment job strategy, and App Service traffic splitting can be used to implement the same pattern at the infrastructure level. We will use the **`canary`** strategy key in a later subsection of this chapter when we configure traffic weighting for our staging slot.

Blue-Green Deployment with App Service Slots

In a blue-green deployment, we maintain two production-equivalent environments, referred to as blue and green. At any given moment, one environment serves all live traffic while the other hosts the new version being prepared for release. When the new version is verified, traffic is switched instantly and atomically between the two environments. If the new version has a critical defect, traffic is switched back to the previous environment with equal speed, restoring the previous state without requiring a new deployment.

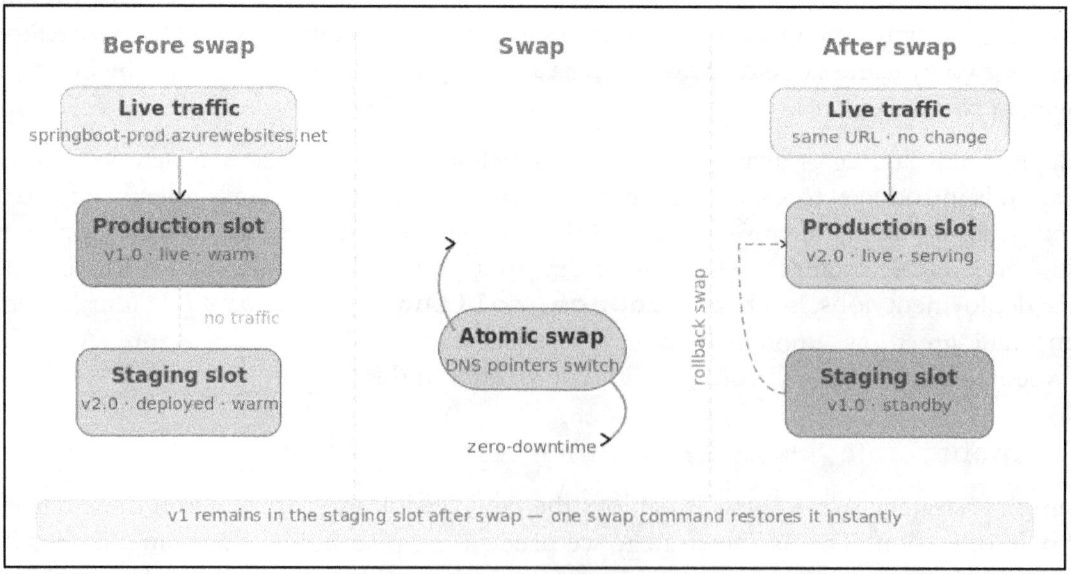

Fig 4.1: Blue-Green Deployment with App Service Slot Swap

Natively, the Azure App Service implements this pattern through deployment slots. Every App Service instance can have one or more named slots in addition to the default production slot.

Each slot is a fully independent App Service instance with its own URL, its own configuration, and its own application state. The swap operation exchanges the content and settings of two slots atomically, with App Service performing a warm-up of the new slot before completing the swap. The result is a zero-downtime deployment where the production slot never serves uninitialised code.

In our setup, the production App Service has two slots. The ***production*** slot serves live traffic. The ***staging-slot*** slot receives every deployment from the pipeline. After deployment to ***staging-slot*** completes and a manual approval gate is satisfied, the pipeline performs the swap that promotes ***staging-slot*** to ***production***. The old production content moves automatically to ***staging-slot***, where it remains available for an instant rollback if needed.

Provisioning Infrastructure with Bicep

As Microsoft's domain-specific language for declaring Azure infrastructure, Bicep compiles to ARM JSON at deployment time. It compiles to ARM JSON at deployment time, which means every resource type available in ARM is equally available in Bicep, but the authoring experience is dramatically cleaner. Bicep files are shorter, read more naturally, support first-class modules for reuse, provide IntelliSense through the Bicep VS Code extension, and eliminate the redundant verbosity of raw JSON. For all new projects, Microsoft recommends Bicep over ARM JSON templates, and we follow that recommendation throughout this book. We address the relationship between Bicep and ARM more fully in a dedicated subsection at the end of this section.

Installing Bicep CLI and Extension

The Bicep CLI is included in the Azure CLI starting from version 2.20.0. Because we installed Azure CLI in Chapter 1, we already have the Bicep CLI available. So at first, we will verify its presence and being up to date:

```
az bicep version
```

This prints the installed version. If an upgrade is available, we install it with the following.

```
az bicep upgrade
```

```
Bicep CLI version 0.29.47 (a6c24e2222)
```

We also install the Bicep extension for VS Code. In the Extensions pane we search for ***Bicep*** and install the extension published by ***Microsoft***. This extension provides syntax highlighting, IntelliSense for all Azure resource types and their properties, real-time validation, and a decompiler that converts existing ARM JSON to Bicep. We will use the decompiler later in this chapter when we discuss ARM template migration.

Writing Bicep Template for App Service

We can now create an **infra/** directory in our repository to store all infrastructure definitions. We can add **infra/**** to the CI trigger's path include list so that infrastructure changes always run the pipeline, while still excluding documentation changes as we configured in Chapter 3.

```
mkdir -p infra
touch infra/appservice.bicep
```

We then open **infra/appservice.bicep** in VS Code and write the following Bicep template. This template provisions an App Service Plan and two App Service instances, like the one for staging and one for production. The production instance also receives a deployment slot named **staging-slot** for our blue-green deployment pattern.

```
@description('Azure region for all resources')
param location string = resourceGroup().location
@description('Environment prefix used in resource names')
param envPrefix string = 'springboot'
@description('App Service Plan SKU')
@allowed(['B1', 'B2', 'S1', 'S2', 'P1v3'])
param skuName string = 'B1'
var planName = '${envPrefix}-plan'
var stagingAppName = '${envPrefix}-staging'
var productionAppName = '${envPrefix}-prod'
resource appServicePlan 'Microsoft.Web/serverfarms@2023-01-01' = {
  name: planName
  location: location
  sku: {
    name: skuName
    tier: skuName == 'B1' ? 'Basic' : 'Standard'
  }
  properties: {
    reserved: true  // Required for Linux
  }
}
resource stagingApp 'Microsoft.Web/sites@2023-01-01' = {
```

```
  name: stagingAppName
  location: location
  properties: {
    serverFarmId: appServicePlan.id
    siteConfig: {
      linuxFxVersion: 'JAVA|17-java17'
      appSettings: [
        { name: 'SPRING_PROFILES_ACTIVE', value: 'staging' }
      ]
    }
    httpsOnly: true
  }
}
resource productionApp 'Microsoft.Web/sites@2023-01-01' = {
  name: productionAppName
  location: location
  properties: {
    serverFarmId: appServicePlan.id
    siteConfig: {
      linuxFxVersion: 'JAVA|17-java17'
      appSettings: [
        { name: 'SPRING_PROFILES_ACTIVE', value: 'production' }
      ]
    }
    httpsOnly: true
  }
}
resource stagingSlot 'Microsoft.Web/sites/slots@2023-01-01' = {
  parent: productionApp
  name: 'staging-slot'
  location: location
  properties: {
    serverFarmId: appServicePlan.id
```

```
    siteConfig: {
      linuxFxVersion: 'JAVA|17-java17'
    }
    httpsOnly: true
  }
}
output stagingUrl string =
'https://${stagingApp.properties.defaultHostName}'
output productionUrl string =
'https://${productionApp.properties.defaultHostName}'
output stagingSlotUrl string =
  'https://${productionApp.name}-staging-slot.azurewebsites.net'
```

In the above template, several Bicep-specific features appear:

- The **@description** decorator documents each parameter inline, which VS Code surfaces as a tooltip when we hover over the parameter name elsewhere in the file.
- The **@allowed** decorator on **skuName** restricts the permitted values to a list we control, preventing accidental deployments to expensive premium tiers.
- The **var** declarations compute resource names from the **envPrefix** parameter, ensuring that staging and production names always follow the same naming convention without duplication.
- The **resource** keyword declares an Azure resource with its type, API version, name, and properties as a single coherent block.

The Bicep resolves the parent reference at compile time and generates the correct ARM resource ID and dependency declaration automatically. The **output** declarations at the bottom expose the App Service URLs so that the pipeline can read them after deployment and use them for smoke testing.

Creating ARM Service Connection

Before our pipeline can deploy to Azure, it needs an authenticated connection to our Azure subscription. At this point, we create this as a service connection in Azure DevOps. We will now navigate to ***Project Settings*** > ***Service connections*** > ***New service connection*** and select ***Azure Resource Manager***. On the next screen we select ***Workload identity federation (automatic)***, which is the recommended authentication method as of 2025. It creates a federated identity credential in Azure Active Directory that the pipeline uses without storing a long-lived secret. We name the service connection **springboot-azure** and note this name precisely, as it appears in every deployment task in our pipeline file.

Creating Resource Group and Deploying Bicep Template

We provision the resource group and deploy the Bicep template once manually from the VS Code terminal to confirm the infrastructure is correct before we automate it through the pipeline.

```
az group create --name SpringBootRG --location eastus
```

We then run the Bicep deployment, passing **`envPrefix`** as a parameter override. The **`--what-if`** flag performs a dry run and shows us exactly what Azure will create without actually creating anything.

```
az deployment group create \
  --resource-group SpringBootRG \
  --template-file infra/appservice.bicep \
  --parameters envPrefix=springboot skuName=B1 \
  --what-if
```

After we review the what-if output and confirm it matches our intent, we run the same command without **`--what-if`** to perform the actual deployment.

```
az deployment group create \
  --resource-group SpringBootRG \
  --template-file infra/appservice.bicep \
  --parameters envPrefix=springboot skuName=B1
```

After we submit the deployment, the Azure provisions all four resources in the correct dependency order, namely the App Service Plan first, then both App Service instances, and finally the deployment slot. The terminal prints a summary when the deployment completes, including the output values we declared in the template.

```
  provisioningState: Succeeded
  outputs:
    stagingUrl:     { value: https://springboot-staging.azurewebsites.net
}
    productionUrl:  { value: https://springboot-prod.azurewebsites.net }
    stagingSlotUrl: { value: https://springboot-prod-staging-
slot.azurewebsites.net }
```

Adding Bicep Deployment Stage to Pipeline

With the infrastructure verified manually, we add a **ProvisionInfra** stage to our **azure-pipelines.yml** that runs before the **Staging** deployment stage. This stage deploys the Bicep template automatically on every pipeline run, which is safe because Bicep deployments are idempotent. Here, running the same template twice against the same resource group produces the same result without duplicating resources.

```
- stage: ProvisionInfra
  displayName: 'Provision App Service infrastructure with Bicep'
  dependsOn: Build
  condition: and(succeeded(), eq('${{ parameters.runDeployment }}', true))
  jobs:
  - job: DeployBicep
    displayName: 'Deploy Bicep template'
    pool:
      vmImage: 'ubuntu-latest'
    steps:
    - task: AzureCLI@2
      displayName: 'Deploy infra/appservice.bicep to SpringBootRG'
      inputs:
        azureSubscription: 'springboot-azure'
        scriptType: 'bash'
        scriptLocation: 'inlineScript'
        inlineScript: |
          az deployment group create \
            --resource-group SpringBootRG \
            --template-file infra/appservice.bicep \
            --parameters envPrefix=springboot skuName=B1 \
            --mode Incremental
```

The **AzureCLI@2** task authenticates using our **springboot-azure** service connection and then runs the inline Bash script as an authenticated Azure CLI session. The **--mode Incremental** flag tells Azure Resource Manager to add or update resources described in the template without touching resources in the resource group that the template does not mention. This is the safest mode for pipeline deployments because it prevents accidental deletion of manually created resources during development.

Deploying Application to App Service

With the infrastructure provisioned, we now replace the placeholder deployment steps in the **Staging** and **Production** stages with real **AzureWebApp@1** tasks. Each task downloads the **springboot-api** artifact published by the **Build** stage and deploys it to the correct App Service instance. This is the build-once, deploy-many pattern in practice. Here, the same **.jar** file that passed all CI checks is the exact artifact that lands in both staging and production.

Deploying to Staging App Service

So, we will now update the **Staging** stage in **azure-pipelines.yml**. The **dependsOn** now references **ProvisionInfra** instead of **Build**, since provisioning must complete before we can deploy to the freshly created App Service. The deployment job downloads the artifact, verifies the **.jar** file is present, and then deploys it using the **AzureWebApp@1** task.

```
- stage: Staging
  displayName: 'Deploy to Staging'
  dependsOn: ProvisionInfra
  condition: and(succeeded(), eq('${{ parameters.runDeployment }}', true))
  jobs:
  - deployment: DeployStaging
    displayName: 'Deploy Spring Boot to springboot-staging'
    pool:
      vmImage: 'ubuntu-latest'
    environment: 'staging'
    strategy:
      runOnce:
        deploy:
          steps:
          - download: current
            artifact: $(artifactName)
            displayName: 'Download springboot-api artifact'
          - script: |
              echo "Artifact contents:"
              ls $(Pipeline.Workspace)/$(artifactName)/
            displayName: 'Verify artifact before deployment'
```

```
        - task: AzureWebApp@1
          displayName: 'Deploy JAR to springboot-staging App Service'
          inputs:
            azureSubscription: 'springboot-azure'
            appType: 'webAppLinux'
            appName: 'springboot-staging'
            package: '$(Pipeline.Workspace)/$(artifactName)/*.jar'
            runtimeStack: 'JAVA|17-java17'
            startUpCommand: 'java -jar /home/site/wwwroot/*.jar'
```

The **appType: 'webAppLinux'** input is required for Linux-based App Service instances. The **startUpCommand** tells App Service how to invoke the Spring Boot fat JAR. Without this command, App Service may default to a Tomcat configuration that does not apply to our embedded-server packaging.

Adding Post-Deployment Smoke Test

After deploying to staging, we add a smoke test step that calls the API's health endpoint and verifies it returns an HTTP 200 response. A smoke test is not a substitute for the full test suite, which already ran in the **Build** stage, but it confirms the deployment itself succeeded and the application started correctly on the App Service instance. With this ready, we add the smoke test as an additional step in the **runOnce.deploy.steps** block, after the **AzureWebApp@1** task.

```
        - script: |
            echo "Running smoke test against staging..."
            sleep 30  # Allow App Service to start the JVM
            STATUS=$(curl -s -o /dev/null -w '%{http_code}' \
              https://springboot-
staging.azurewebsites.net/api/tutorials)
            echo "HTTP status: $STATUS"
            if [ "$STATUS" != "200" ]; then
              echo "Smoke test FAILED. Expected 200, got $STATUS"
              exit 1
            fi
            echo "Smoke test PASSED."
          displayName: 'Smoke test staging deployment'
```

```
        env:
          BRANCH_NAME: $(Build.SourceBranchName)
```

The script waits 30 seconds after the **`AzureWebApp@1`** task reports success, allowing the JVM inside the App Service container to initialise fully. Spring Boot applications typically take between 10 and 20 seconds to start depending on the number of beans loaded, so a 30-second buffer is conservative but safe. The **`curl`** command calls the **`/api/tutorials`** endpoint and captures only the HTTP status code. A response of **`200`** confirms the application is alive and the REST layer is responding. Any other status causes the script to exit with code 1, which fails the pipeline step and prevents the production deployment from proceeding.

Deploying to Production with Blue-Green Swap

The **`Production`** stage uses the blue-green pattern we discussed earlier. Rather than deploying directly to the production App Service, we deploy to the **`staging-slot`** and then perform an App Service slot swap. The swap is atomic. Here, the App Service routes all traffic from the old production content to the new content simultaneously, with no intermediate state where some requests go to the old version and others go to the new version. We proceed to update the **`Production`** stage as follows.

```
- stage: Production
  displayName: 'Deploy to Production (blue-green via slot swap)'
  dependsOn: Staging
  condition: and(succeeded(), eq('${{ parameters.runDeployment }}', true))
  jobs:
  - deployment: DeployProduction
    displayName: 'Deploy to staging-slot and swap to production'
    pool:
      vmImage: 'ubuntu-latest'
    environment: 'production'
    strategy:
      runOnce:
        deploy:
          steps:
          - download: current
            artifact: $(artifactName)
            displayName: 'Download springboot-api artifact'
          - task: AzureWebApp@1
```

```
          displayName: 'Deploy JAR to production staging-slot'
          inputs:
            azureSubscription: 'springboot-azure'
            appType: 'webAppLinux'
            appName: 'springboot-prod'
            deployToSlotOrASE: true
            resourceGroupName: 'SpringBootRG'
            slotName: 'staging-slot'
            package: '$(Pipeline.Workspace)/$(artifactName)/*.jar'
            runtimeStack: 'JAVA|17-java17'
            startUpCommand: 'java -jar /home/site/wwwroot/*.jar'
        - task: AzureAppServiceManage@0
          displayName: 'Swap staging-slot to production'
          inputs:
            azureSubscription: 'springboot-azure'
            action: 'Swap Slots'
            webAppName: 'springboot-prod'
            resourceGroupName: 'SpringBootRG'
            sourceSlot: 'staging-slot'
            swapWithProduction: true
```

In the above, the **`deployToSlotOrASE: true`** input on the **`AzureWebApp@1`** task combined with **`slotName: 'staging-slot'`** directs the deployment to the slot rather than the production slot. After the JAR is deployed and the JVM has started inside the slot, the **`AzureAppServiceManage@0`** task performs the swap. The **`swapWithProduction: true`** input tells App Service to swap the named source slot with the production slot, which is the default and most common swap configuration. After the swap completes, **`staging-slot`** holds the previous production version, ready for an immediate rollback if the new production deployment reveals an unexpected issue.

Managing Environments, Approval Gates, and Checks

The Azure DevOps Environments are named containers that represent a deployment target. When a pipeline's **`deployment`** job references an environment by name, the Azure DevOps records the deployment history for that environment, tracks which pipeline runs deployed to it and when, and enforces any approval or check rules configured on that environment. We created the **staging** and **production** environments as placeholder definitions back in Chapter 2.

In this topic, we will configure them properly with approval gates, business-hours checks, and required reviewer assignments.

Setting up Staging and Production Environments

We will now navigate to ***Pipelines*** > ***Environments*** in the Azure DevOps portal. If the **staging** and **production** environments do not yet exist, we create them by clicking ***New environment***. For each environment we set the name, an optional description, and the resource type. For our App Service deployment we select ***None*** as the resource type because our deployment target is an Azure resource managed through a service connection rather than an Azure DevOps-managed VM or Kubernetes namespace.

With both environments created, the pipeline will automatically record deployment history against them as runs complete. We can view the deployment history for any environment by clicking it on the Environments page. The history shows every pipeline run that deployed to the environment, the branch and commit that triggered it, the person who triggered or approved it, and the outcome.

Configuring Approval Gates on Production Environment

We then click on the **production** environment and navigate to the ***Approvals and checks*** tab. We can now click **+** ***Add*** and select ***Approvals*** from the list of check types.

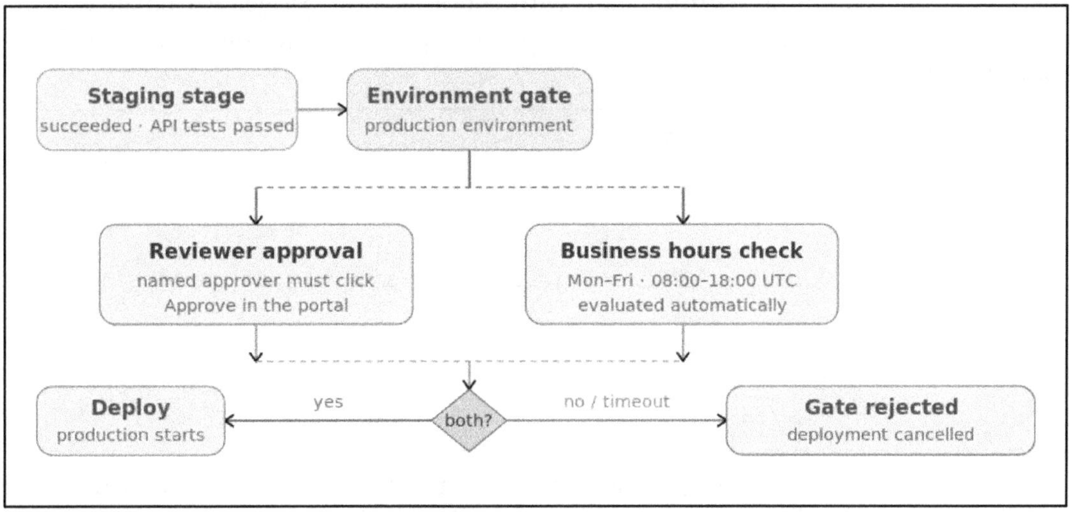

Fig 4.2: Production Environment Approval Gate

On the approval configuration panel, we add the names or Azure Active Directory group identifiers of the people authorised to approve production deployments. We also configure the following additional settings to make the approval gate practical:

- We then set ***Instructions to approvers*** to a short message such as ***"Review the staging smoke test results and SonarCloud quality gate before approving."*** This message appears in the approval notification email and in the pipeline run UI, so approvers know exactly what to check before clicking Approve.
- We then set ***Timeout*** to ***1440 minutes*** (24 hours), which gives approvers a full business day to respond. If the timeout expires without an approval or rejection, the pipeline stage is automatically cancelled, which is safer than allowing it to proceed unreviewed.
- We also tick ***Allow approvers to approve their own runs*** only if our team is small enough that the same person who triggers the pipeline may also be the only available approver. For larger teams this option should remain unticked to enforce the four-eyes principle.

Observing Approval Gate in Action

After this, we then commit and push the updated **`azure-pipelines.yml`** file to trigger a full pipeline run as shown below:

```
git add azure-pipelines.yml infra/appservice.bicep

git commit -m "Complete CD pipeline: Bicep infra, App Service deploy, slot swap, approval gate"

git push azure main
```

The pipeline runs through **`Build`**, **`ProvisionInfra`**, and **`Staging`** automatically. When it reaches the **`Production`** stage, execution pauses. The pipeline run page shows the **`Production`** stage tile in a ***Waiting*** state with a notification badge. An email is sent to all configured approvers with a direct link to the approval page. The terminal view of the waiting stage looks like the following:

```
Stage: Build                SUCCEEDED    3m 22s

Stage: ProvisionInfra       SUCCEEDED      48s

Stage: Staging              SUCCEEDED    2m 14s

  Smoke test PASSED. HTTP 200 from springboot-staging.azurewebsites.net

Stage: Production           WAITING FOR APPROVAL

  Pending approval from: [your-approver-name]

  Timeout: 23h 59m remaining
```

After an approver reviews the staging smoke test results and the SonarCloud dashboard and is satisfied with the build quality, they click ***Approve*** on the pipeline run page. The **`Production`** stage resumes immediately, deploys the **`.jar`** to **`staging-slot`**, and performs the slot swap. The entire production deployment, including the swap, completes in under two minutes.

Feature Flags and Progressive Delivery with Azure App Configuration

With approval gates and deployment slots, we have full control over when and how a new version of the application reaches production. The feature flags give us control over which features within that version are visible to which users after deployment. A feature flag is a boolean configuration value stored externally to the application that the application reads at runtime to decide whether to execute a code path. Through a simple flag toggle, an operator can expose a new feature to internal users first, then to a percentage of external users, and finally to everyone, all without deploying new code.

Azure App Configuration is a managed service that stores key-value configuration pairs and feature flags for applications. It integrates natively with Spring Boot through the **spring-cloud-azure-appconfiguration-config** library, which reads configuration values from App Configuration at application startup and refreshes them at a configurable interval. This allows us to change a feature flag value in the Azure portal and have every running instance of our application pick up the change within seconds, without a redeployment.

Provisioning Azure App Configuration with Bicep

We proceed to add an App Configuration resource to our **infra/appservice.bicep** template. App Configuration has a free tier that provides 10 MB of storage and 1,000 requests per day, which is sufficient for development and small production workloads. We append the following resource declaration to the existing Bicep file.

```
resource appConfig 'Microsoft.AppConfiguration/configurationStores@2023-
03-01' = {
  name: '${envPrefix}-appconfig'
  location: location
  sku: {
    name: 'free'
  }
  properties: {
    disableLocalAuth: false
  }
}
output appConfigEndpoint string = appConfig.properties.endpoint
```

We also add an App Configuration key-value and feature flag directly through the Bicep template. This ensures that every time the infrastructure is provisioned, the initial flags exist in a known state rather than requiring manual portal configuration.

```
resource searchFeatureFlag
'Microsoft.AppConfiguration/configurationStores/keyValues@2023-03-01' = {
  parent: appConfig
  name: '.appconfig.featureflag~2FenableSearchByTitle'
  properties: {
    value: '{"id":"enableSearchByTitle","description":"Enable search by
title API","enabled":false}'
    contentType: 'application/vnd.microsoft.appconfig.ff+json;charset=utf-
8'
  }
}
```

The **enableSearchByTitle** flag corresponds to the **findByTitleContaining** method we added to **TutorialService** in Chapter 3.

At startup, the flag is set to **false**, which means the endpoint will return a **404** or a controlled error response when the feature is disabled. When we are ready to expose the search feature to users, we toggle the flag to **true** in the App Configuration portal without deploying any new code.

Adding Configuration Dependency to Spring Boot

We will now open **pom.xml** and add the Spring Cloud Azure App Configuration starter and the Spring Cloud Azure BOM to manage version alignment.

```
<dependencyManagement>
  <dependencies>
    <dependency>
      <groupId>com.azure.spring</groupId>
      <artifactId>spring-cloud-azure-dependencies</artifactId>
      <version>5.14.0</version>
      <type>pom</type>
      <scope>import</scope>
    </dependency>
  </dependencies>
</dependencyManagement>
<dependencies>
```

```
  <!-- existing dependencies above -->
  <dependency>
    <groupId>com.azure.spring</groupId>
    <artifactId>spring-cloud-azure-appconfiguration-config</artifactId>
  </dependency>
  <dependency>
    <groupId>com.azure.spring</groupId>
    <artifactId>spring-cloud-azure-feature-management-web</artifactId>
  </dependency>
</dependencies>
```

In the above, the **spring-cloud-azure-appconfiguration-config** starter handles the connection to Azure App Configuration and the automatic refresh of configuration values. The **spring-cloud-azure-feature-management-web** starter provides the **@FeatureGate** annotation and the **FeatureManager** bean that our controller will use to check flag state at request time.

Here, we do not pin explicit versions because both are governed by the **spring-cloud-azure-dependencies** BOM we declared in **dependencyManagement**.

Configuring Application to Connect App Configuration

We then open **src/main/resources/application.properties** and add the App Configuration connection properties. Now here, rather than hardcoding the endpoint URL, we use a Spring Boot property placeholder that reads from an environment variable, and set this environment variable in the App Service configuration through our Bicep template, so the application receives the correct endpoint automatically in each environment.

```
spring.cloud.azure.appconfiguration.stores[0].endpoint=${AZURE_APPCONFIG_E
NDPOINT}
spring.cloud.azure.appconfiguration.stores[0].feature-flags.enabled=true
spring.cloud.azure.appconfiguration.refresh-interval=30s
```

The **refresh-interval** property of **30s** tells the library to poll App Configuration every 30 seconds for updated values. When an operator toggles a feature flag in the portal, every running application instance picks up the change within 30 seconds. This is the key advantage of feature flags over deployment-based feature exposure, where the feedback loop between enabling a feature and seeing it live is measured in seconds, not minutes.

Gating Search Endpoint Behind Feature Flag

Next, we then update **`TutorialController.java`** to inject **`FeatureManager`** bean and gate the search endpoint behind the **`enableSearchByTitle`** flag.

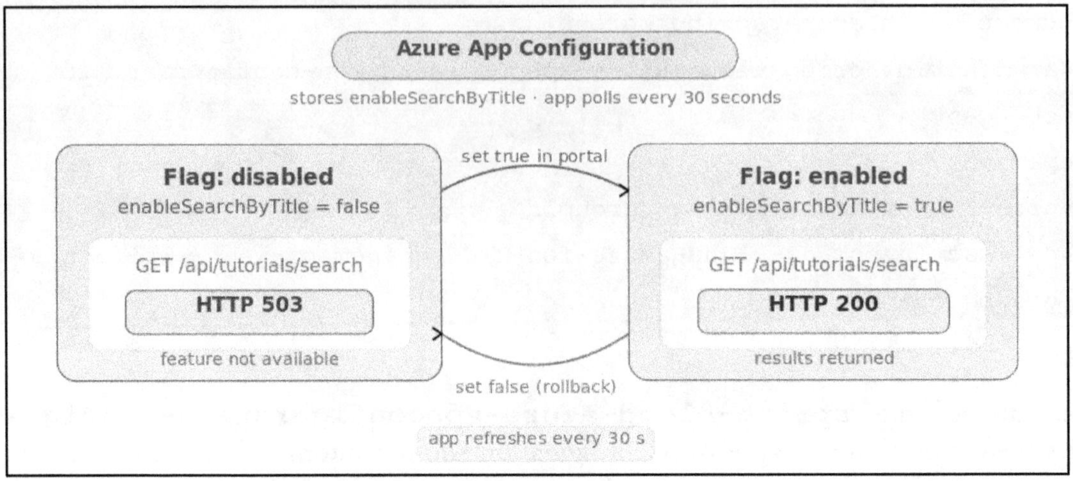

Fig 4.3: Feature Flag State Diagram

When the flag is disabled, the endpoint returns a **`503 Service Unavailable`** response with a message explaining that the feature is not yet available. When the flag is enabled, the endpoint delegates to **`TutorialService.findByTitleContaining()`** as normal.

```
import com.azure.spring.cloud.feature.management.FeatureManager;
import org.springframework.http.HttpStatus;
import org.springframework.http.ResponseEntity;
// Add to existing TutorialController class
@Autowired
private FeatureManager featureManager;
@GetMapping("/tutorials/search")
public ResponseEntity<?> searchByTitle(@RequestParam String title) {
    if (!featureManager.isEnabled("enableSearchByTitle")) {
        return ResponseEntity
            .status(HttpStatus.SERVICE_UNAVAILABLE)
            .body("Search by title is not yet available.");
    }
    List<Tutorial> results =
        tutorialService.findByTitleContaining(title);
    return ResponseEntity.ok(results);
```

```
}
```

In the above, the **featureManager.isEnabled("enableSearchByTitle")** call checks the current state of the flag in real time. If the flag value changed since the last refresh, the library returns the updated value on the next call, within the 30-second refresh window. This means the same deployed binary can expose or hide the search feature purely by toggling a value in the App Configuration portal, which is exactly the progressive delivery capability we set out to build.

Committing Feature Flag Changes and Running Full Pipeline

After this, we then commit all the changes from this section together and push them to **main** to trigger a complete end-to-end pipeline run.

```
git add infra/appservice.bicep pom.xml \
        src/main/resources/application.properties \

src/main/java/com/bezkoder/spring/jpa/h2/controller/TutorialController.jav
a
git commit -m "Add Bicep infra, App Service deploy, slot swap, and feature
flag"
git push azure main
```

The pipeline runs through all five stages. After the **Staging** smoke test passes and a reviewer approves the **Production** gate, the slot swap completes and the application is live.

With the **enableSearchByTitle** flag set to **false** in App Configuration, the **/api/tutorials/search** endpoint returns **503** to all callers. To enable the feature for a selected set of internal testers, we navigate to the App Configuration portal, and we find the **enableSearchByTitle** flag, and toggle it to **true**. Within 30 seconds every running instance of the application exposes the search endpoint without a single new deployment.

Summary

Throughout this chapter, we transformed our three-stage pipeline from a structural skeleton into a fully operational continuous delivery system. We started by discussing the three native Azure Pipelines deployment strategies, **runOnce**, **rolling**, and **canary**, and the blue-green pattern implemented at the infrastructure level via App Service deployment slots. We then wrote a Bicep template in **infra/appservice.bicep** that provisions an App Service Plan, a staging App Service instance, a production App Service instance, and a **staging-slot** on the production instance, all parameterised and idempotent.

Later, we created an Azure Resource Manager service connection using workload identity federation, added a **ProvisionInfra** stage to the pipeline that deployed the Bicep template on every run, and updated the **Staging** and **Production** stages with real **AzureWebApp@1** deployment tasks. We then configured the **production** environment in Azure DevOps with a required approval gate, a 24-hour timeout, and a business-hours check that restricts deployments to weekday working hours. Finally, we introduced Azure App Configuration as a feature flag store, provisioned it through Bicep, added the Spring Cloud Azure dependencies to **pom.xml**, and gated the **findByTitleContaining** search endpoint behind the **enableSearchByTitle** feature flag.

Chapter 5
Managing Dependencies with Azure Artifacts

Overview

So far, we had a fully operational continuous delivery pipeline that builds our App, enforces quality and security gates, and deploys it to Azure App Service through a slot-swap blue-green strategy. One important aspect of that pipeline that we treated as a given is dependency resolution, where Maven downloads every library our application needs from the public Maven Central repository at build time. For small projects that works fine, but for teams building at scale it introduces several risks. A public registry can serve a package that was quietly altered after we last used it, a dependency can disappear if its author removes it, or network policies in a secure environment may block outbound access to public registries entirely.

The Azure Artifacts keeps the capability to solve all these problems by acting as a private, managed package registry that our team controls. In this chapter, we will configure Azure Artifacts feeds for the four ecosystems our project touches, like Maven for our App, **npm** for any frontend assets, PyPI for Python utility scripts in our pipeline, and NuGet for shared .NET libraries in a hypothetical multi-stack organisation. We also configure upstream sources so that each feed proxies the corresponding public registry, giving us a single trusted source for all dependencies. We then wire every feed into our **`azure-pipelines.yml`** file, configure package retention policies, and walk through version pinning, upgrading, and rolling back packages in a way that keeps the CI pipeline stable at every step.

Getting Started with Azure Artifacts

As the package management service inside Azure DevOps, the Azure Artifacts hosts private feeds for multiple protocol types. It hosts private feeds for five protocol types, which are Maven, **npm**, NuGet, Python (PyPI), and Universal Packages. A feed is a named, versioned store of packages that enforces access control separately from the broader Azure DevOps project. The producers push packages to a feed; consumers pull packages from it. A single feed can hold packages of multiple protocol types when the feed is configured in multi-protocol mode, but in practice most teams create one feed per ecosystem so that access policies, retention rules, and upstream configurations remain clean and purposeful.

The most powerful feature of Azure Artifacts feeds is the **upstream source system**. An upstream source is a pointer to a public or external registry, such as Maven Central, npmjs.com, PyPI.org, or nuget.org, that the feed proxies on behalf of its consumers. When a developer requests a package that does not yet exist in the private feed, the feed fetches it from the upstream source, stores a cached copy in the private feed, and serves it to the consumer. On every subsequent request for the same package version, the feed serves the cached copy rather than contacting the public registry again. This gives teams a guaranteed stable copy of every package version they have ever used, immune to deletion or modification by the upstream author.

Now here, every package stored in an Azure Artifacts feed is subject to a retention policy that automatically deletes old package versions after a configurable number of days or after the total count of versions for a given package exceeds a threshold. The retention policies keep feed storage under control without requiring manual housekeeping. The packages that should be kept indefinitely, such as the version currently in production, can be promoted to a ***Release*** view or marked with the ***Keep forever*** flag to exempt them from automatic deletion.

In the following, we will configure all these options as we build each feed.

Creating Maven Feed

At this point, we navigate to our **SpringBootAPI** project in Azure DevOps and click ***Artifacts*** in the left-hand navigation. The Artifacts hub opens on a list of all existing feeds in the project. We then click ***+ New feed*** to create our first feed. On the new feed dialog we fill in the following values.

```
Name          : SpringBootDependencies
Visibility    : Members of GitforGits organisation (private)
Upstream sources: Include packages from public sources (enable upstream)
Scope         : Project  (SpringBootAPI)
```

Here, we are enabling ***Include packages from public sources*** to automatically add Maven Central and the Google Android Maven repository as upstream sources for this feed. We can also customise the upstream list after the feed is created, but accepting the defaults here ensures that the feed can resolve any Maven dependency our Spring Boot project might need from the moment it exists. After clicking ***Create***, the Azure DevOps provisions the feed within seconds and opens the feed's detail page.

Configuring Feed Permissions

Every feed has its own permission model independent of the project's general access settings. So, we click ***Feed settings*** in the top right of the feed page and navigate to the ***Permissions*** tab. The default configuration grants the project's ***Contributors*** group the ***Contributor*** role on the feed, which allows them to push and pull packages. The ***Project Administrators*** group receives the ***Owner*** role. For our team, this default is sufficient. In larger organisations where package publishing should be restricted to the CI pipeline only and developers should be able to pull but not push, we would change the Contributors group to the ***Reader*** role and add the build service account identity with the ***Contributor*** role.

Connecting Maven to Azure Artifacts Feed

To authenticate Maven against our private feed, we need to supply credentials in two places, one is the **~/.m2/settings.xml** file on our local machine for manual development work, and the other is **azure-pipelines.yml** file for pipeline builds. We will handle the pipeline authentication in a dedicated subsection. For local development, we first generate a Personal Access Token that Maven will use as a password.

With this ready, we navigate to ***User settings*** in the top right corner of the Azure DevOps portal, select ***Personal access tokens***, and click ***+ New Token***. We give the token the name **maven-local-dev** and grant it the ***Packaging: Read and Write*** scope. We copy the token value immediately because it will not be displayed again. We then open **~/.m2/settings.xml** in VS Code and add the server entry below, replacing **YOUR_PAT_TOKEN** with the value we just copied.

```
<settings>
  <servers>
    <server>
      <id>SpringBootDependencies</id>
      <username>GitforGits</username>
      <password>YOUR_PAT_TOKEN</password>
    </server>
  </servers>
</settings>
```

In the above, the **<id>** value **SpringBootDependencies** must match exactly the **id** values we will use in the **pom.xml** repository and distribution management sections. Any mismatch between the server ID in **settings.xml** and the repository ID in **pom.xml** causes Maven to skip authentication and produce a **401 Unauthorized** error when it tries to contact the feed. This ID pairing is the most common configuration mistake teams make when first connecting Maven to Azure Artifacts, so we establish the naming convention here and keep it consistent throughout all subsequent configuration steps.

Configuring 'pom.xml' for Azure Artifacts

Now, we will proceed to open **pom.xml** and add the repository declaration and distribution management block that point Maven at our feed. The repository URL is available on the feed's ***Connect to feed*** page. There, we click that button, select ***Maven***, and copy the URL shown under the ***Project setup*** section:

```
<repositories>
  <repository>
    <id>SpringBootDependencies</id>
<url>https://pkgs.dev.azure.com/GitforGits/SpringBootAPI/_packaging/Spring
BootDependencies/maven/v1</url>
```

```
    <releases><enabled>true</enabled></releases>
    <snapshots><enabled>true</enabled></snapshots>
  </repository>
</repositories>
<distributionManagement>
  <repository>
    <id>SpringBootDependencies</id>

<url>https://pkgs.dev.azure.com/GitforGits/SpringBootAPI/_packaging/Spring
BootDependencies/maven/v1</url>
  </repository>
</distributionManagement>
```

Here, the **<repositories>** block tells Maven to search our Azure Artifacts feed when resolving dependencies declared in **<dependencies>**. Because we enabled upstream sources when we created the feed, the Maven Central packages are served through this feed URL as well. The **<distributionManagement>** block tells Maven where to push packages when we run **mvn deploy**, which is the command we use later in this chapter to publish our application as a versioned artifact to the feed.

Authenticating Pipeline to Maven Feed

When the pipeline's **Maven@3** task runs on a Microsoft-hosted agent, it has no access to our local **settings.xml** file. We need to authenticate the agent to the feed using the **MavenAuthenticate@0** task, which reads the **springboot-azure** service connection we created in Chapter 4 and injects the correct credentials into the Maven settings automatically.

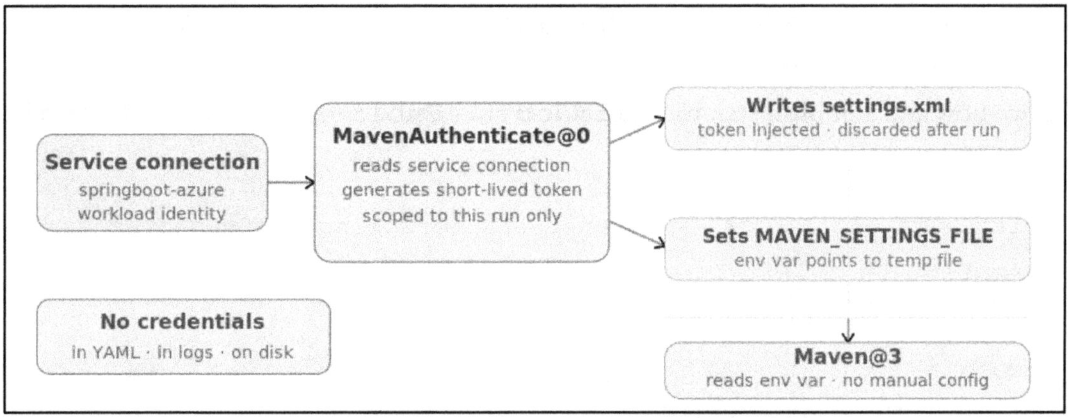

Fig 5.1: MavenAuthenticate@0 Credential Injection Flow

So here, we will now add this task at the very beginning of the **BuildJob** steps, before any Maven task runs.

```
steps:
- task: MavenAuthenticate@0
  displayName: 'Authenticate Maven to Azure Artifacts feed'
  inputs:
    artifactsFeeds: 'SpringBootDependencies'
- task: AdvancedSecurity-CodeQL-Init@1
  displayName: 'Initialise CodeQL database'
  inputs:
    languages: 'java'
# ... remaining steps unchanged from Chapter 4
```

In the above, the **MavenAuthenticate@0** task generates a temporary **settings.xml** file on the agent, populating it with a short-lived token scoped to the current pipeline run. It then sets the **MAVEN_SETTINGS_FILE** environment variable so that all subsequent Maven invocations on the same agent automatically pick up the generated settings without any additional configuration in the **Maven@3** task inputs.

This is the correct and most secure approach because no long-lived PAT ever touches the pipeline YAML file or the agent's file system beyond the duration of a single run.

Publishing Application JAR to Maven Feed

Once Maven is authenticated, we can publish the compiled application artifact to the feed as a versioned Maven package. It allows other services or pipelines in our organisation to depend on a specific version of our Spring Boot API as a library, or to download a known good release without rebuilding the source.

So here, we now add a publish step to **BuildJob** after **PublishBuildArtifacts@1** task:

```
- task: Maven@3
  displayName: 'Publish versioned JAR to SpringBootDependencies feed'
  inputs:
    mavenPomFile: 'pom.xml'
    goals: 'deploy'
    options: '-DskipTests'
    publishJUnitResults: false
```

```
        javaHomeOption: 'JDKVersion'
        jdkVersionOption: '1.17'
        mavenVersionOption: 'Default'
```

in the above, we pass **-DskipTests** because the tests already ran in the earlier **Maven@3** step. If we run them again during **mvn deploy**, it would double the build time without adding any new information. The **deploy** goal reads the version from the **<version>** element in **pom.xml** and pushes the artifact to the distribution repository we configured in the **<distributionManagement>** block.

After the step completes, the artifact appears in the **SpringBootDependencies** feed under the group ID and artifact ID declared in **pom.xml**. The next is that, we commit all the changes we have made to **pom.xml** and **azure-pipelines.yml** and push them to **main** to trigger a pipeline run.

```
git add pom.xml azure-pipelines.yml
git commit -m "Configure Azure Artifacts Maven feed and pipeline authentication"
git push azure main
```

After the run completes, we navigate to the **SpringBootDependencies** feed in the Artifacts hub. The feed page shows the newly published package with its group ID, artifact ID, version number, and the date it was published.

Following is going to be the terminal output once the deploy step confirms that the publish has succeeded:

```
[INFO] --- maven-deploy-plugin:3.1.1:deploy (default-deploy) ---
[INFO] Uploading to SpringBootDependencies:
[INFO]   https://pkgs.dev.azure.com/GitforGits/SpringBootAPI/_packaging/
[INFO]       SpringBootDependencies/maven/v1/com/bezkoder/
[INFO]       spring-boot-3-rest-api-example/0.0.1-SNAPSHOT/
[INFO]       spring-boot-3-rest-api-example-0.0.1-SNAPSHOT.jar
[INFO] Uploaded to SpringBootDependencies: 42.3 kB at 1.2 MB/s
[INFO] BUILD SUCCESS
```

Setting up npm Feed

The **npm** is the package manager for the Node.js ecosystem and the most widely used package manager in the world by volume. Even in a Java-first project like our App, development workflows through build tools, linters, documentation generators, and frontend asset pipelines. In a microservices architecture where our Spring Boot API is accompanied by a React or Angular frontend, the npm dependency management becomes directly critical to the overall build.**npmdevelopment workflows through build tools, linters, documentation generators, and frontend asset pipelines. In a microservices architecture where our Spring Boot API is accompanied by a React or Angular frontend, the npm dependency management becomes directly critical to the overall build.** appears in modern development workflows through build tools, linters, documentation generators, and frontend asset pipelines. In a microservices architecture where our Spring Boot API is accompanied by a React or Angular frontend, the npm dependency management becomes directly critical to the overall build.

So here ,we will now create a dedicated **npm** feed in Azure Artifacts so that all **npm** packages our pipelines consume are served from our private registry, with npmjs.com proxied as an upstream source.

Creating 'npm' Feed

At first, we will return to the Artifacts hub and click **+ *New feed*** again. And then, we will fill in the following values for the **npm** feed.

```
Name         : SpringBootNpm
Visibility   : Members of GitforGits organisation (private)
Upstream sources: Include packages from public sources (npmjs.com)
Scope        : Project  (SpringBootAPI)
```

After clicking ***Create***, we open the feed's ***Connect to feed*** page and select ***npm*** from the protocol list. The portal shows a pre-populated **`.npmrc`** configuration snippet tailored to our organisation and feed. We will copy this snippet because we will use it in the next step.

Configuring '.npmrc' for Local Development

The **npm** reads registry configuration from a **`.npmrc`** file that can exist at the user level (**`~/.npmrc`**) or at the project level (**`.npmrc`** in the repository root). For local development we configure the user-level file so that it applies to all projects on our machine.

So here, we will open **`~/.npmrc`** in VS Code and add the following lines, replacing **`YOUR_PAT_TOKEN_BASE64`** with the Base64-encoded value of our PAT. And, we can generate the encoded value by running the command shown below.

```
echo -n ':YOUR_PAT_TOKEN' | base64
```

The **`-n`** flag suppresses the trailing newline that **`echo`** would otherwise append, which would corrupt the Base64 encoding. We copy the output of this command and paste it into the **`~/.npmrc`** file.

```
registry=https://pkgs.dev.azure.com/GitforGits/SpringBootAPI/_packaging/Sp
ringBootNpm/npm/registry/
always-auth=true
//pkgs.dev.azure.com/GitforGits/SpringBootAPI/_packaging/SpringBootNpm/npm
/registry/:username=GitforGits
//pkgs.dev.azure.com/GitforGits/SpringBootAPI/_packaging/SpringBootNpm/npm
/registry/:_password=YOUR_PAT_TOKEN_BASE64
//pkgs.dev.azure.com/GitforGits/SpringBootAPI/_packaging/SpringBootNpm/npm
/registry/:email=not-used@example.com
```

With the above configuration, any **`npm install`** command we run locally will route through the **`SpringBootNpm`** feed. If the package is already cached in the feed, it is served immediately. If not, the feed fetches it from npmjs.com, caches it, and serves the cached copy.

Authenticating Pipeline to 'npm' Feed

For pipeline builds we use the **`npmAuthenticate@0`** task, which works analogously to **`MavenAuthenticate@0`**. It injects a short-lived token into the project-level **`.npmrc`** file on the agent before any **`npm install`** or **`npm publish`** command runs. We then create a project-level **`.npmrc`** file in the repository root that declares the feed registry without any credentials. The **`npmAuthenticate@0`** task adds the credentials at pipeline runtime.

```
cat > .npmrc << 'EOF'
registry=https://pkgs.dev.azure.com/GitforGits/SpringBootAPI/_packaging/Sp
ringBootNpm/npm/registry/
always-auth=true
EOF
```

At this point, we add the **`npmAuthenticate@0`** task to any pipeline job that runs **`npm`** commands. For our current pipeline, this would appear in a hypothetical frontend build job. The task configuration below shows the standard pattern.

```
- task: npmAuthenticate@0
  displayName: 'Authenticate npm to SpringBootNpm feed'
  inputs:
    workingFile: '.npmrc'
```

After authentication, any subsequent **`npm install`**, **`npm ci`**, or **`npm publish`** command in the same job context uses the injected credentials automatically.

Setting up Python PyPI Feed

In general, the python packages appear at several places in our DevOps workflow. Our current pipeline already uses **yamllint**, which is a Python tool we installed in Chapter 2. As we add more Python-based pipeline utilities, testing helpers, or data-processing scripts in later chapters, if we have a private PyPI feed, then it is going to ensure that those tools are served from a stable, controlled source. Hence, for organisations that publish internal Python libraries shared across multiple teams, a private PyPI feed is equally essential for the same reasons that justify a private Maven feed.

Creating PyPI Feed

We will first click + ***New feed*** in the Artifacts hub and fill in the following values.

```
Name          : SpringBootPython
Visibility    : Members of GitforGits organisation (private)
Upstream sources: Include packages from public sources (PyPI.org)
Scope         : Project  (SpringBootAPI)
```

After the feed is created, we then open ***Connect to feed*** and select ***pip***. The portal then shows the pip index URL and the twine upload URL that we use for consuming and publishing packages respectively.

Configuring pip for Local Development

Next, we will configure pip to use our Azure Artifacts feed as its index by adding a **pip.conf** entry. On Linux, this file lives at **~/.config/pip/pip.conf**. After this, we open the file and add the following configuration:

```
[global]
index-url =
https://GitforGits:YOUR_PAT_TOKEN@pkgs.dev.azure.com/GitforGits/SpringBoot
API/_packaging/SpringBootPython/pypi/simple/
```

After this, the **pip install** command routes through the **SpringBootPython** feed. We then verify the configuration is working by installing **yamllint** from our feed rather than directly from PyPI.org.

```
pip install yamllint --break-system-packages
```

The first time we install a package, pip downloads it from PyPI.org through the feed's upstream proxy and caches it.

```
Looking in indexes: https://pkgs.dev.azure.com/GitforGits/SpringBootAPI/
    _packaging/SpringBootPython/pypi/simple/
Collecting yamllint
  Downloading .../yamllint-1.35.1-py3-none-any.whl (66 kB)
Successfully installed yamllint-1.35.1
```

The aboce is going to be the terminal output showing the feed URL in the download line. It thereby confirms that the proxy is working.

Authenticating Pipeline to PyPI Feed

For pipeline jobs that need to install Python packages, we use the **PipAuthenticate@1** task. It injects the Azure Artifacts feed credentials into the pip environment for the duration of the pipeline job, following the same pattern as **MavenAuthenticate@0** and **npmAuthenticate@0**. The configuration below shows how to add it to any job that calls pip.

```
- task: PipAuthenticate@1
  displayName: 'Authenticate pip to SpringBootPython feed'
  inputs:
    artifactFeeds: 'SpringBootAPI/SpringBootPython'
    onlyAddExtraIndex: false
```

Setting **onlyAddExtraIndex: false** replaces the default PyPI.org index with our Azure Artifacts feed as the sole index. This means the agent can only install packages that exist in our feed, either because we published them there or because the upstream proxy has cached them. If we set it to **true**, then it would add the feed as an extra index alongside PyPI.org, which is appropriate in environments where we want to allow packages from the public registry for packages not in our feed.

Setting up NuGet Feed

In .NET ecosystem, the NuGet is the tool we rely on. In organisations that run Java and .NET services side by side, a shared NuGet feed allows .NET teams to follow exactly the same private-feed-with-upstream-proxy pattern we have established for Maven, **npm**, and Python.

Even for a Java-only project, the NuGet feed configuration is worthwhile. And it is because the shared DevOps tooling like code generation utilities or contract-first API client generators arrives as NuGet packages.

So here in this topic, we will configure the NuGet feed as a complete reference for mixed-stack teams.

Creating NuGet Feed

To begin with, we first click **+ *New feed*** in the Artifacts hub and provide the following values.

```
Name          : SpringBootNuGet
Visibility    : Members of GitforGits organisation (private)
Upstream sources: Include packages from public sources (nuget.org)
Scope         : Project  (SpringBootAPI)
```

After the feed is created, we open ***Connect to feed*** and select ***NuGet.exe***. The portal shows feed URL as below:

https://pkgs.dev.azure.com/GitforGits/SpringBootAPI/_packaging/SpringBootNuGet/nuget/v3/index.json

We just have to copy this URL for use to the **nuget.config** file.

Configuring 'nuget.config' for Local Development

Next, we then create a **nuget.config** file in the repository root. This file is checked into source control so that every developer and every pipeline agent read the same feed configuration without any machine-specific setup beyond authentication.

```
<?xml version="1.0" encoding="utf-8"?>
<configuration>
  <packageSources>
    <clear />
    <add key="SpringBootNuGet"
value="https://pkgs.dev.azure.com/GitforGits/SpringBootAPI/_packaging/SpringBootNuGet/nuget/v3/index.json" />
  </packageSources>
</configuration>
```

In the above, the **<clear />** element removes all previously configured package sources before adding ours. The developer's machine does not silently fall back to nuget.org if the Azure Artifacts feed is temporarily unreachable.

Pushing and Consuming NuGet Packages

For a natural .NET project, that publishes a shared library to the **SpringBootNuGet** feed, the pipeline commonly use **NuGetAuthenticate@1** task followed by **NuGetCommand@2** tasks for restore, pack, and push operations. The **NuGetAuthenticate@1** task, like its counterparts for Maven, **npm**, and pip, injects short-lived credentials into the NuGet configuration for the duration of the job.

The following YAML fragment shows the complete pattern for a .NET pipeline job that restores dependencies, builds the project, packs the output, and publishes the package.

```yaml
- job: BuildAndPublishNuGet
  displayName: 'Build and publish NuGet package'
  pool:
    vmImage: 'ubuntu-latest'
  steps:
  - task: NuGetAuthenticate@1
    displayName: 'Authenticate NuGet to SpringBootNuGet feed'
  - task: NuGetCommand@2
    displayName: 'Restore NuGet packages'
    inputs:
      command: 'restore'
      feedsToUse: 'config'
      nugetConfigPath: 'nuget.config'
  - task: DotNetCoreCLI@2
    displayName: 'Build the .NET project'
    inputs:
      command: 'build'
      arguments: '--configuration Release'
  - task: NuGetCommand@2
    displayName: 'Pack the .NET project as NuGet package'
    inputs:
      command: 'pack'
      packagesToPack: '**/*.csproj'
      versioningScheme: 'byBuildNumber'
  - task: NuGetCommand@2
    displayName: 'Push NuGet package to SpringBootNuGet feed'
    inputs:
      command: 'push'
```

```
    packagesToPush: '$(Build.ArtifactStagingDirectory)/*.nupkg'
    nuGetFeedType: 'internal'
    publishVstsFeed: 'SpringBootAPI/SpringBootNuGet'
```

In the above, the **versioningScheme: 'byBuildNumber'** input on the pack task uses the pipeline's build number as the package version, which creates a monotonically increasing version for every successful build. This is appropriate for continuous deployment scenarios where every build that passes CI should be publishable. For projects that follow semantic versioning, **versioningScheme** can be set to **byEnvVar** and a specific version number supplied through a pipeline variable, giving the team full control over the published version string.

Configuring Upstream Sources and Proxying External Registries

We enabled upstream sources when we created each feed, which adds the default public registries automatically. For most teams this default configuration is sufficient. However, there are scenarios where we need to add, remove, or customise upstream sources after a feed has been created.

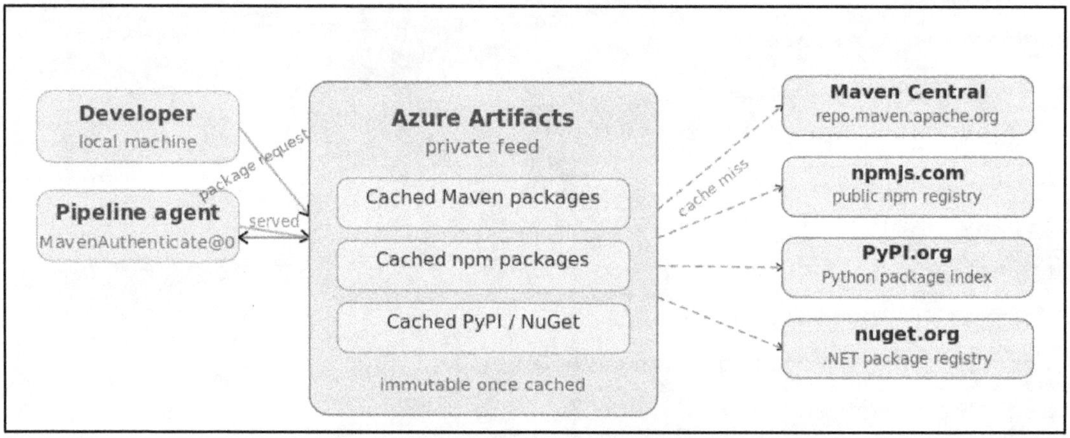

Fig 5.2: Azure Artifacts Upstream Proxy Architecture

In this section, we will learn to manage upstream sources for **SpringBootDependencies** Maven feed, because Maven's upstream source management is the most nuanced of the four ecosystems we have configured.

Adding Upstream Sources

We then navigate to **SpringBootDependencies** feed and open ***Feed settings* > *Upstream sources***. The page shows Maven Central and the Google Android Maven repository. For our Spring Boot project, both are relevant. If our project also depends on packages published to the

Spring Releases or Spring Milestones repositories, then we can add those as custom upstreams by clicking ***Add upstream source*** and selecting ***Custom URL***:

```
Upstream source type : Custom
Protocol             : Maven
Name                 : Spring Releases
Upstream URL         : https://repo.spring.io/release
```

After clicking ***Save***, the feed begins proxying the Spring Releases repository. Any Maven request for a package that does not exist in Maven Central will now also be attempted against Spring Releases before failing with a **`package not found`** error.

Exploring Package Caching Behaviour

The first time a package version is requested from an upstream source, the Azure Artifacts fetches it from the external registry, stores a permanent copy in the private feed, and serves the copy to the requester. Every subsequent request for the same package and version is served from the private feed without contacting the upstream. This is the caching behaviour, and it has two important implications that every team should understand.

The first implication is that package versions are immutable once cached. If a library author releases version **`3.2.1`** of a package, then discovers a security flaw and replaces the **`3.2.1`** binary on Maven Central with a patched binary without bumping the version number, our feed will continue to serve the original cached binary. This is actually the desired behaviour for reproducibility, wher our builds will produce the same output regardless of what happens upstream. If we need the patched binary, we either wait for the author to release version **`3.2.2`** and update our **`pom.xml`**, or we manually delete the cached version from the feed to force a fresh fetch on the next build.

The second implication is that packages cached from upstream sources consume storage against our Azure Artifacts storage quota. The free tier provides 2 GB of storage, which is ample for most teams. For organisations with very large dependency trees or many feeds, the retention policy we configure in the next section helps keep storage consumption under control by removing old versions of cached upstream packages that are no longer referenced by any active build.

Configuring Package Retention Policies

The retention policies tell Azure Artifacts how many versions of a package to keep before automatically deleting the oldest.

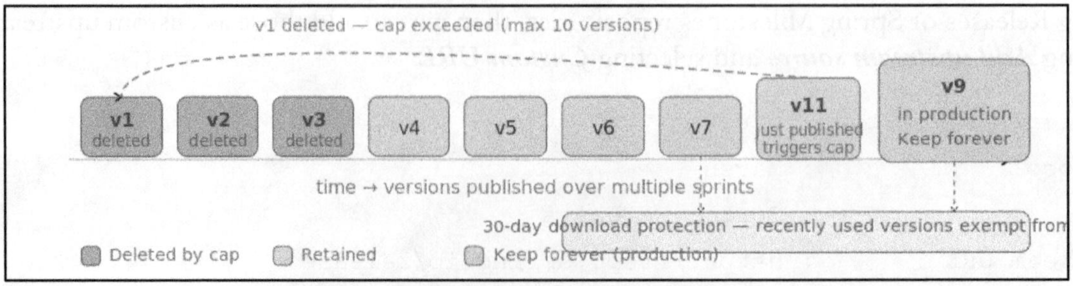

Fig 5.3: Package Retention Policy Timeline

We can now configure them at the feed level by navigating to ***Feed settings* > *Retention policies***. There are two settings are available. The ***Maximum number of versions per package*** deletes old versions once the total version count for a given package exceeds the limit. The ***Number of days to keep recently downloaded packages*** exempts recently downloaded versions from deletion, ensuring that a version actively being used by a pipeline is not removed mid-build.

For our **SpringBootDependencies** feed, we can set the values as follows.

```
Maximum versions per package          : 10
Days to keep recently downloaded      : 30
```

With the above settings, the Azure Artifacts keeps the 10 most recent versions of every package and retains any version that was downloaded within the last 30 days regardless of how many total versions exist.

And, for packages pinned to a specific version in our **pom.xml**, those versions will be downloaded on every pipeline run and therefore protected by the 30-day rule. The 10-version cap then cleans up old snapshots and development versions that are no longer referenced by any active build.

Managing Package Versions and Dependencies

A package management system is only as valuable as its ability to guarantee reproducible builds. Reproducibility requires that we pin every dependency to a specific, immutable version rather than relying on floating version ranges or latest-version resolution. In this section we establish the version pinning conventions for Maven, demonstrate how to upgrade a dependency safely through the CI pipeline, and show how to roll back a problematic upgrade without manual intervention beyond a single **git revert**.

Pinning Package Versions

Our **pom.xml** already pins every Spring Boot dependency version through the Spring Boot parent POM, which acts as a bill of materials. The parent POM declares tested and compatible versions for every library in the Spring ecosystem, so we benefit from version pinning without having to maintain individual version numbers. For any library that falls outside the Spring Boot BOM, we declare the version explicitly in the **<dependency>** block. The pattern below shows the correct way to declare a versioned dependency for an internal shared library we publish to **SpringBootDependencies**.

```
<dependency>
  <groupId>com.gitforgits</groupId>
  <artifactId>shared-validation-library</artifactId>
  <version>2.3.1</version>
</dependency>
```

We avoid version ranges such as **[2.3.0,2.4.0)** for shared library dependencies in production code. The version ranges cause different pipeline runs to produce different build outputs depending on which package versions were available in the feed at the time of each run. For developer-facing tooling where we want minor patch updates automatically, version ranges are acceptable. For application dependencies that affect the deployed binary, explicit pinning is always the correct choice.

Upgrading Dependency via CI Pipeline

When a new version of the Spring Boot parent POM is released, or when a new version of a pinned library is available, we perform the upgrade through a feature branch and pull request rather than directly on **main**. This ensures that the CI pipeline validates the upgraded dependency before the change reaches the protected branch.

```
git checkout -b feature/upgrade-shared-validation-library
```

We then open **pom.xml**, change the version from **2.3.1** to **2.4.0**, save the file, and verify the build passes locally.

```
mvn clean install
```

If the local build succeeds, we commit the change and push the branch.

```
git add pom.xml
git commit -m "Upgrade shared-validation-library from 2.3.1 to 2.4.0"
git push azure feature/upgrade-shared-validation-library
```

At this point, we open a pull request against **main**. The PR trigger fires the pipeline automatically, running the full test suite with the upgraded dependency. If all tests pass and the SonarCloud quality gate is satisfied, the reviewer approves the pull request and the upgrade merges cleanly. If a test fails because the new version introduced a breaking change, the pull request remains open, the reviewer requests changes, and we update the code to accommodate the new API before re-pushing to the feature branch.

Rolling Back Problematic Dependency

If an upgrade that passed all pipeline checks causes an issue that only manifests in production, or if a post-merge problem is detected during staging smoke testing, we roll back the dependency by reverting the commit that introduced the upgrade. The **`git revert`** command creates a new commit that undoes the changes of the target commit without rewriting history, which is the correct approach for a protected branch where history rewriting is disallowed.

```
# Find the commit hash of the upgrade
git log --oneline -5
# Revert the upgrade commit
git revert <commit-hash>
# Push the revert commit to main via a pull request
git push azure feature/rollback-shared-validation-library
```

The revert commit triggers a pipeline run on the feature branch. The pipeline validates that the rollback compiles and all tests pass with the reverted version. After a reviewer approves the pull request, the rollback merges to **`main`** and the next pipeline run on **`main`** deploys the application with the stable **`2.3.1`** version restored. The entire rollback process, from identifying the problematic commit to a verified deployment of the stable version, can complete within a single pipeline cycle of approximately five minutes.

Summary

Throughout this chapter we built a complete private package registry ecosystem on top of Azure Artifacts. We created four feeds, like the **`SpringBootDependencies`** for Maven, **`SpringBootNpm`** for **npm**, **`SpringBootPython`** for PyPI, and **`SpringBootNuGet`** for NuGet. Each feed was configured with upstream sources pointing to the corresponding public registry, transforming the feed into a transparent proxy that caches every package version it serves and makes it permanently available regardless of changes to the upstream source.

We authenticated each feed from both local development machines and pipeline agents using correct authentication task for each ecosystem. All authentication tasks use short-lived tokens scoped to the current pipeline run, so no long-lived credential ever appears in our YAML file or persists on the agent's file system beyond the duration of a single job.

We also configured a retention policy on the Maven feed to limit version accumulation, explained the immutable caching behaviour of upstream proxied packages, and walked through adding a custom upstream source for Spring milestone releases. And lastly, we established version pinning conventions, demonstrating a safe dependency upgrade workflow through a feature branch and pull request, and showing how a **`git revert`** command triggers the pipeline to validate and deploy a rollback automatically.

Chapter 6
QA Testing with Azure Test Plans

Overview

So far, the **`Build`** stage already runs seven JUnit unit tests, a SonarCloud quality gate, a CodeQL security scan, and a dependency vulnerability scan. Those automated checks validate correctness and security at the code level. In this chapter we will learn to add the complementary testing layer, which includes structured manual testing through Azure Test Plans, API contract testing through Newman running inside our pipeline, exploratory testing through the browser extension, and finally the integration of GitHub Advanced Security alerts with Azure Boards work items so that security findings receive the same sprint-level tracking as any other bug.

Later, we will walk through activating and configuring Azure Test Plans, which includes writing structured test cases linked to work items, executing them through the Test Runner, and reviewing results. We then build a Postman collection that tests the live REST API endpoints of our App, export it, add it to the repository, and wire it into the pipeline using Newman so that API contract tests run automatically on every build. Throughout the chapter, our **`azure-pipelines.yml`** continues to grow, and every test result, whether generated by JUnit, Newman, or the manual Test Runner, converges into the single Tests tab of each pipeline run summary.

Getting Started with Azure Test Plans

As the testing service within Azure DevOps, the Azure Test Plans provides a structured environment It provides a structured environment for creating test plans, organising test cases into suites, assigning them to testers, executing them through the Test Runner, and tracking outcomes against sprint milestones. Unlike the unit tests we wrote in Chapter 3, which verify individual Java methods in isolation, test plans target the running application from the outside, validating that user-facing workflows and API contracts behave correctly in a deployed environment. The two testing layers are complementary, not redundan. The unit tests run fast and catch regressions at the code level. The test plan cases run against a real deployment and catch integration failures and user-experience issues that unit tests cannot see.

Activating Azure Test Plans

The Azure Test Plans requires either the Basic + Test Plans license or the Visual Studio Enterprise subscription for each user who will create and run test cases. The users who only need to run tests assigned to them by others can do so with a basic license using the Test Runner in the browser.

So now, we will navigate to ***Organisation Settings*** > ***Billing*** and confirm that the ***Test Plans*** service is enabled for our organisation. If it is not, we click ***Set up billing***, link an Azure subscription, and toggle ***Paid*** next to Azure Test Plans. For the purposes of this chapter, the basic manual testing features we use are available on the free tier, and only the advanced parameterised test execution requires a paid license.

After the billing is confirmed, we then proceed to navigate to our project and click ***Test Plans*** in the left navigation. If this is the first time Test Plans has been accessed in the project, the portal greets us with an empty state page and a ***New Test Plan*** prompt.

Creating Test Plan and Structuring Test Suites

So, we click ***New Test Plan*** and fill in the following values.

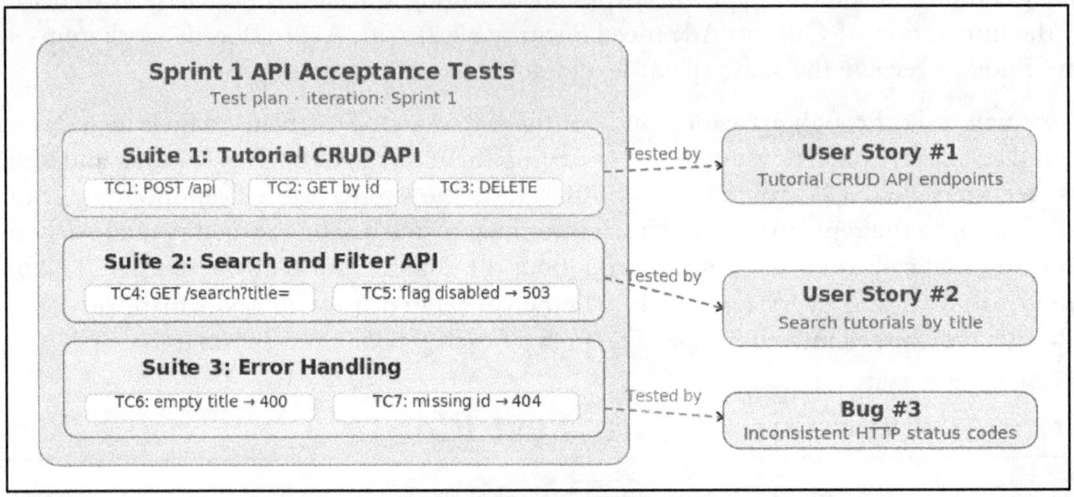

Fig 6.1: Test Plan and Suite Hierarchy

When we associate the test plan with a sprint iteration, it links its test cases to the same timebox that governs our Azure Boards work items. It thereby gives the project manager a single sprint burndown that reflects both development work and testing progress.

```
Name       : Sprint 1 API Acceptance Tests
Area path  : SpringBootAPI
Iteration  : SpringBootAPI\Sprint 1
```

Now here, inside the new test plan, we create three test suites to organise our cases by concern. With this ready, we then click ***New Suite*** on the left panel three times and name the suites as follows:

```
Suite 1 : Tutorial CRUD API
Suite 2 : Search and Filter API
Suite 3 : Error Handling and Edge Cases
```

In the above, the ***Tutorial CRUD API*** suite covers the four core endpoints of our application:

- creating a tutorial,
- retrieving all tutorials,

- retrieving a tutorial by ID, and
- deleting a tutorial.

The ***Search and Filter API*** suite covers the **`GET /api/tutorials/search`** endpoint we added in Chapter 3 and protected behind the **`enableSearchByTitle`** feature flag in chapter 4.

Linking Test Plans to Azure Boards Work Items

Before we begin to create individual test cases, at first, we will link the test suites to the work items in our Azure Boards backlog that correspond to the features being tested. This linkage creates bidirectional traceability, like from a user story we can see which test cases validate it, and from a test case we can see which requirement it satisfies.

After this, we proceed to navigate to ***Boards*** > ***Backlogs*** and confirm that work items for our tutorial CRUD feature and search feature exist in the Sprint 1 iteration. If they do not yet exist, we create them then:

```
Work Item 1 : [User Story]  Tutorial CRUD API endpoints
Work Item 2 : [User Story]  Search tutorials by title
Work Item 3 : [Bug]         Validation errors return inconsistent HTTP
status codes
```

Now back in Test Plans, we select the ***Tutorial CRUD API*** suite and click ***New Test Case***. On the test case form, we scroll to the ***Links*** tab and click ***Add link***, choosing ***Tested by*** as the link type and selecting the ***Tutorial CRUD API endpoints*** work item as the target. It creates the traceability relationship. And, we repeat this for each suite and its corresponding work item.

Setting up Test Plans for Manual Testing

Each test case in Azure Test Plans is a structured document that specifies a sequence of actions a tester should perform, the expected outcome of each action, and any test data required. The Test Runner presents these steps one by one during execution, allowing the tester to pass or fail each step individually and capture screenshots, notes, or bug reports as they go.

So here, in this section, we will write the manual test cases for our tutorial API, execute them against the staging App Service we deployed in Chapter 4, and review the results.

Creating Structured Test Cases for CRUD API

To begin with, we will first select the ***Tutorial CRUD API*** suite and click ***New Test Case***. The test case editor opens with fields for the title, steps, and expected results. We then create the first test case for the POST endpoint.

```
Title   : Create a new tutorial with valid input
Priority: 1
Step 1  Action   : Send POST request to https://springboot-staging.azurewebsites.net/api/tutorials
        Body     : { "title": "Azure DevOps Basics", "description": "CI/CD with Azure", "published": false }
        Expected : HTTP 201 Created; response body contains id, title, description, published=false
Step 2  Action   : Send GET request to /api/tutorials/{id} using the id from Step 1
        Expected : HTTP 200 OK; response body matches the created tutorial
Step 3  Action   : Verify the tutorial appears in GET /api/tutorials
        Expected : HTTP 200 OK; response array contains at least one item with title "Azure DevOps Basics"
```

After this, we can save the test case and create three more:

- one for **GET /api/tutorials/{id}** with a known ID,
- one for **PUT /api/tutorials/{id}** updating the **published** field to **true**, and
- one for **DELETE /api/tutorials/{id}**.

Each test case follows the same structure, of a clear title that describes the scenario, numbered steps with an action and an expected result, and a priority rating that tells the tester which cases to run first if time is constrained. Once all four cases are saved, the ***Tutorial CRUD API*** suite shows four test cases with status ***Not Run***.

Next, we then move to the ***Error Handling and Edge Cases*** suite and add two test cases that are difficult to cover exhaustively with unit tests.

```
Title   : Retrieve a tutorial that does not exist
Priority: 2
Step 1  Action   : Send GET request to /api/tutorials/99999
        Expected : HTTP 404 Not Found
Step 2  Action   : Verify the response body is empty or contains an appropriate error message
        Expected : Response body is either empty or contains { "message": "Not found Tutorial with id 99999" }
Title   : Create a tutorial with an empty title
Priority: 2
```

```
Step 1  Action   : Send POST request to /api/tutorials with body { 
"title": "", "description": "No title" }
        Expected : HTTP 400 Bad Request
Step 2  Action   : Verify the response contains a validation error message
        Expected : Response body indicates that the title field is 
required
```

Executing Manual Tests with Test Runner

We then select all six test cases in the ***Tutorial CRUD API*** and ***Error Handling and Edge Cases*** suites and click ***Run for web application***. The Test Runner opens in a new browser tab alongside the staging application at ***https://springboot-staging.azurewebsites.net***. The left panel of the Test Runner shows the first test case with each step listed sequentially. We begin working through the steps.

For each step, we need to perform the said action, observe the result, and click either ***Pass*** or ***Fail*** in the Test Runner panel. At this point, we use a REST client such as the **`curl`** command or the Postman desktop application to send the API requests. After passing all three steps of the first test case, we mark the overall test case as ***Passed*** and move to the next. When we reach test case 6, which submits an empty title, the application currently returns HTTP 200 with an empty title stored rather than HTTP 400. This is a bug. We then click ***File a bug*** inside the Test Runner.

Later, the bug filing dialog pre-populates the title, the steps to reproduce, and a screenshot from the Test Runner session. So there, we will add a description, set the priority to ***2***, link the bug to the ***Validation errors return inconsistent HTTP status codes*** work item we created earlier, and save. After this, the bug appears in Azure Boards as a work item in the current sprint, and visible to the developer who owns the sprint backlog.

Reviewing Test Results and Coverage Reports

Now that we are ready, we will navigate back to ***Test Plans*** and click on the ***Sprint 1 API Acceptance Tests*** plan. The plan summary page will then show the overall pass rate across all suites, a breakdown by tester, and a per-suite progress bar. Post this, we then proceed to click ***Charts*** to view the pass/fail distribution as a pie chart and the test case status over time as a trend line. These charts are available as dashboard widgets in Azure DevOps, meaning we can add them to the project dashboard that the product owner and stakeholders see daily.

We can also navigate to ***Boards > Work Items*** and open the ***Tutorial CRUD API endpoints*** user story. Here, the ***Tests*** tab on the work item shows all four test cases linked to it, their current status, and the date of the last execution. This bidirectional view is what makes the linkage between test plans and work items valuable. A stakeholder reviewing the user story can see instantly whether the feature has been tested and what the test outcome was, without needing to navigate to the Test Plans hub separately.

Automating API Tests with Postman and Newman

The Test Runner is quite a valuable tool for executing exploratory, user-acceptance, and regression scenarios that require human judgment. For API contract tests, where the expected request and response shapes are precisely defined and do not vary, the automation can gives us faster feedback and able to remove the possibility of human error in the execution. And, Postman is the most widely used tool for designing REST API tests. Its collection format packages requests and their assertions into a portable JSON file, and Newman is the command-line runner that executes those collections in a headless environment such as a pipeline agent.

Creating Postman Collection

To start with, we will open the Postman desktop application and create a new collection named ***Spring Boot API Contract Tests***. We then add four requests to the collection, one for each of the CRUD endpoints our application exposes. Here, each request includes test scripts in the ***Tests*** tab that validate the response status code, content type header, and key fields in the response body.

```
Method : POST
URL    : {{baseUrl}}/api/tutorials
Body   : {
           "title": "Newman Test Tutorial",
           "description": "Created by automated Newman run",
           "published": false
         }
Tests tab (JavaScript):
  pm.test('Status is 201', () => { pm.response.to.have.status(201); });
  pm.test('Response has id', () => {
    const body = pm.response.json();
    pm.expect(body).to.have.property('id');
    pm.collectionVariables.set('tutorialId', body.id);
  });
  pm.test('Title matches', () => {
    pm.expect(pm.response.json().title).to.eql('Newman Test Tutorial');
  });
```

In the above, the call **`pm.collectionVariables.set('tutorialId', body.id)`** stores the ID returned by the server into a Postman collection variable. The subsequent requests in the collection reference this variable as **`{{tutorialId}}`**, so the GET, PUT, and DELETE requests all operate on the specific resource created in Request 1. This chained variable pattern makes the collection self-contained, wherein it creates its own test data, validates it, and cleans it up within a single run, requiring no pre-seeded database state.

```
Method : GET
URL    : {{baseUrl}}/api/tutorials/{{tutorialId}}
Tests tab:
  pm.test('Status is 200', () => { pm.response.to.have.status(200); });
  pm.test('ID matches', () => {

pm.expect(pm.response.json().id).to.eql(pm.collectionVariables.get('tutori
alId'));
  });
Method : PUT
URL    : {{baseUrl}}/api/tutorials/{{tutorialId}}
Body   : {
           "title": "Newman Test Tutorial",
           "description": "Updated by Newman",
           "published": true
         }
Tests tab:
  pm.test('Status is 200', () => { pm.response.to.have.status(200); });
  pm.test('Published is true', () => {
    pm.expect(pm.response.json().published).to.be.true;
  });
Method : DELETE
URL    : {{baseUrl}}/api/tutorials/{{tutorialId}}
Tests tab:
  pm.test('Status is 204', () => { pm.response.to.have.status(204); });
```

In addition, we also create a Postman environment named ***Staging*** with a variable **`baseUrl`** set to ***https://springboot-staging.azurewebsites.net***. It separates the environment-specific base URL from the collection definition, thereby it allows the same collection to run against any environment by simply swapping the environment file. In the pipeline we will pass the staging environment file to Newman so it targets the correct App Service instance.

Exporting Collection and Environment files

We will now export both files from Postman by clicking the collection name, selecting ***Export***, and choosing ***Collection v2.1***. We will repeat the process for the environment by clicking ***Environments***, selecting ***Staging***, clicking the three-dot menu, and choosing ***Export***. And, we can now save both files into a **postman/** directory in our repository.

```
mkdir -p postman
# Move exported files into the directory
# SpringBootAPIContractTests.postman_collection.json
# Staging.postman_environment.json
git add postman/
git commit -m "Add Postman collection and Staging environment for Newman"
git push azure main
```

Adding Newman API Test Stage to Pipeline

Next, we then add a new stage named **APITests** to our **azure-pipelines.yml** file. This stage runs after **Staging** and before **Production**, meaning the API contract tests execute against the live staging App Service that was deployed by the previous stage. If any Postman assertion fails, the **APITests** stage fails, which in turn prevents the **Production** stage from running due to the **condition: succeeded()** guard.

```
- stage: APITests
  displayName: 'API contract tests against staging'
  dependsOn: Staging
  condition: and(succeeded(), eq('${{ parameters.runDeployment }}', true))
  jobs:
  - job: RunNewman
    displayName: 'Run Postman collection with Newman'
    pool:
      vmImage: 'ubuntu-latest'
    steps:
    - task: NodeTool@0
      displayName: 'Use Node.js 20.x'
      inputs:
        versionSpec: '20.x'
```

```
    - script: npm install -g newman newman-reporter-junitfull
      displayName: 'Install Newman and JUnit reporter'
    - script: |
        mkdir -p $(System.DefaultWorkingDirectory)/newman-results
        newman run
postman/SpringBootAPIContractTests.postman_collection.json \
          --environment postman/Staging.postman_environment.json \
          --reporters cli,junitfull \
          --reporter-junitfull-export \
            $(System.DefaultWorkingDirectory)/newman-results/newman-
results.xml
      displayName: 'Execute Postman collection against staging'
      env:
        BASE_URL: https://springboot-staging.azurewebsites.net
    - task: PublishTestResults@2
      displayName: 'Publish Newman test results to Azure Pipelines'
      condition: always()
      inputs:
        testResultsFormat: 'JUnit'
        testResultsFiles: '$(System.DefaultWorkingDirectory)/newman-
results/newman-results.xml'
        testRunTitle: 'Postman API Contract Tests - Staging'
        failTaskOnFailedTests: true
```

Now here, there are several details in this stage which needs our immediate attention. The **newman-reporter-junitfull** package is a third-party Newman reporter that produces more detailed JUnit XML than the built-in **junit** reporter, including individual assertion names as separate test cases rather than grouping all assertions under the request name. This produces more actionable failure messages in the Azure DevOps Tests tab.

The **condition: always()** on the **PublishTestResults@2** task ensures that test results are published even when the Newman run fails. Without this condition, a failed Newman run would skip the publish step, leaving the Tests tab empty and making it impossible to see which specific assertions failed. With **condition: always()**, the XML report is always uploaded, and **failTaskOnFailedTests: true** then causes the step to fail the job based on the test results in the report, not based on Newman's exit code alone.

Running Pipeline and Reviewing Newman Results

Later, we commit the updated pipeline file and push it to **main** to trigger a full pipeline run.

```
git add azure-pipelines.yml
git commit -m "Add Newman API contract test stage after Staging
deployment"
git push azure main
```

Now here, the pipeline runs through **Build**, **ProvisionInfra**, **Staging**, and then **APITests**. After Newman completes, the stage log shows the collection run summary, and the Tests tab on the run summary page shows the Newman results alongside the JUnit test results from the **Build** stage.

```
Newman run complete.
Spring Boot API Contract Tests
  Tutorial CRUD Workflow
    POST /api/tutorials            200ms    4/4 assertions passed
    GET  /api/tutorials/{id}        95ms    2/2 assertions passed
    PUT  /api/tutorials/{id}       110ms    2/2 assertions passed
    DELETE /api/tutorials/{id}      88ms    1/1 assertions passed
Requests:   4 total, 4 succeeded
Assertions: 9 total, 9 passed
Duration:   1.2s
```

All these nine assertions pass. The **APITests** stage completes successfully and the **Production** stage is now eligible to proceed after the approval gate is satisfied. The Tests tab on the run summary page shows two test run groups, one is ***JUnit Tests*** from the Build stage with seven unit tests, and the other is ***Postman API Contract Tests - Staging*** from the APITests stage with nine assertions. Overall, both the groups are shown with their pass rates and durations, which ultimately gives us a complete picture of automated test coverage across the pipeline.

Integrating Test Results into Azure Pipelines

The Azure Pipelines aggregates test results from any task that publishes a **PublishTestResults@2** or **PublishTestResults@3** output, regardless of the test framework that generated the results. The JUnit XML from Maven, JUnit XML from Newman, NUnit XML from .NET, and TRX files from Visual Studio Test are all valid inputs. Now here, the pipeline engine parses each format and stores the results in a common model accessible through the Tests tab, the Analytics tab, and the REST API.

So, in this section, we will examine the integrated test view across all three test sources we have configured.

Viewing Automated Test Results in Pipeline Run

At this point, we open the most recent pipeline run on the Azure DevOps portal and click the ***Tests*** tab. The page shows a summary row for each test run published during the pipeline, with columns for the run name, the pass percentage, the total test count, and the duration.

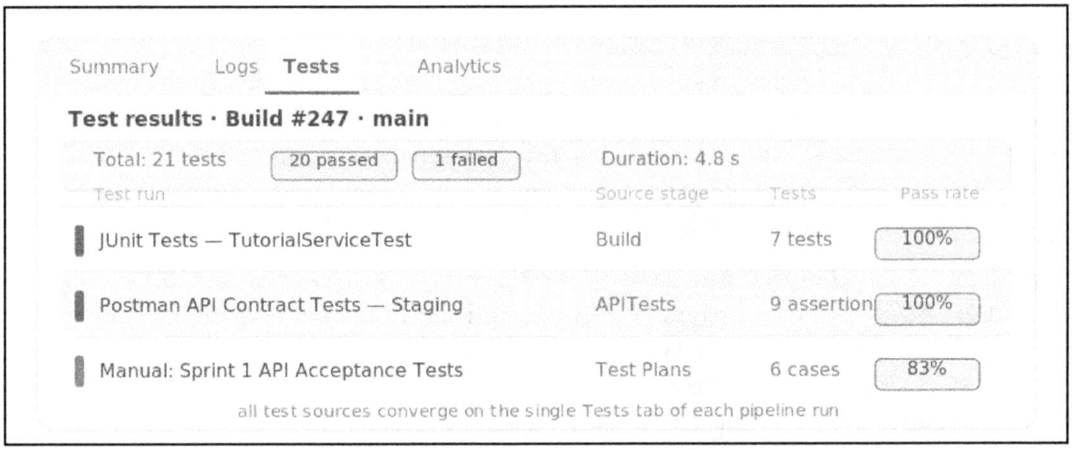

Fig 6.2: Integrated Test Results in Pipeline Tests Tab

In the above, we see two rows at this point:

- one for the Maven unit test run published by **`Maven@3`** in the **`Build`** stage, and
- one for the Newman run published by **`PublishTestResults@2`** in the **`APITests`** stage.

If we click any row, it then expands it to show individual test cases. For the Newman run, each Postman request appears as a test case, and each assertion within that request appears as a sub-test. This granularity is provided by the **`newman-reporter-junitfull`** reporter.

For the Maven run, each JUnit test method appears as an individual test case grouped under its class name. If any test fails in a future pipeline run, the failing test row appears highlighted in red and we can click it to see the full stack trace or assertion message without scrolling through log files manually.

Connecting Manual Test Results to Pipeline

Manual test results from Azure Test Plans are not automatically included in the pipeline run's Tests tab, because manual tests are executed independently of a pipeline trigger. However, we can associate a manual test run with a specific build by navigating to ***Test Plans*** > ***Runs***, finding the manual test run we completed earlier, and clicking ***Update analysis***. On the update dialog we link the run to the most recent pipeline build by selecting it from the ***Associated build*** dropdown.

After linking, the manual test run appears in the Tests tab of that pipeline build alongside the automated results. The combined view shows automated test results from the CI run and manual test results from the tester's session as a unified pass rate for the build. This aggregated view is what allows quality dashboards to report a single quality signal for each sprint. Like, if a build has 95% automated test coverage passing and 5 manual acceptance tests, all passing, the dashboard reflects the complete picture rather than reporting automation and manual results in separate silos.

Using Pipeline Analytics to Track Test Health Over Time

The ***Analytics*** tab on the pipeline page shows trend data across all recent runs. The ***Test failures*** chart plots the number of failing tests per run over time, making it immediately visible if a recent change introduced a regression. The ***Test duration*** chart shows whether test execution time is growing, which is an early warning sign that the test suite is accumulating slow tests that will eventually impede developer productivity. So here, we can check both charts regularly as we add more test cases throughout the book.

For more detailed analytics, we can navigate to ***Boards*** > ***Analytics views*** and create a custom view that filters on work items of type ***Test Case*** and field ***Outcome*** equals ***Failed*** over the last 14 days. We can pin this view as a ***Widget*** to the project dashboard. The widget also shows a running total of failing test cases across all test plans, alerting the team immediately when manual or automated failures are accumulating without being addressed.

Performing Exploratory Testing

The concept of exploratory testing is of utmost importance as it validates the unknown scenarios. It could be the edge cases that no one thought to write a test case for, or the interaction patterns that only emerge when a tester uses the application the way a real user would, or may be the combinations of inputs and states that are too numerous to enumerate in advance. The Azure Test Plans supports exploratory testing through a browser extension that records every action, screenshot, and note the tester takes during an unscripted session, and links the findings to work items in Azure Boards.

Installing Test and Feedback Browser Extension

For this, we open the Chrome browser and navigate to Chrome Web Store. We can search for ***Test and Feedback*** and install the extension published by ***Microsoft***. After installation, the extension icon will appear in the browser toolbar as a small flask symbol. We can then proceed to click the icon and sign in with the same Azure DevOps account we use for the **`GitforGits`** organisation. In the extension's settings panel, we select ***Connected*** mode and choose the **`SpringBootAPI`** project. The connected mode links every finding from our exploratory session directly to work items and test plans in that project.

Starting Exploratory Testing Session

Next, we will click the Test and Feedback extension icon and click ***Start session***. The extension prompts us to specify what we are exploring. We then click ***Explore work item*** and select the ***Tutorial CRUD API endpoints*** user story. This creates a traceability link between the session and the work item from the start. The extension toolbar shows a red recording indicator confirming the session is active.

After this, we navigate to the staging App Service URL in the same browser and begin exploring the API. Here, we can use the browser's built-in developer tools to send requests directly from the console, simulating a frontend application consuming the API.

We can try the following scenarios in sequence:

```
Scenario 1 : POST /api/tutorials with a very long title (500+ characters)
             Observe: Does the application truncate, reject, or store the
full string?
Scenario 2 : PUT /api/tutorials/{id} with a body that omits the title
field
             Observe: Does the application return 400, or silently nullify
the title?
Scenario 3 : GET /api/tutorials with no data in the database
             Observe: Does the application return 200 with an empty array,
or 404?
Scenario 4 : DELETE /api/tutorials/{id} twice in succession with the same
ID
             Observe: Does the second delete return 404, or 204 again?
```

In the above, during Scenario 2 we can discover that submitting a **`PUT`** body without a title field causes the application to set the title to **`null`** silently and return HTTP 200. This is an unintended behaviour. Here, the application should either require the title field in update requests or preserve the existing title when it is absent.

So here, next, we click ***File a bug*** in the Test and Feedback toolbar.

Filing Bugs from Exploratory Session

The bug filing dialog opens with the session recording pasted in automatically. The extension captures the URL we were on, the browser console output, and a screenshot of the current page.

After this, we then fill in the following fields:

```
Title        : PUT /api/tutorials/{id} silently nullifies title when field
omitted
Priority     : 2
Severity     : 2 - High
```

```
Area path    : SpringBootAPI
Iteration    : SpringBootAPI\Sprint 1
Repro steps : (auto-populated by extension)
System info : (auto-populated by extension)
```

At this point, we click ***Save***. The bug appears immediately in Azure Boards as a work item in Sprint 1, linked to the exploratory session and to the ***Tutorial CRUD API endpoints*** user story. A developer on the team can open the bug, see the exact sequence of HTTP requests and responses captured by the extension, and reproduce the issue without asking the tester for further information. This self-documenting quality of exploratory testing bugs is one of the primary reasons why the Azure Test Plans' extension is more productive than a manual bug template filled in after the fact.

Ending Session and Reviewing Findings

Now, after completing all four exploratory scenarios, we can click the Test and Feedback extension icon and click ***End session***. The extension then generates a session summary report showing every action recorded, every screenshot taken, every note made, and every bug filed during the session. This report is finally saved to the **`SpringBootAPI`** project under ***Test Plans*** > ***Runs*** with the session name and the associated work item visible.

The two bugs which we filed during the chapter, the missing input validation on empty title for POST and the silent null-assignment on PUT, are now tracked in Sprint 1 as work items. The developer is generally responsible for those endpoints, which they can pick them up from the board, fix the validation logic in **`TutorialController.java`**, add corresponding unit tests to **`TutorialServiceTest.java`**, and push a pull request. The CI pipeline will then validate the fix automatically, the manual test cases will be re-run in the next Test Runner session, and the Newman collection will verify the corrected HTTP status codes in the next pipeline run. This is truly the full quality loop, wherein the test plans surface issues, the pipeline validates fixes, and both converge on the same work item in Azure Boards.

Linking Advanced Security Alerts to Work Items

In the previous chapter 3, we enabled GitHub Advanced Security for Azure DevOps and configured the CodeQL code scanning, dependency scanning, and secret scanning tasks in our pipeline. Now, these scans produce security alerts visible under ***Repos*** > ***Advanced Security***. Until now those alerts have existed in isolation from our sprint planning. A developer looking at the Azure Boards sprint backlog would not see pending security remediation work unless they separately navigated to the Advanced Security hub.

In this section, we will link the security alerts to Azure Boards work items so that security findings become first-class backlog items, prioritised and tracked alongside feature work and bugs.

Navigating Advanced Security Alerts

So, for this, we will first navigate to ***Repos > Advanced Security*** in the Azure DevOps portal. The Alerts page then shows three tabs. They are ***Dependencies***, ***Code scanning***, and ***Secret scanning***. So here, we first click ***Dependencies*** to review the dependency scan results from our most recent pipeline run. The page lists every dependency with a known CVE, the severity level, the affected package name and version, the recommended fixed version, and the file in the repository that references the vulnerable dependency.

For a freshly scaffolded Spring Boot project using the most recent Spring Boot parent POM, the dependency scan may show zero critical alerts. If alerts are present, they are most likely in transitive dependencies pulled in by the parent POM. We will demonstrate the linking workflow using one of these alerts regardless of whether it is critical or informational, because the process is identical for all severity levels.

Linking Alert to Work Item

With this ready, we can then click any alert row to open its detail view. The detail view shows the full CVE description, the impact assessment, the affected code location or dependency reference, and the recommended remediation steps.

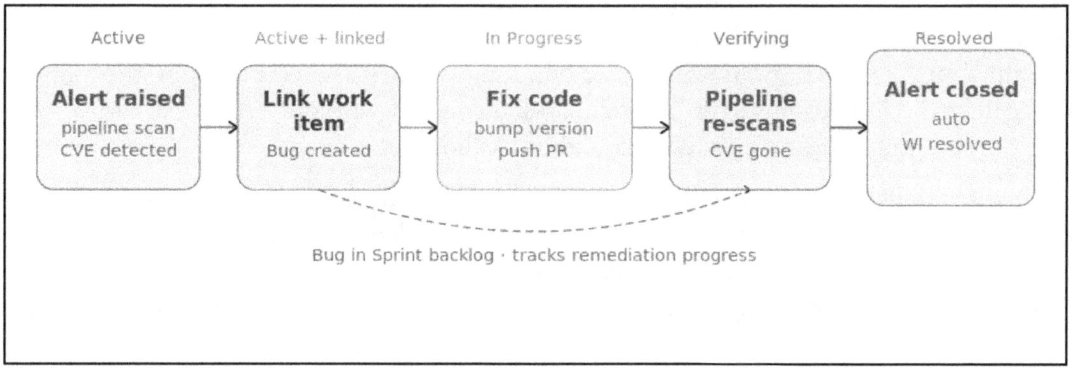

Fig 6.3: Security Alert Lifecycle

On the right-hand panel, we see a ***Linked work items*** section. We proceed here to click ***Create work item*** to generate a new Azure Boards work item pre-populated with the alert details. The Azure DevOps creates a Bug work item with the CVE identifier as the title, the full alert description in the repro steps field, and the severity mapped to the work item priority. The work item is automatically linked to the alert with the relationship type ***Found in***. We assign the bug to the current sprint iteration and to the developer who owns the dependency in question. We will now click ***Save***. The bug now appears on the sprint backlog alongside the exploratory testing bugs we filed earlier in this chapter.

The bidirectional link created by this workflow means that when the developer fixes the vulnerability by updating the dependency version in `pom.xml` and pushing a pull request, the next pipeline run re-runs the dependency scan. If the scan no longer detects the CVE, the alert status in Advanced Security changes from ***Active*** to ***Closed*** automatically. The linked work item can then be resolved by the developer in Azure Boards, completing the traceability chain from alert detection through remediation to verified closure.

Linking Existing Work Items to Alerts

If a work item already exists for a known vulnerability, perhaps because the security team flagged it through another channel before the pipeline scan was configured, then we can link the existing work item to the alert rather than creating a duplicate.

And, on the alert detail page, instead of clicking ***Create work item***, we click ***Link work item*** and search for the existing work item by ID or title. The Azure DevOps will then create the same ***Found in*** relationship between the alert and the existing work item. It gives the same closure tracking without the overhead of duplicate backlog entries.

Summary

Throughout this chapter, we built a complete quality assurance layer on top of the CI/CD pipeline and application we have been developing since Chapter 1. We started by activating and configuring Azure Test Plans in the **`SpringBootAPI`** project, creating a test plan named ***Sprint 1 API Acceptance Tests*** with three suites organized. We then wrote six structured test cases covering the CRUD API endpoints and error handling scenarios, executed them through the Test Runner against the live staging App Service, and filed a bug directly from the runner when we discovered that empty titles were accepted without validation.

Later, we then built a Postman collection of four chained requests with nine assertions that validate the API contract of our App. We exported the collection and a staging environment file to the repository, added a new **`APITests`** stage to **`azure-pipelines.yml`** that runs after the **`Staging`** deployment using Newman, and configured **`PublishTestResults@2`** with **`condition: always()`** to ensure results are always uploaded to the Tests tab regardless of the run outcome. We also performed an exploratory testing session using the Test and Feedback browser extension, discovering a second validation bug where the **`PUT`** endpoint silently accepts a body without a title field and sets the title to **`null`**. Finally, we linked GitHub Advanced Security dependency alert to a new Bug work item in Azure Boards, and therefore we completed the traceability chain from automated security detection through sprint-level tracking to verified remediation.

CHAPTER 7

INFRASTRUCTURE AUTOMATION WITH AZURE PIPELINES

Overview

So far, we built the pipeline, tested, scanned, and deployed the App to Azure App Service through a blue-green slot swap, and our staging environment was validated by both JUnit unit tests and Newman API contract tests before every production deployment. In this chapter, we will try to go deeper into infrastructure automation, introducing Terraform as a complementary IaC tool alongside Bicep and explaining when each one is the appropriate choice. In this, we will containerise the App with Docker, push the image to Azure Container Registry, and deploy it to AKS.

Later, we then add Flyway database migrations to our application so that schema changes are versioned, automated, and applied in the correct order across every environment. We integrate the Flyway migration step into the pipeline so that every deployment carries the matching schema version alongside the application binary. And lastly, we then conclude the chapter by configuring disaster recovery using failover groups and automated backups, with the backup step wired into the pipeline so that a verified database snapshot always accompanies a successful production deployment. Every infrastructure resource we provision in this chapter extends the **`infra/`** directory we created in Chapter 4 and builds on the **`SpringBootRG`** resource group and **`springboot-azure`** service connection that are already in place.

Terraform and Bicep

In Chapter 4, we established Bicep as our primary IaC language for provisioning Azure resources. The Bicep is the right choice when all infrastructure targets Azure and the team wants the tightest possible integration with the Azure Resource Manager API, including first-class support for all resource types on the day they are released.

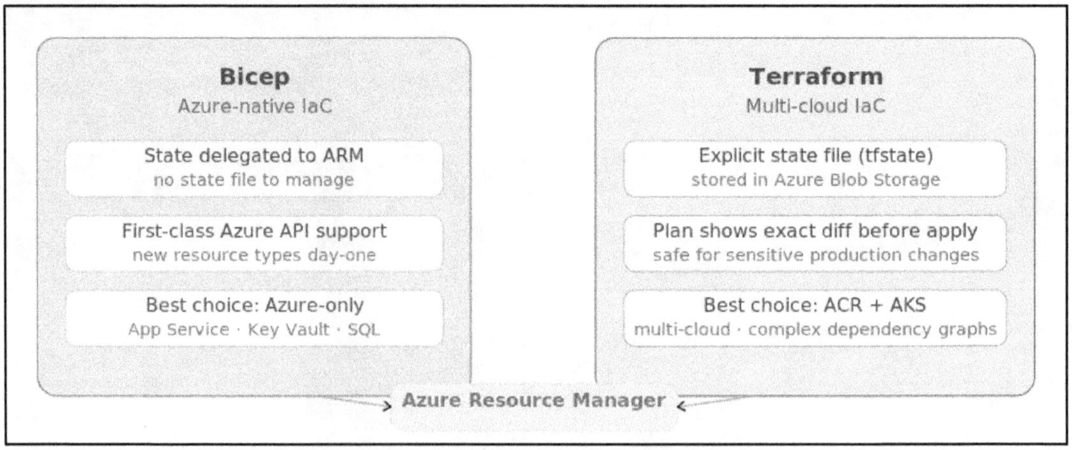

Fig 7.1: Terraform and Bicep: Key Differences

Terraform is the right choice when the team manages infrastructure across multiple cloud providers, when the team already has a significant Terraform investment, or when the team needs Terraform's explicit state management model for resources that are difficult to express as idempotent ARM deployments. Both tools are in active use in the industry and both are valid choices for Azure infrastructure. We learn both here so that we can make an informed decision for each project.

The fundamental difference between Terraform and Bicep is how they track state. The Bicep delegates state to the Azure Resource Manager in which the ARM knows what resources exist, so Bicep simply describes the desired state and ARM reconciles reality with the description on every deployment. The Terraform maintains its own state file, a JSON document that records every resource it has created, their current attributes, and the dependencies between them. This explicit state file enables Terraform's **`plan`** command to show a precise diff between the current state and the desired state before any change is applied, which many teams find reassuring for production infrastructure. The trade-off is that the state file must be stored securely, versioned, and locked during concurrent pipeline runs.

Installing and Verifying Terraform CLI

The Terraform CLI is already available on Microsoft-hosted Ubuntu agents. We can verify its presence by running:

```
terraform version
```

This prints the installed version. For new local installations, the official HashiCorp APT repository is the recommended source.

```
wget -O - https://apt.releases.hashicorp.com/gpg | sudo gpg --dearmor -o
/usr/share/keyrings/hashicorp-archive-keyring.gpg
echo "deb [arch=$(dpkg --print-architecture) signed-
by=/usr/share/keyrings/hashicorp-archive-keyring.gpg] \
  https://apt.releases.hashicorp.com $(lsb_release -cs) main" \
  | sudo tee /etc/apt/sources.list.d/hashicorp.list
sudo apt update && sudo apt install terraform -y
```

```
Terraform v1.9.5
on linux_amd64
```

Configuring Terraform Authentication with Service Principal

The Terraform communicates with Azure through the **`azurerm`** provider. The provider supports several authentication methods. For pipeline use, we can create a dedicated Service Principal with Contributor rights on our resource group, store its credentials as pipeline secret variables, and pass them to Terraform through environment variables. We can now create the Service Principal using the Azure CLI we configured in Chapter 1.

```
az ad sp create-for-rbac \
  --name terraform-springboot-sp \
  --role Contributor \
  --scopes /subscriptions/$(az account show --query id -o tsv)/resourceGroups/SpringBootRG \
  --output json
```

The above command returns a JSON object containing **appId**, **password**, and **tenant**. We can store these values as secret pipeline variables in our Azure DevOps project under ***Pipelines*** > ***Library*** > + ***Variable group***. We can name the group **terraform-credentials** and add four variables, marking each as secret.

```
ARM_CLIENT_ID          : <appId from output>        (secret)
ARM_CLIENT_SECRET      : <password from output>     (secret)
ARM_TENANT_ID          : <tenant from output>       (secret)
ARM_SUBSCRIPTION_ID : <your subscription id>  (secret)
```

Now, when these four environment variables are present in the shell, the **azurerm** provider reads them automatically without requiring any explicit **provider** block configuration beyond **features {}**. This means our Terraform files contain no credentials, no subscription IDs, and no tenant IDs. All the sensitive values travel through the pipeline variable group as secrets that are masked in logs and never written to disk on the agent.

Writing Terraform Configuration

Next, we then create a **terraform/** directory inside the existing **infra/** directory and add **main.tf** for resource definitions, **variables.tf** for input variable declarations, and **backend.tf** for remote state configuration. The separation of these concerns helps us to keep each file focused and readable.

```
mkdir -p infra/terraform
touch infra/terraform/main.tf infra/terraform/variables.tf infra/terraform/backend.tf
```

At this point, we can open **infra/terraform/backend.tf** first and configure the Azure Storage backend for remote state. The storage of Terraform state file in Azure Blob Storage ensures that concurrent pipeline runs can acquire a state lock, that the state is not lost if the pipeline agent is recycled, and that multiple team members share the same view of provisioned resources.

```
terraform {
  required_version = ">= 1.5.0"
  required_providers {
    azurerm = {
      source  = "hashicorp/azurerm"
      version = "~> 3.110"
    }
  }
  backend "azurerm" {
    resource_group_name  = "SpringBootRG"
    storage_account_name = "springboottfstate"
    container_name       = "tfstate"
    key                  = "springboot-aks.tfstate"
  }
}
```

In the above, the **storage_account_name** value **springboottfstate** refers to the storage account we created with the Azure CLI in Chapter 1.

Next, we then create the blob container that will hold the state file.

```
az storage container create \
  --name tfstate \
  --account-name springboottfstate \
  --auth-mode login
```

After this, we then open **infra/terraform/variables.tf** and declare the input variables:

```
variable "location" {
  type        = string
  default     = "eastus"
  description = "Azure region for all resources"
}
```

```
variable "resource_group_name" {
  type    = string
  default = "SpringBootRG"
}
variable "aks_node_count" {
  type    = number
  default = 2
}
variable "aks_vm_size" {
  type    = string
  default = "Standard_DS2_v2"
}
variable "acr_name" {
  type    = string
  default = "springbootacr"
}
```

Next, we then write **infra/terraform/main.tf**. This file provisions Azure Container Registry and an AKS cluster, two resources that are easier to manage with Terraform than with Bicep because of Terraform's explicit dependency graph and the richer set of AKS helper arguments available in the **azurerm** provider.

```
provider "azurerm" {
  features {}
}
# Azure Container Registry
resource "azurerm_container_registry" "acr" {
  name                = var.acr_name
  resource_group_name = var.resource_group_name
  location            = var.location
  sku                 = "Basic"
  admin_enabled       = false
}
# AKS Cluster
resource "azurerm_kubernetes_cluster" "aks" {
```

```
  name                = "springboot-aks"
  location            = var.location
  resource_group_name = var.resource_group_name
  dns_prefix          = "springbootaks"
  kubernetes_version  = "1.30"
  default_node_pool {
    name       = "default"
    node_count = var.aks_node_count
    vm_size    = var.aks_vm_size
  }
  identity {
    type = "SystemAssigned"
  }
  network_profile {
    network_plugin    = "azure"
    load_balancer_sku = "standard"
  }
  tags = {
    Environment = "production"
    ManagedBy   = "terraform"
  }
}
# Grant AKS pull access to ACR
resource "azurerm_role_assignment" "aks_acr_pull" {
  scope                = azurerm_container_registry.acr.id
  role_definition_name = "AcrPull"
  principal_id         =
azurerm_kubernetes_cluster.aks.kubelet_identity[0].object_id
}
output "acr_login_server" {
  value = azurerm_container_registry.acr.login_server
}
output "aks_kube_config" {
```

```
  value     = azurerm_kubernetes_cluster.aks.kube_config_raw
  sensitive = true
}
```

In the above, the **azurerm_role_assignment** resource grants the AKS cluster's managed identity the **AcrPull** role on the Container Registry. This means every node in the cluster can pull images from our private registry without any additional credential configuration in the Kubernetes deployment manifests. The managed identity approach eliminates the service principal secret rotation burden that plagued older AKS-to-ACR integrations.

Adding Terraform Pipeline Stage

Next, we will add a **ProvisionAKS** stage to **azure-pipelines.yml** that runs Terraform init, plan, and apply in sequence. This stage depends on the **Build** stage and runs in parallel with **ProvisionInfra** because both stages provision independent resources. We also link the **terraform-credentials** variable group to the pipeline so that the Terraform environment variables are injected automatically.

```
variables:
  - group: terraform-credentials
  - name: mavenGoals
    value: 'clean install'
  - name: artifactName
    value: 'springboot-api'
- stage: ProvisionAKS
  displayName: 'Provision ACR and AKS with Terraform'
  dependsOn: Build
  condition: and(succeeded(), eq('${{ parameters.runDeployment }}', true))
  jobs:
  - job: TerraformApply
    displayName: 'Terraform init, plan, apply'
    pool:
      vmImage: 'ubuntu-latest'
    steps:
    - task: AzureCLI@2
      displayName: 'Export Terraform credentials to environment'
      inputs:
```

```
      azureSubscription: 'springboot-azure'
      scriptType: 'bash'
      scriptLocation: 'inlineScript'
      addSpnToEnvironment: true
      inlineScript: |
        echo "##vso[task.setvariable
variable=ARM_CLIENT_ID]$servicePrincipalId"
        echo "##vso[task.setvariable
variable=ARM_CLIENT_SECRET;issecret=true]$servicePrincipalKey"
        echo "##vso[task.setvariable variable=ARM_TENANT_ID]$tenantId"
        echo "##vso[task.setvariable variable=ARM_SUBSCRIPTION_ID]$(az
account show --query id -o tsv)"
  - script: |
      cd infra/terraform
      terraform init
    displayName: 'Terraform init'
    env:
      ARM_CLIENT_ID:          $(ARM_CLIENT_ID)
      ARM_CLIENT_SECRET:      $(ARM_CLIENT_SECRET)
      ARM_TENANT_ID:          $(ARM_TENANT_ID)
      ARM_SUBSCRIPTION_ID: $(ARM_SUBSCRIPTION_ID)
  - script: |
      cd infra/terraform
      terraform plan -out=tfplan -input=false
    displayName: 'Terraform plan'
    env:
      ARM_CLIENT_ID:          $(ARM_CLIENT_ID)
      ARM_CLIENT_SECRET:      $(ARM_CLIENT_SECRET)
      ARM_TENANT_ID:          $(ARM_TENANT_ID)
      ARM_SUBSCRIPTION_ID: $(ARM_SUBSCRIPTION_ID)
  - script: |
      cd infra/terraform
      terraform apply -auto-approve tfplan
    displayName: 'Terraform apply'
```

```
    env:
      ARM_CLIENT_ID:        $(ARM_CLIENT_ID)
      ARM_CLIENT_SECRET:    $(ARM_CLIENT_SECRET)
      ARM_TENANT_ID:        $(ARM_TENANT_ID)
      ARM_SUBSCRIPTION_ID: $(ARM_SUBSCRIPTION_ID)
```

In the above, all the four **ARM_*** environment variables are passed explicitly to each Terraform script step using the **env** key. This is the injection-safe pattern we established in Chapter 3, in which the sensitive values never appear in the inline script body and are never accessible to injected commands. The **addSpnToEnvironment: true** input on the **AzureCLI@2** task exposes the service connection's underlying service principal credentials as special variables **$servicePrincipalId** and **$servicePrincipalKey** within the inline script scope, which we then promote to Azure DevOps task-level variables with the **##vso[task.setvariable]** logging command.

Containerising App with Docker

With ACR and AKS provisioned by Terraform, we will now containerise our App so that it can run inside a Kubernetes pod. The containerisation packages the application binary, its runtime dependencies, and its configuration into a single, immutable image that runs identically on a developer laptop, a CI pipeline agent, and a production Kubernetes node. The image we build in this section uses the same **.jar** file that our **Build** stage already produces and publishes as a pipeline artifact, so we do not build the application a second time. We will also download the artifact, wrap it in a Docker image, and push the image to ACR.

Writing Dockerfile

So, let us begin. We will first create a **Dockerfile** in the root of the repository. We will be using Eclipse Temurin Java 17 slim image for production Spring Boot containers as shown below:

```
FROM eclipse-temurin:17-jre-jammy
# Create a non-root user for security
RUN groupadd --gid 1001 springboot \
  && useradd --uid 1001 --gid springboot --shell /bin/bash --create-home
springboot
WORKDIR /app
# Copy the fat JAR produced by Maven
COPY target/*.jar app.jar
# Switch to non-root user
```

```
USER springboot
# Expose the Spring Boot default port
EXPOSE 8080
# Start the application
ENTRYPOINT ["java", "-Djava.security.egd=file:/dev/./urandom", "-jar",
"/app/app.jar"]
```

We then run the container as a non-root user through the **`USER springboot`** instruction, as it is a mandatory security practice for production containers. If a vulnerability in the application allowed an attacker to execute arbitrary commands inside the container, the attacker would land as the **`springboot`** user with no write access outside **`/home/springboot`** and **`/app`**, rather than as root with the ability to modify the container filesystem or escape to the host. The **`-Djava.security.egd`** JVM argument reduces startup time on Linux systems where the default entropy source may be slow to initialise.

We will also add a **`.dockerignore`** file to the repository root to prevent unnecessary files from being sent to the Docker build context.

```
cat > .dockerignore << 'EOF'
.git
.gitignore
*.md
docs/
infra/
postman/
azure-pipelines.yml
EOF
```

Building and Testing Docker Image Locally

With this ready, we now build the image locally to confirm the Dockerfile is correct before involving the pipeline. For thiws, we will first ensure the **`.jar`** is present in the **`target/`** directory by running a Maven build, then we build the Docker image.

```
mvn clean package -DskipTests
docker build -t springboot-app:local .
```

Next, we then proceed to run the image locally to verify it starts correctly.

```
docker run -p 8080:8080 --name springboot-local springboot-app:local
```

```
...
2025-07-15T10:00:12.345Z  INFO --- Tomcat started on port(s): 8080
2025-07-15T10:00:12.567Z  INFO --- Started SpringBoot3RestApiApplication
in 3.4s
```

Here, the application starts inside the container on port 8080 exactly as it does locally. We can stop the container with **docker stop springboot-local && docker rm springboot-local** and proceed.

Adding Docker Build and Push Stage to Pipeline

Next, we then add **BuildImage** stage to **azure-pipelines.yml** that runs after the **ProvisionAKS** to ensure ACR exists before we push to it. This stage downloads the **springboot-api** pipeline artifact produced in the **Build** stage, places the **.jar** in the **target/** directory where the Dockerfile expects it, builds the Docker image, and pushes it to ACR with the specific build number and **latest** tag.

```
- stage: BuildImage
  displayName: 'Build and push Docker image to ACR'
  dependsOn: ProvisionAKS
  condition: and(succeeded(), eq('${{ parameters.runDeployment }}', true))
  jobs:
  - job: DockerBuildPush
    displayName: 'Docker build and ACR push'
    pool:
      vmImage: 'ubuntu-latest'
    steps:
    - download: current
      artifact: $(artifactName)
      displayName: 'Download JAR artifact'
    - script: |
        mkdir -p target
        cp $(Pipeline.Workspace)/$(artifactName)/*.jar target/
      displayName: 'Stage JAR for Docker build context'
    - task: AzureCLI@2
      displayName: 'Build Docker image and push to ACR'
      inputs:
```

```
        azureSubscription: 'springboot-azure'
        scriptType: 'bash'
        scriptLocation: 'inlineScript'
        inlineScript: |
          ACR_SERVER=$(az acr show --name springbootacr --query
loginServer -o tsv)
          az acr login --name springbootacr
          docker build -t $ACR_SERVER/springboot-api:$(Build.BuildId) \
                       -t $ACR_SERVER/springboot-api:latest .
          docker push $ACR_SERVER/springboot-api:$(Build.BuildId)
          docker push $ACR_SERVER/springboot-api:latest
          echo "##vso[task.setvariable
variable=ACR_IMAGE;isOutput=true]$ACR_SERVER/springboot-
api:$(Build.BuildId)"
      name: DockerPush
```

From the above, the **az acr login** command authenticates the Docker daemon to our private registry using the **springboot-azure** service connection's identity, which already has the **AcrPush** role through the service connection configuration. The image is then tagged with **$(Build.BuildId)**, which is the immutable Azure DevOps build number, ensuring that every image pushed to ACR is uniquely identifiable and traceable back to the pipeline run that produced it. And, the output variable **ACR_IMAGE** carries the fully qualified image reference forward to the deployment stages.

Deploying Containerised App to AKS

With the Docker image in ACR and the AKS cluster running, we can now deploy the application by applying a Kubernetes manifest. The manifest can define a deployment that manages two replicas of our container, a Service that exposes the deployment through an Azure Load Balancer, and a ConfigMap that supplies environment-specific configuration without baking values into the image.

Writing Kubernetes Deployment Manifest

To begin with, we will first create a **k8s/** directory in the repository and add the manifest file.

```
mkdir -p k8s
touch k8s/springboot-deployment.yaml
apiVersion: v1
```

```yaml
kind: ConfigMap
metadata:
  name: springboot-config
  namespace: default
data:
  SPRING_PROFILES_ACTIVE: "kubernetes"
  AZURE_APPCONFIG_ENDPOINT: "$(APPCONFIG_ENDPOINT)"
---
apiVersion: apps/v1
kind: Deployment
metadata:
  name: springboot-deployment
  namespace: default
spec:
  replicas: 2
  selector:
    matchLabels:
      app: springboot-api
  template:
    metadata:
      labels:
        app: springboot-api
    spec:
      containers:
      - name: springboot-api
        image: PLACEHOLDER_IMAGE
        ports:
        - containerPort: 8080
        envFrom:
        - configMapRef:
            name: springboot-config
        resources:
          requests:
```

```yaml
            memory: "256Mi"
            cpu:    "250m"
          limits:
            memory: "512Mi"
            cpu:    "500m"
        readinessProbe:
          httpGet:
            path: /api/tutorials
            port: 8080
          initialDelaySeconds: 30
          periodSeconds: 10
---
apiVersion: v1
kind: Service
metadata:
  name: springboot-service
  namespace: default
spec:
  type: LoadBalancer
  ports:
  - port: 80
    targetPort: 8080
  selector:
    app: springboot-api
```

In the above, the **`PLACEHOLDER_IMAGE`** string is intentional, and the pipeline replaces it with the actual ACR image reference at deployment time using **`sed`**. The **`readinessProbe`** polls the **`/api/tutorials`** endpoint every 10 seconds starting 30 seconds after the container starts. The Kubernetes will not route traffic to a pod until the probe returns HTTP 200, which prevents the load balancer from sending user requests to a pod that has not yet finished initialising the Spring application context.

Adding AKS Deployment Stage to Pipeline

Next, we then add a **`DeployAKS`** stage that runs after **`BuildImage`**. It retrieves the AKS credentials, substitutes the image placeholder in the manifest, and applies it to the cluster.

```
- stage: DeployAKS
  displayName: 'Deploy to AKS'
  dependsOn: BuildImage
  condition: and(succeeded(), eq('${{ parameters.runDeployment }}', true))
  jobs:
  - deployment: DeployToAKS
    displayName: 'Apply Kubernetes manifest'
    pool:
      vmImage: 'ubuntu-latest'
    environment: 'aks-production'
    strategy:
      runOnce:
        deploy:
          steps:
          - task: AzureCLI@2
            displayName: 'Get AKS credentials and deploy manifest'
            inputs:
              azureSubscription: 'springboot-azure'
              scriptType: 'bash'
              scriptLocation: 'inlineScript'
              inlineScript: |
                az aks get-credentials \
                  --resource-group SpringBootRG \
                  --name springboot-aks \
                  --overwrite-existing
                ACR_SERVER=$(az acr show --name springbootacr --query
loginServer -o tsv)
                IMAGE=$ACR_SERVER/springboot-api:$(Build.BuildId)
                sed "s|PLACEHOLDER_IMAGE|$IMAGE|g" k8s/springboot-
deployment.yaml \
                  | kubectl apply -f -
                kubectl rollout status deployment/springboot-deployment --
timeout=300s
```

In the above, the **kubectl rollout status** command blocks until the deployment reports all desired replicas as ready or until the 300-second timeout expires. If any pod fails to start within that window, the rollout status command exits with a non-zero code, which fails the pipeline step and triggers the natural rollback mechanism, because the Kubernetes deployment tracks revision history, we can roll back to the previous stable image by running **kubectl rollout undo deployment/springboot-deployment** from any authenticated terminal.

Database Migrations with Flyway

Our App currently uses an H2 in-memory database, which is appropriate for development and unit testing but unsuitable for production because it does not persist data between restarts.

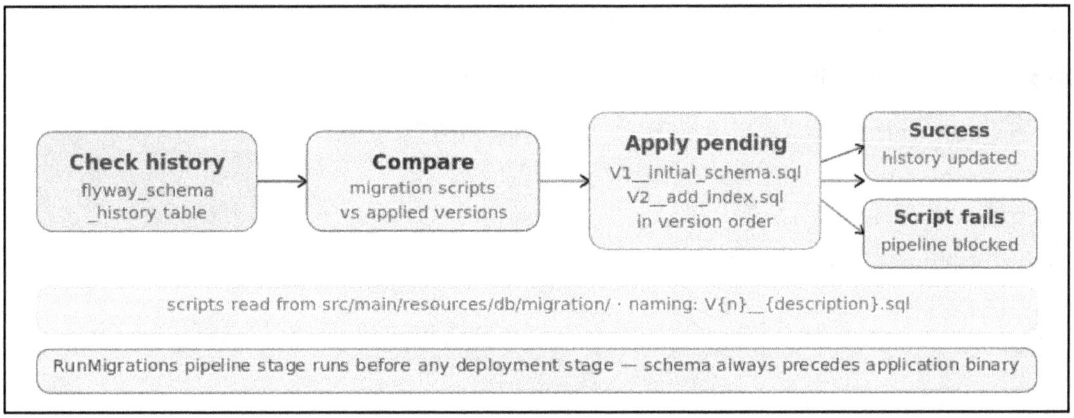

Fig 7.2: Flyway Migration Execution Flow

In this topic, we will learn to configure the application to connect to an Azure SQL Database in production, add Flyway to manage schema version control, write the initial migration script, and automate the migration step in the pipeline so that every deployment carries the correct schema version alongside the application binary.

Provisioning Azure SQL Database

To start with, we will first extend the **infra/appservice.bicep** to provision an Azure SQL Server and a database. Here, we will declare the SQL administrator password as a Bicep parameter so that it is supplied at deployment time as a pipeline secret rather than appearing in the template file.

```
@secure()
param sqlAdminPassword string
param sqlAdminLogin string = 'springbootadmin'
resource sqlServer 'Microsoft.Sql/servers@2023-08-01-preview' = {
```

```
  name: '${envPrefix}-sqlserver'
  location: location
  properties: {
    administratorLogin: sqlAdminLogin
    administratorLoginPassword: sqlAdminPassword
    minimalTlsVersion: '1.2'
  }
}
resource sqlDatabase 'Microsoft.Sql/servers/databases@2023-08-01-preview'
= {
  parent: sqlServer
  name: 'springbootdb'
  location: location
  sku: {
    name: 'GP_S_Gen5_1'
    tier: 'GeneralPurpose'
  }
  properties: {
    autoPauseDelay: 60
    minCapacity: json('0.5')
  }
}
resource sqlFirewallAzure 'Microsoft.Sql/servers/firewallRules@2023-08-01-
preview' = {
  parent: sqlServer
  name: 'AllowAzureServices'
  properties: {
    startIpAddress: '0.0.0.0'
    endIpAddress: '0.0.0.0'
  }
}
output sqlConnectionString string =
```

```
'jdbc:sqlserver://${sqlServer.properties.fullyQualifiedDomainName}:1433;da
tabase=springbootdb;encrypt=true;trustServerCertificate=false'
```

In the above, the **@secure()** decorator on **sqlAdminPassword** prevents Bicep from logging the value in deployment history or ARM output. The **GP_S_Gen5_1** SKU selects the serverless tier with auto-pause after 60 minutes of inactivity, which is cost-efficient for development and staging workloads. And, the firewall rule with start and end address both set to **0.0.0.0** which then permits the connections from pipeline agents and App Service instances without opening the database to all public internet addresses.

Adding Flyway to App

Next, we will now add the Flyway Spring Boot starter and the Microsoft SQL Server JDBC driver to **pom.xml**. Here, both are managed by the Spring Boot BOM, so no version declarations are needed.

```
<dependency>
  <groupId>org.flywaydb</groupId>
  <artifactId>flyway-sqlserver</artifactId>
</dependency>
<dependency>
  <groupId>com.microsoft.sqlserver</groupId>
  <artifactId>mssql-jdbc</artifactId>
  <scope>runtime</scope>
</dependency>
```

Now, when the **flyway-sqlserver** dependency is on the classpath, Spring Boot's auto-configuration detects it and automatically runs all pending migrations in **src/main/resources/db/migration/** at application startup. The migrations run before any Spring Data JPA repository is initialised. At this point, we configure the datasource in **application.properties** using placeholders that read from environment variables, which are injected differently in each environment.

```
spring.datasource.url=${SPRING_DATASOURCE_URL:jdbc:h2:mem:testdb}
spring.datasource.username=${SPRING_DATASOURCE_USERNAME:sa}
spring.datasource.password=${SPRING_DATASOURCE_PASSWORD:}
spring.flyway.enabled=true
spring.flyway.baseline-on-migrate=true
```

```
spring.jpa.hibernate.ddl-auto=validate
```

In the above script, the **:jdbc:h2:mem:testdb** default value preserves the existing H2 in-memory behaviour for local development and unit testing when the **SPRING_DATASOURCE_URL** environment variable is not set.

When the application runs in a deployed environment where those variables are set through App Service application settings or Kubernetes ConfigMap, it connects to Azure SQL instead. So here, we are setting the **spring.jpa.hibernate.ddl-auto=validate** which then tells the Hibernate to verify if the schema matches the JPA entity definitions.

Writing Flyway Migration

Next, is to create the migrations directory and the first migration file. The Flyway naming conventions require migration files to follow a specific pattern, which is something like **V{version}__{description}.sql**, where **V** is a literal prefix, the version is a number, and the description uses underscores for spaces.

```
mkdir -p src/main/resources/db/migration
touch src/main/resources/db/migration/V1__initial_schema.sql
-- Initial schema for the Tutorial REST API
-- Applied by Flyway on first application startup against Azure SQL
Database
CREATE TABLE tutorials (
    id          BIGINT IDENTITY(1,1) PRIMARY KEY,
    title       NVARCHAR(255) NOT NULL,
    description NVARCHAR(1000),
    published   BIT NOT NULL DEFAULT 0,
    created_at  DATETIME2 DEFAULT SYSUTCDATETIME()
);
CREATE INDEX idx_tutorials_title ON tutorials(title);
```

Now in the above script, the **BIGINT IDENTITY(1,1)** column type is the Azure SQL equivalent of an auto-incrementing primary key. The **NVARCHAR** is preferred over **VARCHAR** for Azure SQL databases to ensure proper Unicode support for tutorial titles in any language. The index on **title** accelerates the **findByTitleContaining** query we added in Chapter 3, which performs a **LIKE** search on that column.

Automating Flyway Migrations

So, we will now add a **RunMigrations** stage to the pipeline that runs after **ProvisionInfra** and before the application deployment stages. This stage connects to the Azure SQL Database using the Flyway CLI and applies any pending migrations. Now here, when we run the migrations as a dedicated pipeline stage, rather than relying solely on Spring Boot's startup auto-migration, it gives us the visibility into migration success or failure before the application binary is deployed, and allows us to run migrations against a database without needing the application to be running.

```
- stage: RunMigrations
  displayName: 'Apply Flyway database migrations'
  dependsOn: ProvisionInfra
  condition: and(succeeded(), eq('${{ parameters.runDeployment }}', true))
  jobs:
  - job: FlywayMigrate
    displayName: 'Flyway migrate against Azure SQL'
    pool:
      vmImage: 'ubuntu-latest'
    steps:
    - script: |
        wget -qO- https://repo1.maven.org/maven2/org/flywaydb/flyway-
commandline/10.15.0/flyway-commandline-10.15.0-linux-x64.tar.gz \
          | tar xz
        sudo ln -sf $(pwd)/flyway-10.15.0/flyway /usr/local/bin/flyway
        flyway -version
      displayName: 'Install Flyway 10 CLI'
    - task: AzureCLI@2
      displayName: 'Run Flyway migrate'
      inputs:
        azureSubscription: 'springboot-azure'
        scriptType: 'bash'
        scriptLocation: 'inlineScript'
        inlineScript: |
          SQL_SERVER=$(az sql server show \
            --name springboot-sqlserver \
            --resource-group SpringBootRG \
```

```
            --query fullyQualifiedDomainName -o tsv)
          flyway \
            -
url="jdbc:sqlserver://$SQL_SERVER:1433;database=springbootdb;encrypt=true"
\
            -user=$(SQL_ADMIN_LOGIN) \
            -password=$(SQL_ADMIN_PASSWORD) \
            -locations="filesystem:src/main/resources/db/migration" \
            migrate
      env:
        SQL_ADMIN_LOGIN:    $(SQL_ADMIN_LOGIN)
        SQL_ADMIN_PASSWORD: $(SQL_ADMIN_PASSWORD)
```

So here in the above, the database credentials **$(SQL_ADMIN_LOGIN)** and **$(SQL_ADMIN_PASSWORD)** are stored as secret pipeline variables. The **env** block on the **AzureCLI@2** task passes them to the inline script as environment variables, following the injection-safe pattern established in Chapter 3. The Flyway reads the SQL files from the **src/main/resources/db/migration/** directory in the checked-out repository, applies any migrations whose version numbers are higher than the highest version recorded in the **flyway_schema_history** table, and exits with a non-zero code if any migration fails, which fails the pipeline stage.

Configuring Disaster Recovery in Azure Pipelines

A deployment pipeline that produces a verified, tested release is only half of a resilient production system. The other half is the ability to recover from infrastructure failure quickly and predictably.

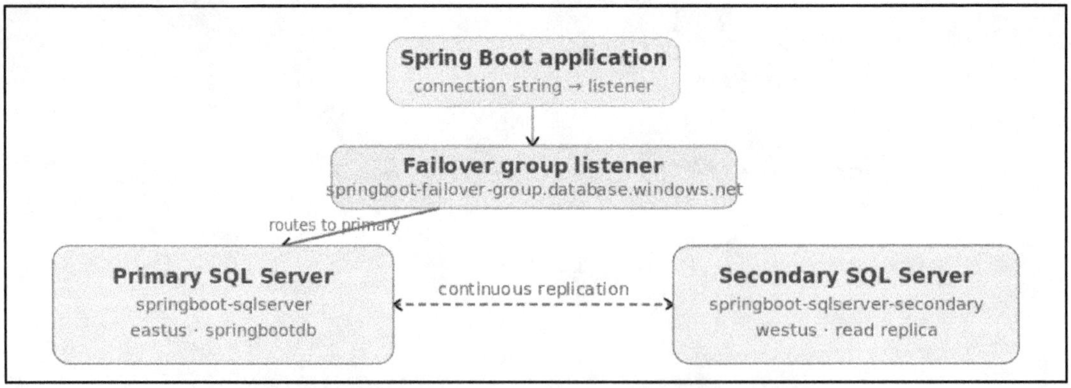

Fig 7.3: Azure SQL Failover Group and Disaster Recovery

In this section we configure two disaster recovery mechanisms, one is the automated database backups with point-in-time restore capability, and the other is Azure SQL failover group that replicates the database to a secondary region and can switch traffic automatically if the primary region becomes unavailable. Both mechanisms are integrated into the pipeline so that the backup step runs after every successful production deployment and the failover configuration is applied consistently across environments.

Configuring Automated Database Backups

The Azure SQL Database automatically performs full, differential, and transaction-log backups on a schedule determined by the service tier. For our General Purpose serverless tier, full backups run weekly, differential backups run every 12 hours, and log backups run every 5 to 10 minutes. These automatic backups support point-in-time restore to any second within the retention period, which defaults to 7 days for the General Purpose tier and can be extended up to 35 days.

In addition to the automatic backups, we add a pipeline step that exports the database as a BACPAC file to our Azure Blob Storage account after every successful production deployment. This gives us a deployment-aligned backup that we can restore to the exact state the database was in immediately after a known good deployment, which is more useful than a time-based backup when investigating a data corruption issue introduced by a specific release.

```
        - task: AzureCLI@2
          displayName: 'Export post-deployment database backup to Blob
Storage'
          inputs:
            azureSubscription: 'springboot-azure'
            scriptType: 'bash'
            scriptLocation: 'inlineScript'
            inlineScript: |
              TIMESTAMP=$(date -u +%Y%m%dT%H%M%SZ)
              az sql db export \
                --resource-group SpringBootRG \
                --server springboot-sqlserver \
                --name springbootdb \
                --admin-user $(SQL_ADMIN_LOGIN) \
                --admin-password $(SQL_ADMIN_PASSWORD) \
                --storage-key $(STORAGE_KEY) \
                --storage-key-type StorageAccessKey \
```

```
                --storage-uri
"https://springboottfstate.blob.core.windows.net/backups/springbootdb-
${TIMESTAMP}.bacpac"
          env:
            SQL_ADMIN_LOGIN:     $(SQL_ADMIN_LOGIN)
            SQL_ADMIN_PASSWORD: $(SQL_ADMIN_PASSWORD)
            STORAGE_KEY:         $(STORAGE_KEY)
```

The **TIMESTAMP** variable creates a unique filename for each backup, incorporating the UTC date and time in ISO 8601 format. The **STORAGE_KEY** secret variable holds the storage account access key and is stored in the pipeline variable group alongside the SQL credentials. After several weeks of production deployments, the **backups** container will accumulate one BACPAC file per deployment. With this ready, we configure a Blob Storage lifecycle policy to delete files older than 90 days to prevent unbounded storage growth.

Setting up Azure SQL Failover Groups

A failover group synchronises an Azure SQL Database to a secondary server in a different Azure region. If the primary server becomes unavailable due to a regional outage, traffic automatically redirects to the secondary server, and the application can continue operating against the replica with minimal interruption. We proceed to configure the failover group through the Azure CLI and capture its endpoint for use in our connection string.

```
# Create the secondary SQL Server in a different region
az sql server create \
  --name springboot-sqlserver-secondary \
  --resource-group SpringBootRG \
  --location westus \
  --admin-user $(SQL_ADMIN_LOGIN) \
  --admin-password $(SQL_ADMIN_PASSWORD)
# Create the failover group linking primary to secondary
az sql failover-group create \
  --name springboot-failover-group \
  --resource-group SpringBootRG \
  --server springboot-sqlserver \
  --partner-server springboot-sqlserver-secondary \
  --failover-policy Automatic \
  --grace-period 1
```

The **--failover-policy Automatic** flag enables automatic failover, meaning Azure SQL triggers the failover without human intervention when the primary server is unavailable for longer than the **--grace-period** minutes. We will now set the grace period to 1 minute to balance protection against brief transient failures with a fast response to genuine regional outages.

With the failover group configured, we update the **SPRING_DATASOURCE_URL** environment variable in our App Service and Container App configurations to point to the failover group listener endpoint rather than the primary server endpoint directly. The listener endpoint is always **springboot-failover-group.database.windows.net**, and it automatically routes connections to whichever server is currently primary. This means the application connection string never needs to change during a failover event.

Automating Failover Testing

A disaster recovery configuration that is never tested is a disaster recovery configuration that may not work when it matters most. We then add a scheduled pipeline that runs a planned failover test once per month during a low-traffic window. The test stage forces the failover group to switch primary to the secondary server, verifies the application responds correctly against the secondary, and then fails back to the original primary.

```
schedules:
- cron: '0 2 1 * *'
  displayName: 'Monthly DR failover test (1st of month, 02:00 UTC)'
  branches:
    include:
      - main
  always: true
```

In the above, the **always: true** flag causes the scheduled run to trigger even if no code changes have been pushed since the last run. Without it, the Azure Pipelines would skip the scheduled run if the branch has not changed. For a DR test that validates infrastructure rather than application code, the skipping is never the correct behaviour, since the infrastructure must be tested on the defined schedule regardless of code activity. The test pipeline stage that uses this schedule would perform the **az sql failover-group set-primary** command against the secondary server, run the Newman collection from Chapter 6 against the application, and then fail back to the original primary using the same command in reverse.

Summary

Throughout this chapter we added the infrastructure automation and operational resilience layer that transforms our delivery pipeline from a deployment tool into a complete infrastructure management system. We introduced Terraform alongside Bicep, explaining the state-management distinction between the two tools and choosing Terraform for the ACR and AKS resources that benefit most from its explicit plan-and-apply workflow. We wrote **infra/terraform/main.tf**, **variables.tf**, and **backend.tf** using current resource types, managed identities instead of hardcoded credentials, and remote state stored in the Azure Blob Storage account we provisioned in Chapter 1.

We wrote a production-ready **Dockerfile** using the Eclipse Temurin Java 17 base image, running the container as a non-root user for security, and added a **.dockerignore** file to keep the build context lean. We added a **BuildImage** stage that downloads the pipeline artifact JAR from the **Build** stage, builds the Docker image, and pushes it to ACR with an immutable build-number tag. We deployed the image to AKS using a Kubernetes manifest with a readiness probe and rolled back capability, and we provisioned Azure Container Apps through Bicep as a simpler managed alternative for teams that do not need full Kubernetes control.

We added Flyway to the application by declaring the **flyway-sqlserver** dependency in **pom.xml**, writing the **V1__initial_schema.sql** migration that creates the **tutorials** table with a title index, and automating the Flyway CLI in a dedicated **RunMigrations** pipeline stage that applies migrations before any application deployment. We finished by configuring post-deployment BACPAC backups, an Azure SQL failover group with automatic failover to a secondary region, and a monthly scheduled DR test pipeline. In Chapter 8 we focus on collaboration and team management, exploring Azure Boards at depth, the GitHub integration we have been using across the book, and DORA metrics for measuring the delivery performance of everything we have built.

CHAPTER 8

COLLABORATION AND TEAM MANAGEMENT IN AZURE DEVOPS

Overview

So far, we have built a Spring Boot REST API from a cloned scaffold into a fully automated, security-scanned, database-migrating, multi-stage delivery pipeline that deploys to Azure App Service, AKS, and Azure Container Apps. Every technical capability we added was pipeline-centric. We focused on what the CI/CD machinery does. This final chapter zooms out to the human layer, which includes how teams plan the work, collaborate on code and pull requests, visualise progress, connect Azure DevOps to GitHub for hybrid workflows, and measure the health of their delivery system using quantitative metrics.

So here, we will start with Azure Boards which we first touched in Chapter 1 when we created the Sprint 1 work items for our test plans. We go deeper here, covering work item types, the Kanban board, sprint planning, swimlanes, and the burndown chart. We then cover the GitHub integration in full, showing how to connect a GitHub repository to Azure Pipelines and how to configure status checks that surface pipeline results directly on GitHub pull requests. After that we configure team workflows with branch policies and approval automations, explore the Azure DevOps Analytics hub and its Power BI connector, and discuss shared pipeline templates and cross-project triggers. We close the chapter, and the book, by introducing DORA metrics, which are the four quantitative indicators that the DevOps Research and Assessment team identified as the most reliable predictors of software delivery performance, and how to measure each one using data already present in our Azure DevOps organisation.

Managing Work Items and Project Boards

As the project planning and work tracking service within Azure DevOps, the Azure Boards holds every feature, bug, user story, task, and impediment Every feature, bug, user story, task, and impediment that our team works on lives in Azure Boards as a typed, versioned, linkable work item. We have been creating work items throughout this book, from the Sprint 1 test cases in Chapter 6 to the security alert bugs linked in that same chapter. In this section we treat Boards more formally, establishing the work item hierarchy, the Kanban board configuration, and the sprint planning workflow that will serve our team as the SpringBootAPI project grows beyond the initial sprint.

Understanding Work Item Hierarchy

Azure Boards organises work using a three-level hierarchy in the Scrum process template we selected in Chapter 1. At the top level, ***Epics*** represent large bodies of work that span multiple sprints or even multiple quarters, such as ***Migrate to containerised deployment*** or ***Implement full observability stack***. Each Epic breaks down into ***Features***, which are deliverable increments within a single release cycle, such as ***AKS deployment pipeline*** or ***Database migration automation***. Each Feature breaks down into ***Product Backlog Items*** (PBIs) in Scrum or ***User Stories*** in Agile, which are the units of work a developer can complete within a sprint, such as

Add Flyway V1 schema migration. Tasks live below PBIs and represent the individual implementation steps a developer takes to complete a story.

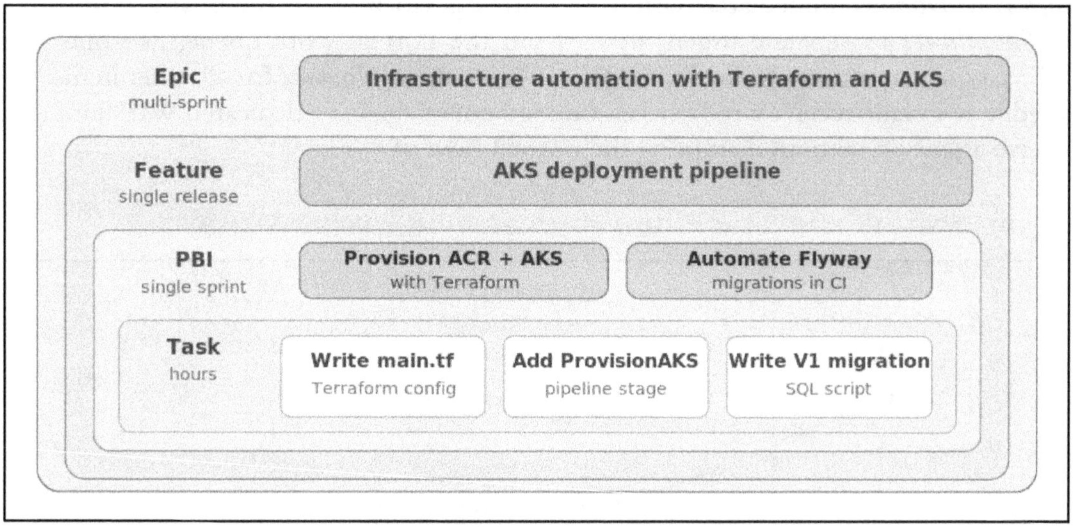

Fig 8.1: Azure Boards Work Item Type Hierarchy

We then navigate to ***Boards > Work Items*** in our **`SpringBootAPI`** project. At this point, we create a Feature named ***Infrastructure automation with Terraform and AKS*** and beneath it we create three Product Backlog Items (PBI) created in chapter 7. We assign each PBI to the current iteration, set the story points to reflect their relative complexity, and link each one to the corresponding pipeline run that validated the work. This linkage is what gives us the audit trail from a stakeholder requirement all the way to the pipeline run that delivered it.

Configuring Kanban Board

We will now navigate to ***Boards > Boards***. The Kanban board displays all active work items as cards arranged in columns that represent the current state of each item. The default Scrum columns are ***New***, ***Active***, ***Resolved***, and ***Closed***. Our team's workflow has a more granular set of states, so we customise the column mapping. So, we click ***Column Options*** and adjust the board columns to the following configuration.

```
Column 1 : New          → maps to state: New
Column 2 : Backlog      → maps to state: Approved
Column 3 : In Progress  → maps to state: Committed
Column 4 : In Review    → maps to state: In Review  (custom state)
Column 5 : Testing      → maps to state: Testing    (custom state)
Column 6 : Done         → maps to state: Done
```

The custom states ***In Review*** and ***Testing*** ensure that a work item is only moved to ***Done*** after it has been through a peer code review and a testing cycle. Any work item that moves directly from ***In Progress*** to ***Done*** is immediately visible as a process violation on the board. With this ready, we add ***Swimlanes*** to separate urgent items from the normal work queue, like one swimlane named ***Expedite*** for critical production bugs and one named ***Normal*** for all other items. Items in the Expedite swimlane receive a red card colour and count against a dedicated WIP limit to ensure they receive attention without disrupting the normal flow of work.

Managing Sprints and Tracking Progress

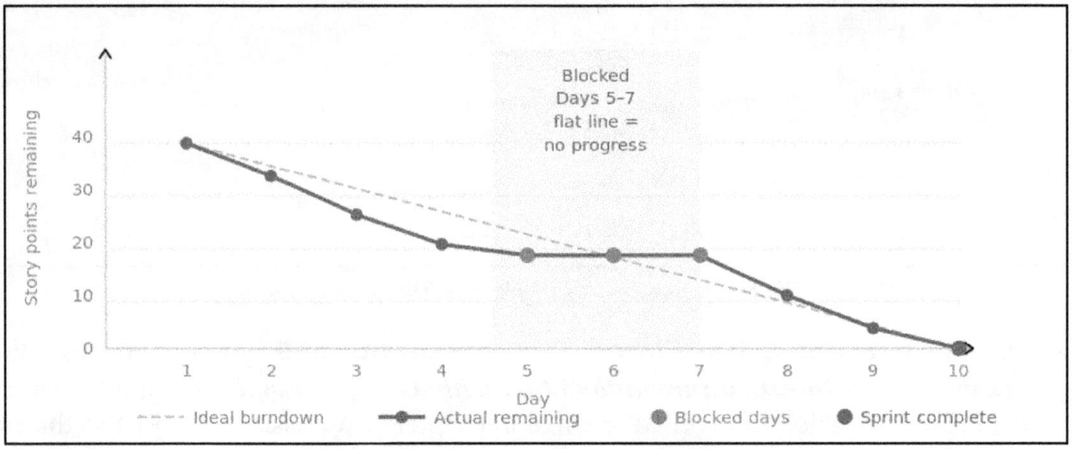

Fig 8.2: Sprint Burndown Chart

We proceed to navigate to ***Boards*** > ***Sprints***. The sprint view shows three tabs, such as Backlog, Taskboard, and Capacity. The ***Backlog*** tab shows all PBIs assigned to the current sprint with their story points and acceptance criteria. The ***Taskboard*** tab shows the individual tasks under each PBI as sticky-note cards, allowing developers to move tasks from ***To Do*** to ***In Progress*** to ***Done*** as they work through the sprint. The ***Capacity*** tab lets us declare each team member's availability in hours per day for the sprint duration, which the burndown chart uses to project whether the sprint scope is achievable given the team's actual capacity.

The ***Sprint Burndown*** chart at the bottom of the Backlog tab updates automatically as work items change state. We will now configure it to burn on story points rather than task count so that the chart reflects the relative weight of remaining work rather than the number of items. A healthy burndown line runs from the total sprint points on day one to zero on the last day of the sprint. A flat line mid-sprint indicates that work is not being completed, which prompts the Scrum Master to investigate whether there is a blocker. A line that drops steeply and then flattens suggests that the team completed simple items early but is now stuck on complex ones.

Using Queries to Track Cross-Sprint Health

In Azure Boards, queries allow us to create saved views of work items filtered by any combination of fields. We then create three standing queries that we add to our project dashboard.

```
Query 1 : 'Open bugs this sprint'
          Work Item Type = Bug
          AND State <> Closed
          AND Iteration = @CurrentIteration
Query 2 : 'Pull requests without linked work items'
          Work Item Type = Task
          AND State = Done
          AND Tags Does Not Contain 'pr-linked'
Query 3 : 'Security alerts awaiting remediation'
          Work Item Type = Bug
          AND Tags Contains 'security-alert'
          AND State <> Closed
```

The third query, targeting bugs tagged **`security-alert`**, surfaces every vulnerability we linked from the GitHub Advanced Security alerts hub in Chapter 6. Any security finding that has been open for more than five days without state movement triggers an automated notification to the security owner, which we configure using Azure DevOps service hooks connected to our team communication channel.

Integrating GitHub with Azure DevOps

We introduced the Azure DevOps and GitHub relationship conceptually in Chapter 1 when we discussed the platform convergence. Throughout this book we have used Azure Repos as our primary Git host and Azure Pipelines as our CI/CD engine, which is the straightforward single-platform configuration. In this section, we connect a GitHub repository as a pipeline source, so that teams who host their source code on GitHub can still use the full Azure Pipelines feature set for their delivery workflows.

Connecting a GitHub Repository to Azure Pipelines

We can now navigate to ***Pipelines*** > ***New Pipeline*** in our **`SpringBootAPI`** project. On the connection type screen we select ***GitHub*** rather than Azure Repos Git. The Azure DevOps immediately redirects us to the GitHub OAuth consent screen. We authorise the Azure Pipelines app on our GitHub account and return to the portal. The Azure DevOps now shows a list of all repositories accessible to our GitHub account. We then select a hypothetical second repository, **`gitforgits/springboot-frontend`**, which represents a React frontend that consumes the API we have been building. At this point, we select ***Starter Pipeline*** and Azure DevOps creates a new **`azure-pipelines.yml`** file at the root of the GitHub repository.

The resulting pipeline is identical in structure to the one we have been building in **`azure-pipelines.yml`** throughout this book. All YAML syntax, all task names, all variable and parameter features work identically regardless of whether the source repository lives in Azure Repos or GitHub. The only operational difference is that Azure DevOps installs a GitHub App on the repository to receive webhook events rather than using the Azure Repos webhook that fires automatically for repositories hosted within the Azure DevOps organisation.

Surfacing Pipeline Status Checks on GitHub Pull Requests

When a pipeline is connected to a GitHub repository, the Azure DevOps automatically reports pipeline run results back to GitHub as status checks on the pull request that triggered the run. Every pull request on **`main`** in the **`springboot-frontend`** repository will show an Azure Pipelines status check in the GitHub Checks tab, with a direct link to the pipeline run in Azure DevOps for detailed log inspection.

We will now configure the GitHub branch protection rule to require the Azure Pipelines status check to pass before a pull request can be merged. So, we navigate to the GitHub repository settings, click ***Branches*** under Code and Automation, click ***Add branch ruleset*** for **`main`**, and tick ***Require status checks to pass before merging***. We search for and add the Azure Pipelines check name, which follows the format **`Azure Pipelines / SpringBootAPI`**. With this rule in place, the branch protection model on GitHub mirrors the branch policy we configured on Azure Repos in Chapter 1, where no code can reach **`main`** without a passing pipeline, and no pipeline result can be bypassed.

Linking GitHub Commits and Pull Requests to Azure Boards Work Items

Azure Boards supports bidirectional linking with GitHub through the Azure Boards app for GitHub.

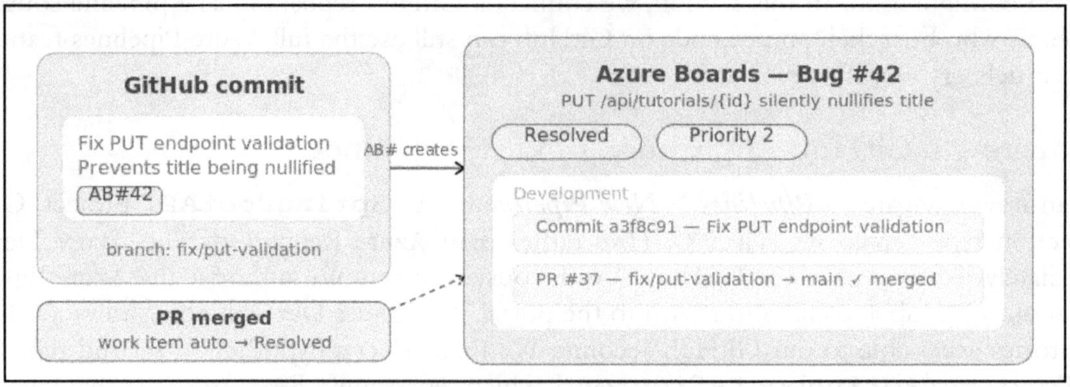

Fig 8.3: Bidirectional GitHub Commit and Work Item Traceability

With this ready, we install the app by navigating to ***Project Settings*** > ***GitHub connections*** and clicking ***New connection***. We authorise the Azure Boards app on our GitHub organisation and select the **`gitforgits/springboot-frontend`** repository.

With the connection established, any GitHub commit message that contains the syntax **`AB#<work-item-id>`** automatically creates a link between the commit and the Azure Boards work item. For example, a commit message of **`Add search bar component AB#42`** links that commit to work item 42 in Azure Boards. The work item's ***Development*** section then shows the commit, the branch it was on, and a link to the GitHub pull request that merged it. The pull requests that include **`AB#42`** in their title or description create a similar link, and when the pull request is merged, the Azure Boards automatically transitions the linked work item to the ***Resolved*** state if the default transition rules are active.

Managing Notifications and Monitoring Pipeline Runs

Azure DevOps sends notifications when pipeline runs complete, fail, or require approval. We proceed to configure team notifications by navigating to ***Project Settings*** > ***Notifications*** > ***New subscription***. We will now create two notification rules. The first sends an email to the entire development team when any pipeline on **`main`** fails. The second sends a targeted notification to the designated on-call engineer when the **`Production`** stage enters the ***Waiting for approval*** state, so that approval requests are never silently queued overnight without anyone knowing they are pending.

For real-time team alerts, we configure a service hook that posts to a Microsoft Teams or Slack channel. We then navigate to ***Project Settings*** > ***Service hooks*** > ***+ Create subscription***. We can now select ***Microsoft Teams*** or ***Slack*** as the target, choose ***Run stage state changed*** as the trigger event, filter on the **`Production`** stage and the ***Failed*** state, and paste the incoming webhook URL for our team channel. Every failed production deployment now posts a message to the channel immediately, giving the on-call engineer the build number, the pipeline name, and a direct link to the failing stage log.

Setting up Team Workflows

A team workflow defines the rules that govern how work moves through the system, like which branches require review, how many approvers a pull request needs, whether automated checks must pass before a merge is allowed, and how work item states transition as code progresses through the pipeline. We have applied branch policies and approval gates individually at various points in this book. In this section we consolidate those rules into a coherent workflow definition and show how to extend it using Azure DevOps process customisation and work item automation.

Defining and Enforcing Branch Policies

The branch policy we configured on **`main`** in Chapter 1 required one reviewer approval before merging. Now that our team is growing and the codebase is maturing, we strengthen that policy. We then navigate to ***Project Settings*** > ***Repositories*** > **`SpringBootAPI`** > ***Policies*** > **`main`** branch and review the current settings. At this point, we add the following additional policies.

```
Minimum reviewers            : 2 (increased from 1)
Prohibit self-approval       : enabled
Reset votes on new push      : enabled
Require linked work items    : enabled
Required builds              : SpringBootAPI CI (our azure-pipelines.yml)
Comment resolution           : All comments must be resolved before merging
```

The ***prohibit self-approval*** setting means the pull request author cannot count as one of the two required reviewers, enforcing the four-eyes principle. The ***reset votes on new push*** means that if a reviewer approves a pull request and the author then pushes a new commit, all approval votes are reset and the reviewers must re-examine the updated code before the merge proceeds. This prevents the common bypass pattern where a developer obtains approval on a small diff and then pushes a large additional change before the window of approval expires.

The ***require linked work items*** option enforces our policy that every pull request must reference at least one Azure Boards work item. A developer who opens a pull request without linking it to a user story, task, or bug will see a blocking policy violation in the PR overview and will be unable to merge until the link is added. This rule, combined with the commit message **`AB#`** convention for GitHub integration, ensures that every line of code that enters **`main`** is traceable to a planned work item, giving management and audit stakeholders complete visibility into why each change was made.

Customising Work Item Process

We will now navigate to ***Organisation Settings*** > ***Process*** and select the ***Scrum*** process. So, we click ***Product Backlog Item*** to open the work item type editor and add a custom field named ***Definition of Done*** of type ***Text (multiple lines)***. This field gives each PBI an explicit, team-agreed checklist of what must be true before the item is considered complete. It includes tests written and passing, documentation updated, security scan clean, peer review approved, and feature flag configured if applicable.

We also add a custom rule that prevents a PBI from transitioning to the ***Done*** state if the ***Definition of Done*** field is empty. With this ready, we click ***New rule*** in the work item type editor, set the condition to ***Definition of Done field is empty***, and set the action to ***Restrict the transition to Done***. This rule transforms the Definition of Done from a suggestion into an enforced checklist, preventing items from being marked complete without explicit sign-off on each acceptance criterion.

Automating Work Item State Transitions with Service Hooks

We want the pipeline to automatically advance work item states as deployments succeed. When our **`Staging`** deployment completes successfully, any PBI linked to that build's commits should transition automatically from ***Active*** to ***Testing***. When the **`Production`** deployment completes, those same PBIs should move to ***Resolved***. We proceed to implement this through Azure DevOps service hooks and a simple Azure Function that receives the webhook payload and calls the Azure DevOps REST API.

We will now navigate to ***Project Settings*** > ***Service hooks*** > ***+ Create subscription*** and select ***Azure Functions*** as the target. We choose ***Run stage state changed*** as the trigger, filter on the **`Staging`** stage and the ***Succeeded*** state, and supply the URL of an Azure Function we deploy separately. The Function reads the build ID from the webhook payload, queries the Azure DevOps API for work items associated with that build's commits, and issues a PATCH request to transition each qualifying work item from ***Active*** to ***Testing***. This closes the automation loop of code merged to **`main`** moves work items to ***Active***, a successful staging deployment moves them to ***Testing***, and a successful production deployment moves them to ***Resolved***.

Tracking Project Progress with Azure DevOps Analytics

As a built-in, near-real-time reporting engine, the Azure DevOps Analytics stores a queryable copy of all work item, pipeline, test, and deployment data for the organisation. Unlike the classic Azure DevOps reports that required warehouse synchronisation, Analytics is always current and supports OData queries directly from the portal or from Power BI. Every dashboard widget we add in this section reads from the Analytics service, and every chart we build in Power BI connects to the same data source through the Azure DevOps Power BI connector.

Setting up Project Dashboard

We then navigate to ***Overview*** > ***Dashboards*** and create a new dashboard named ***Sprint Health***. We can now set the dashboard as the project's default so that every team member sees it when they open the Azure DevOps portal. We then click ***Edit*** and add the following widgets using the ***+ Add widget*** panel.

```
Widget 1  : Sprint Burndown, tracks story points remaining in current sprint
Widget 2  : Work Items, shows open / active / resolved counts by type
Widget 3  : Velocity, plots story points completed per sprint for last 6 sprints
Widget 4  : Test Results Trend, plots unit test pass rate per pipeline run
Widget 5  : Build History, shows last 10 runs of the main CI pipeline with status
```

```
Widget 6  : Deployment Frequency, shows number of production deployments
per week
Widget 7  : Failed Builds, counts of failed pipeline runs this sprint
Widget 8  : Active Bugs, count of open bugs tagged security-alert
```

The ***Deployment Frequency*** widget in Widget 6 is not a standard out-of-the-box widget; we configure it as a ***Query Tile*** that counts completed pipeline runs against the **`Production`** stage environment within the current sprint date range. This is our first step toward DORA metrics measurement, which we formalise in the dedicated section later in this chapter.

Using Velocity and Capacity Reports

The ***Velocity*** report is accessible from ***Boards*** > ***Analytics*** > ***Velocity***. It plots the total story points completed against the total points committed for each of the last ten sprints. For a team new to Azure DevOps, the first two or three sprints often show a large gap between committed and completed because estimates are calibrated poorly. The velocity report makes this pattern visible and gives the Scrum Master concrete data to present in the sprint retrospective. After four or five sprints, the completed line stabilises, and the team can use the average completed points as a planning benchmark for future sprints.

The ***Cumulative Flow Diagram*** is the most powerful analytics view for identifying bottlenecks in the team's workflow. It is accessible from ***Boards*** > ***Analytics*** > ***Cumulative Flow***. The diagram plots the count of work items in each state over time as stacked areas. A healthy CFD shows all bands expanding at roughly the same rate, indicating work is flowing smoothly through each state. A widening band in ***In Review*** or ***Testing*** indicates a bottleneck at that state, where work is accumulating faster than it is being processed. We pin the CFD to the Sprint Health dashboard as a second-tab widget so that the team reviews it every Monday standup.

Exporting Data to Power BI

For stakeholder reporting that goes beyond the built-in dashboard widgets, we connect the Azure DevOps project to Power BI using the official Azure DevOps connector. At this point, we open Power BI Desktop, click ***Get Data***, search for ***Azure DevOps***, and enter our organisation URL ***https://dev.azure.com/GitforGits*** and project name **`SpringBootAPI`**. The Power BI loads all available Analytics entities, like work items, iterations, areas, pipelines, test runs, and deployments. We then select the work item and pipeline run entities and click ***Load***.

So, we create a Power BI report page named ***Delivery Executive Summary*** with four visuals. The first is a card visual showing the total number of production deployments in the last 30 days. The second is a line chart showing the pipeline pass rate over the same period. The third is a bar chart showing the distribution of work items by state and type. The fourth is a table listing all open bugs with their age in days and their priority. We publish the report to the Power BI service and share the URL with stakeholders so they can view it directly in their browser without needing Power BI Desktop or Azure DevOps credentials. We schedule the data refresh to run daily at 07:00 so the report always reflects the previous day's state when stakeholders check it at the start of their working day.

Collaborating across Teams with Shared Pipelines

As our organisation grows and additional microservices join the SpringBootAPI ecosystem, each new service needs its own pipeline. Without a shared structure, each service team would define its own pipeline from scratch, leading to inconsistent quality gates, different security scan configurations, and no guarantee that the Maven build template or the Newman API test stage follow the same standards as the original. In Chapter 2 we introduced YAML pipeline templates as a reusability mechanism within a single repository. In this section we scale that mechanism to the organisational level using a shared template repository that all service pipelines reference.

Creating a Shared Pipeline Template Repository

With this ready, we create a new Azure Repos repository named **pipeline-templates** inside the **GitforGits** organisation. This repository holds the reusable YAML templates that any service pipeline can reference. We proceed to add the following files to the repository, extracted and generalised from the **azure-pipelines.yml** and **templates/maven-build-steps.yml** files we wrote in Chapter 2.

```
pipeline-templates/
├── steps/
│   ├── maven-build.yml          ← Maven build, test, SonarCloud, GHAzDO
│   ├── docker-build-push.yml    ← Docker build and ACR push
│   ├── newman-api-tests.yml     ← Newman collection runner
│   └── flyway-migrate.yml       ← Flyway migration runner
├── stages/
│   ├── build-stage.yml          ← complete Build stage
│   ├── staging-stage.yml        ← Staging deployment stage
│   └── production-stage.yml     ← Production deployment with approval gate
└── pipelines/
    └── spring-boot-full.yml     ← full pipeline composing all stages
```

Each file in **steps/** is a step template that accepts parameters for the values that differ between Maven goals, artifact name, ACR image name, the Postman collection path, and the database connection details. Each file in **stages/** is a stage template that composes one or more step templates. The **pipelines/spring-boot-full.yml** file is a complete pipeline definition that a new service team can use by creating a single two-line **azure-pipelines.yml** in their own repository that extends this template.

```
resources:
  repositories:
  - repository: pipelineTemplates
    type: git
    name: GitforGits/pipeline-templates
    ref: refs/heads/main
extends:
  template: pipelines/spring-boot-full.yml@pipelineTemplates
  parameters:
    artifactName: 'payments-api'
    acrImageName: 'payments-api'
    sonarProjectKey: 'GitforGits_PaymentsAPI'
    postmanCollection:
'postman/PaymentsAPIContractTests.postman_collection.json'
    postmanEnvironment: 'postman/Staging.postman_environment.json'
```

The **extends** keyword is Azure Pipelines' template inheritance mechanism. It requires the consumer pipeline to use the extended template as its root structure, which means the service team cannot add arbitrary stages or steps outside the template. This is a security and governance feature, where an organisation security administrator can require that all pipelines in sensitive repositories extend from an approved template, preventing a developer from adding an ad-hoc **script** step that exfiltrates secrets or deploys to an unauthorised environment.

Configuring Cross-Project Pipeline Triggers

In a microservices architecture, the deployment of one service may need to trigger integration tests or downstream deployments in a dependent service. For example, when the SpringBootAPI pipeline successfully deploys to production, the frontend service pipeline should run its end-to-end tests against the new API version to confirm the contract has not broken. We will now configure this cross-project trigger in the frontend service's **azure-pipelines.yml** file.

```
resources:
  pipelines:
  - pipeline: SpringBootAPIProduction
    project: SpringBootAPI
```

```
    source: 'SpringBootAPI'
    trigger:
      stages:
      - Production
trigger: none
# This pipeline runs only when SpringBootAPI's Production stage succeeds.
# It then executes the frontend integration test suite.
stages:
- stage: IntegrationTests
  displayName: 'Frontend integration tests against new API version'
  jobs:
  - job: RunTests
    pool:
      vmImage: 'ubuntu-latest'
    steps:
    - template: steps/newman-api-tests.yml@pipelineTemplates
      parameters:
        postmanCollection:
'postman/FrontendE2ETests.postman_collection.json'
        postmanEnvironment: 'postman/Production.postman_environment.json'
```

The **`trigger: none`** at the top of the file disables all automatic triggers for this pipeline. The only mechanism that can start a run is the cross-project pipeline resource trigger defined in the **`resources.pipelines`** block. When the **`SpringBootAPI`** pipeline's **`Production`** stage completes successfully, the Azure DevOps automatically queues a new run of the frontend integration pipeline. The run targets the production environment with the just-deployed API version, giving the team immediate feedback on whether the API change broke any frontend contract expectations.

Measuring Team Performance with DORA Metrics

The DevOps Research and Assessment team, after years of surveying tens of thousands of software professionals, identified four metrics that most reliably distinguish high-performing software delivery teams from low-performing ones. These four metrics, collectively called DORA metrics, measure the throughput and stability of a delivery system. Teams that perform well on all four consistently deliver more value, recover from failures faster, and have lower rates of change-induced incidents than teams that do not. At this point in the work, we have built a pipeline and a deployment system that produces all the raw data we need to calculate each DORA metric directly from Azure DevOps.

Understanding Four DORA Metrics

Deployment Frequency measures how often the team deploys code to production. Elite teams deploy multiple times per day; high performers deploy between once per day and once per week; medium performers deploy between once per week and once per month; low performers deploy less than once per month. In Azure DevOps, every successful run of the **`Production`** stage in our pipeline is a production deployment. We measure deployment frequency by counting those runs over a rolling 30-day window.

Lead Time for Changes measures the time from the first commit on a branch to when that commit is running in production. The short lead times indicate a streamlined pipeline and a fast review cycle. Elite teams achieve lead times of under one hour; high performers achieve under one day. In our pipeline, lead time begins when a developer pushes the first commit to a feature branch and ends when the **`Production`** stage for the pull request that merged those commits completes successfully.

Change Failure Rate measures the percentage of production deployments that require a hotfix, a rollback, or any immediate remediation. Elite teams achieve change failure rates below 5%; low performers see rates above 15%. In our pipeline, a change failure is a production deployment followed by a rollback via **`kubectl rollout undo`** or a slot swap reversal, or a hotfix deployment within 24 hours of the original release.

Failed Deployment Recovery Time measures how long it takes to restore service after a production incident or failed deployment. Elite teams restore service in under one hour; low performers take between one week and one month. In our system, recovery time begins when the on-call engineer acknowledges a production alert and ends when a remediation deployment completes and the smoke test confirms the application is healthy.

Measuring Deployment Frequency with Azure DevOps Analytics

We measure deployment frequency by querying the Analytics service for completed pipeline runs that reached the **`Production`** stage with a ***Succeeded*** result. We then navigate to ***Analytics*** > ***Analytics views*** and create a new view named ***Production Deployments*** with the following OData filter applied.

```
Entity        : Pipelines - Pipeline Runs
Filter        : Pipeline name = 'SpringBootAPI'
               AND Stage name = 'Production'
               AND Result     = 'Succeeded'
Date field    : Finish time
```

```
Time range    : Rolling 30 days
```

We can now add a ***Query Tile*** widget to the Sprint Health dashboard that displays the count of rows in this view. The number shown is the deployment frequency for the last 30 days. For a team aiming to reach the ***High*** performance band, the target is 30 or more deployments in a 30-day window, which corresponds to at least one deployment per day on average. Teams new to continuous delivery typically start in the ***Medium*** band at 4 to 12 deployments per month and improve as they reduce manual gates, speed up pipeline execution, and increase confidence in automated test coverage.

Calculating Lead Time Using Pipeline and Work Item Data

The lead time calculation requires joining two data sources, such as the timestamp of the first commit on a feature branch and the timestamp of the completed **`Production`** pipeline run that deployed that commit. The Azure DevOps records both timestamps. We then use the Power BI Azure DevOps connector to pull both datasets and create a calculated column in Power BI.

```
Lead Time (hours) =
  DATEDIFF(
    [FirstCommitTime],
    [ProductionDeploymentFinishTime],
    HOUR
  )
```

At this point, we add a card visual to the Delivery Executive Summary Power BI report that shows the average lead time in hours over the last 30 days. We also add a scatter plot that shows the lead time distribution, with each point representing a single merged pull request. The outliers are immediately visible as points far to the right of the cluster. These outliers are typically associated with long-running feature branches, which is exactly what the short-branch, frequent-integration discipline of continuous integration is designed to prevent.

Tracking Change Failure Rate Through Tagged Deployments

We track change failure rate by adding a standardised tag to any pipeline run that resulted in a production incident. When the on-call engineer determines that a deployment caused an incident requiring immediate remediation, they navigate to the pipeline run in Azure DevOps, click the ellipsis menu, and select ***Add tags***. They add the tag **`incident`**. We then create an Analytics view that counts runs with the **`incident`** tag against the total production deployment count for the same period. The ratio is the change failure rate.

```
Change Failure Rate = (Runs tagged 'incident' / Total Production Runs) *
100
```

```
Example:
  30 production deployments in October
  2 deployments tagged 'incident'
  CFR = (2 / 30) * 100 = 6.7%  → High performer band (< 15%)
```

So, we add a card visual to the Power BI report showing the rolling 90-day change failure rate. A 90-day window is more meaningful than a 30-day window for this metric because a single incident in a 30-day period with only a few deployments can produce a misleadingly high rate. Over 90 days with more deployments, the rate stabilises into a genuine signal about the team's quality practices.

Measuring Failed Deployment Recovery Time with Work Items

Recovery time begins at the moment the team acknowledges a production incident and ends when a remediation deployment restores the service to health. We track both timestamps using a dedicated work item type. With this ready, we add a custom work item type named ***Incident*** to the Scrum process template with three custom fields, which are ***Detected At*** (the time the incident was first observed), ***Acknowledged At*** (the time the on-call engineer accepted ownership), and ***Resolved At*** (the time the service was restored and the smoke test passed).

We proceed to create an Incident work item for every production event and populate these three fields. In Power BI, we calculate the recovery time as **`Resolved At`** minus **`Acknowledged At`** and plot the average over a rolling 90-day window. We also plot the individual incident recovery times as a bar chart sorted by duration, which makes it immediately visible whether recent incidents are being resolved faster than older ones. A downward trend in that chart is the quantitative evidence that our disaster recovery investments from Chapter 7, the automated database backups, the SQL failover group, and the Kubernetes rollback capability, are producing real improvements in operational resilience.

Publishing a DORA Scorecard Dashboard

We will now create a final Power BI report page named ***DORA Scorecard*** that shows all four metrics side by side with their performance band classifications. Each metric is presented as a card visual with a colour-coded band indicator. They are green for ***Elite***, blue for ***High***, yellow for ***Medium***, and red for ***Low***. We then add a target line to each trend chart showing the threshold for the next performance band above our current level.

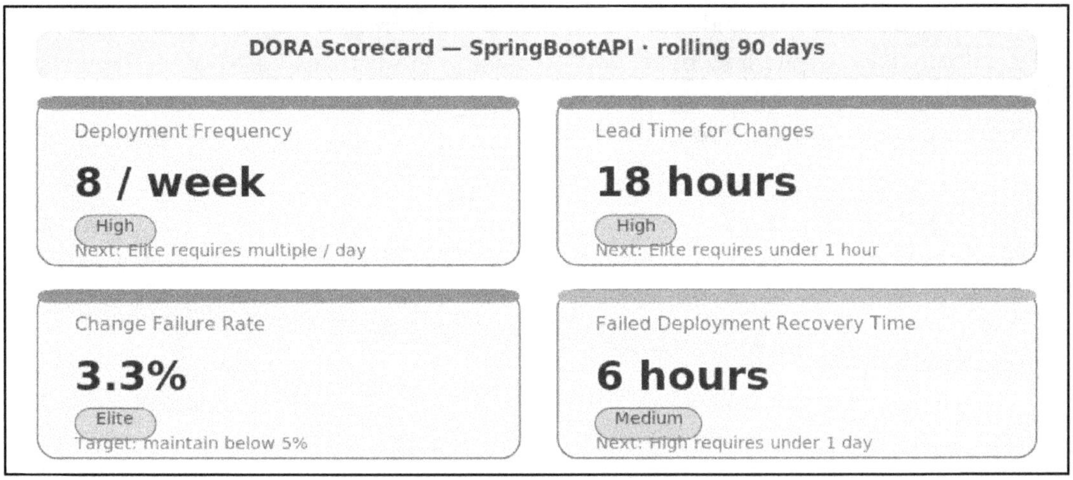

Fig 8.4: DORA Metrics Scorecard

This gives the team a concrete, data-driven goal to work toward in every sprint retrospective, grounded in the same measurements used by thousands of teams worldwide.

Summary

Throughout this final chapter, we completed the human-layer complement to the technical delivery pipeline we built across Chapters 1 through 7. We configured Azure Boards with a properly structured work item hierarchy, customised Kanban board columns, sprint planning workflows, standing queries for sprint health, and an enforced Definition of Done field with a state transition rule. We connected a GitHub repository to Azure Pipelines and configured status checks to surface pipeline results on GitHub pull requests, then linked GitHub commits and pull requests bidirectionally to Azure Boards work items using the **`AB#`** syntax convention.

We strengthened the branch policy on **`main`** with two-reviewer requirements, self-approval prohibition, vote resets on new push, and mandatory work item linkage. We customised the Scrum work item process to add the Definition of Done field and a custom state transition rule. We configured service hooks to post team notifications to Microsoft Teams or Slack when pipeline stages fail or enter the approval waiting state, and we outlined an Azure Function-based automation for transitioning work item states as deployments succeed. We built the Sprint Health dashboard with velocity, burndown, CFD, test results, and deployment frequency widgets, and we connected the project to Power BI for stakeholder-grade executive reporting.

We created a shared **`pipeline-templates`** repository that centralises the Maven build, Docker build, Newman test, and Flyway migration step templates, demonstrated the **`extends`** keyword for template inheritance, and configured cross-project pipeline triggers so that a successful SpringBootAPI production deployment automatically runs the frontend integration test pipeline. Finally, we introduced DORA metrics as the quantitative measurement framework for our delivery system, defined each of the four metrics, and showed how to calculate

Deployment Frequency from Analytics views, Lead Time from a Power BI DAX join, Change Failure Rate from tagged pipeline runs, and Recovery Time from custom Incident work item fields. The result is a DORA Scorecard Power BI page that gives our team a clear, evidence-based view of where we stand and what to improve next.

Chapter 9
Implementing DevSecOps

Overview

Security has been woven into our pipeline across the entire book. In Chapter 3 we enabled GitHub Advanced Security and added CodeQL code scanning, secret scanning, and dependency scanning to the **`Build`** stage. In Chapter 4 we stored sensitive values as secret pipeline variables and used the **`env`** injection pattern to prevent expression injection attacks. In Chapter 5 we proxied all external package registries through private Azure Artifacts feeds to eliminate the supply chain risk of packages disappearing or being tampered with after we first consumed them. In Chapter 6 we linked security alerts from the Advanced Security hub to Azure Boards work items so that vulnerabilities receive sprint-level tracking. In Chapter 7 we ran the Spring Boot container as a non-root user and stored infrastructure credentials through managed identities rather than long-lived secrets.

This chapter consolidates all of those individual security decisions into a coherent DevSecOps model. The DevSecOps is the practice of integrating security controls into every stage of the DevOps lifecycle rather than treating security as a separate gate that software passes through once before release. The underlying idea is simple. It says that the vulnerability found in a developer's IDE costs minutes to fix, and the same vulnerability found in a penetration test after deployment costs days or weeks and may require emergency patching, customer notifications, and regulatory reporting. Earlier detection is always cheaper than later detection, and automation is the only way to make early detection consistent enough to be relied upon.

We organise this chapter around the DevOps lifecycle stages we have worked through in order. For each stage, plan, code, build, test, release, deploy, operate, we identify the security controls that belong there, show how to configure them in our Azure DevOps environment, and wire them into the pipeline so they run automatically without requiring any manual security review step. We also cover GitHub Advanced Security's autofix capability, security campaign bulk remediation, supply chain security with SBOM generation, and the integration of Microsoft Defender for Cloud with our pipeline.

DevSecOps Principles and Shift-Left Security

The term ***shift left*** refers to moving security activities earlier in the development timeline. On a traditional project timeline that reads from left (planning) to right (production), security testing was historically the rightmost activity, where a separate team ran penetration tests and vulnerability scans against a completed application before it was approved for deployment. The shifting left means performing those same checks continuously throughout development, starting from the moment a developer writes their first line of code.

The shift-left model rests on three principles. The first is ***automation over manual review***. Every security check that can be expressed as a rule, a pattern, or a policy should be automated and run on every commit. Manual security reviews are slow, inconsistent, and cannot scale to the frequency of modern continuous delivery.

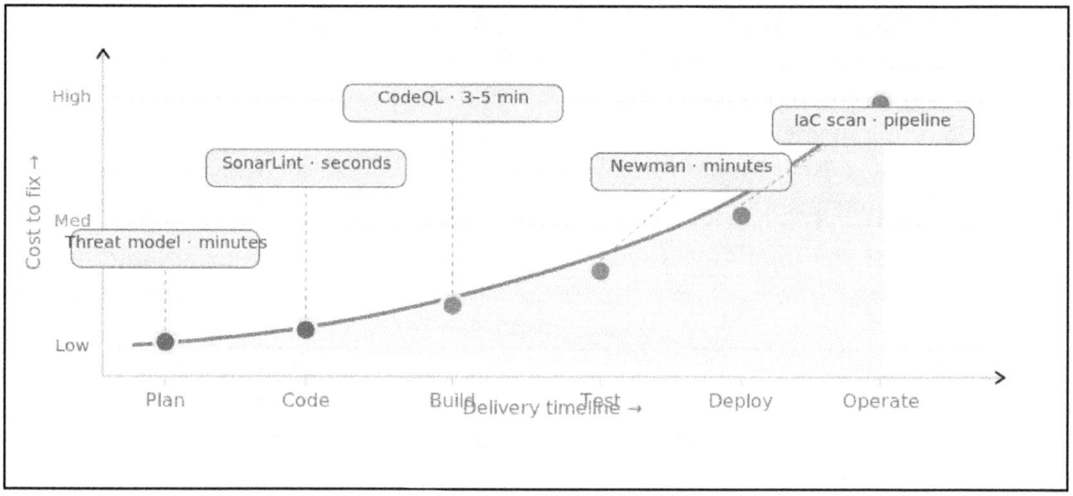

Fig 9.1: Shift-Left Security Cost Curve

The second principle is ***developer ownership***. When a security scan runs in the developer's IDE or on their pull request, the developer who wrote the code sees the finding and fixes it immediately. The security team's role shifts from gatekeeper to enabler, where it defines the rules, configure the tools, and triage complex findings, but the frontline remediation work belongs to the developer who introduced the issue.

The third principle is ***progressive enforcement***. New security controls are introduced gradually with educational feedback before they become pipeline blockers. A rule that immediately fails builds without explanation creates friction; a rule that first warns, then enforces once the team has had time to remediate the existing backlog, creates compliance without hostility.

Throughout the remainder of this chapter we apply these three principles to every security control we configure. Each control is automated, each finding is routed to the developer responsible for the code, and each new enforcement rule is introduced with an appropriate on-ramp period. We also map every security control to the specific DevOps stage where it provides the most value and the least friction, because a control applied at the wrong stage is either ineffective or unnecessarily disruptive.

Security at Plan Stage

Of all security activities, the work that begins at the plan stage is the most cost-effective. A threat model completed before a single line of code is written can eliminate entire vulnerability classes by choosing a different architecture, a different library, or a different data storage strategy. The Azure Boards is our tool for embedding security requirements into sprint planning alongside feature requirements.

Creating Security Work Items from Threat Models

For every new feature that touches authentication, authorisation, data storage, or external API integration, we create a dedicated ***Security Review*** task as a child of the feature's Product Backlog Item. This task represents the lightweight threat modelling exercise the developer or tech lead performs before implementation begins. The Definition of Done field we configured in Chapter 8 includes an explicit ***Threat model completed*** checklist item, so no feature reaches ***In Review*** state without at least one person having thought through the security implications of the design.

We also configure the ***Iteration Goals*** section of each sprint to include a standing security item, in which we ***review and triage all new Advanced Security alerts from the previous sprint***. This item is assigned to the security-aware developer on the team, who is responsible for ensuring that dependency, code scan, and secret scan findings from the prior sprint's pipeline runs are either linked to remediation work items or dismissed with a documented justification. With this as a standing sprint commitment rather than an ad-hoc task, we ensure security debt never accumulates silently across sprints.

Enforcing Security Requirements

The branch policies we configured on **`main`** in Chapter 8 already enforce code review and pipeline passage. We can now add one additional policy that specifically addresses security about a ***required reviewer*** rule that includes our security-aware developer as a mandatory reviewer on any pull request that modifies files in the **`src/main/java/`**, **`infra/`**, or **`k8s/`** directories. It ensures that changes to application code, infrastructure templates, and Kubernetes manifests always receive a security-informed review in addition to the standard functional review.

```
Reviewer group  : Security Champions
Applies to paths:
  src/main/java/**
  infra/**
  k8s/**
  Dockerfile
  .github/**
Bypass allowed  : Off
Review required : Yes
```

In the above, the ***Security Champions*** group is a small team of developers who have received additional security training and act as the first line of security review for the engineering team. They are not a bottleneck, rather they review pull requests within the same SLA as any other reviewer, and their presence on every infrastructure and application code change ensures that a developer with security expertise has seen every modification before it reaches **`main`**.

Security at Code Stage

The code stage is where developers write and edit source files in their IDE. The security controls at this stage produce the fastest possible feedback loop. A finding in VS Code is visible within seconds of writing the vulnerable code, before the developer has even saved the file.

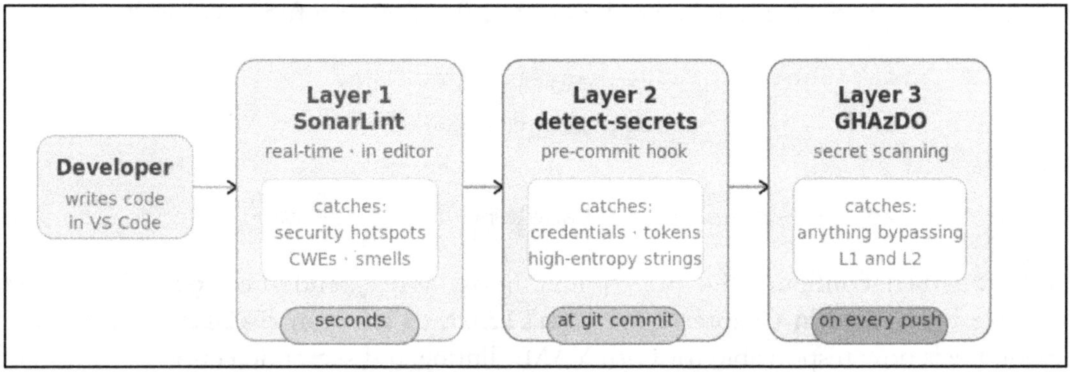

Fig 9.2: Three-Layer Code-Stage Defence

The two primary code-stage security tools in our stack are the SonarLint VS Code extension for real-time static analysis and the **`.gitignore`** and pre-commit hook combination for preventing secrets from ever entering the repository.

Installing and Configuring SonarLint

SonarLint is going to be the IDE companion to SonarCloud. When connected to our **`SpringBootAPI`**, the SonarLint downloads the same ruleset and quality profile that our pipeline uses and applies it to files as we type. A violation that would fail the SonarCloud quality gate on the next pipeline run is flagged with a red underline in the editor right now, allowing us to fix it before we commit.

So here, we will install SonarLint from the VS Code Extensions pane by searching for ***SonarLint*** and installing it. After installation, we connect it to our SonarCloud account, and then open the Command Palette, type **`SonarLint: Connect to SonarCloud`**, and follow the authentication flow. We then select **`GitforGits`** and **`GitforGits_SpringBootAPI`** project, after which the SonarLint downloads the bound quality profile and begins analysing files immediately. The **`Problems`** panel in VS Code then shows SonarLint findings alongside the existing Java and YAML language server findings, each labelled with its rule ID so we can look up the security rationale in the SonarCloud documentation.

Preventing Secrets with Pre-Commit Hook

The secret scanning in the pipeline, which we enabled in Chapter 3, catches credentials that were accidentally committed. However, by the time the pipeline scanner finds a secret, the credential has already entered the repository's commit history, where it can be recovered from **`git log`** even after the file is deleted. The correct defence is to prevent secrets from entering the repository at all, using a pre-commit hook that scans every staged file before the commit is finalised.

So here, we will now use the **detect-secrets** tool, which is a Python-based pre-commit hook developed by Yelp to identify high-entropy strings, API key patterns, and connection string formats in staged files. So, we install it into our project and generate a baseline file that records all currently known false positives so the hook does not flag them on future commits.

```
pip install detect-secrets --break-system-packages
detect-secrets scan > .secrets.baseline
git add .secrets.baseline
git commit -m "Add detect-secrets baseline for pre-commit secret scanning"
```

After this, we then configure the pre-commit hook. We extend the **.git/hooks/pre-commit** file we created in Chapter 2 for **yamllint** to also run **detect-secrets**. This single hook file is now responsible for both YAML linting and secret detection on every commit.

```
#!/bin/bash
set -e
# YAML lint check
yamllint azure-pipelines.yml
if [ $? -ne 0 ]; then
  echo "YAML lint failed. Fix errors before committing."
  exit 1
fi
# Secret scanning check
detect-secrets-hook --baseline .secrets.baseline $(git diff --cached --
name-only)
if [ $? -ne 0 ]; then
  echo "Potential secret detected. Review the finding before committing."
  echo "If it is a false positive, run: detect-secrets scan >
.secrets.baseline"
  exit 1
fi
echo "Pre-commit checks passed."
```

With this hook in place, any commit that contains a string matching a known credential pattern is blocked at the developer's machine before it touches the repository. The error message directs the developer to either remove the credential and replace it with an environment variable or configuration reference, or update the baseline if the finding is a confirmed false positive. This two-line defence, local pre-commit hook plus pipeline secret scanning, creates a defence-in-depth posture where secrets must bypass two independent controls to enter the codebase.

Security at Build Stage

The build stage is where our most comprehensive set of automated security controls runs. As of Chapter 7, the **BuildJob** in our pipeline included CodeQL code scanning, SonarCloud static analysis, and GitHub Advanced Security dependency scanning.

So here, in this section, we will run a review on the full security posture of the build stage, add the GHAzDO autofix capability for code scanning alerts, and introduce security quality gates that fail the build on critical findings.

Reviewing Build-Stage Security Stack

The security controls that currently execute during the **Build** stage run in a specific order designed to avoid redundancy and ensure each tool has the data it needs. With this ready, we review that order now, because understanding why each tool occupies its position is as important as knowing which tools are present.

```
Step 1  : AdvancedSecurity-CodeQL-Init@1
          Purpose : Begins instrumenting the Java compilation for semantic analysis.
          Why here: Must precede compilation to trace data flows through compiled classes.
Step 2  : SonarCloudPrepare@1
          Purpose : Instruments the Maven build for code quality and coverage analysis.
          Why here: Must precede compilation to collect metrics during the build.
Step 3  : Maven@3 (clean install)
          Purpose : Compiles, tests, and packages the application.
          Why here: All analysis tools need a completed compilation to operate on.
Step 4  : AdvancedSecurity-Dependency-Scanning@1
          Purpose : Audits pom.xml against the GitHub Advisory Database.
          Why here: Needs resolved dependency tree from the completed Maven build.
```

```
Step 5  : SonarCloudAnalyze@1 + SonarCloudPublish@1
          Purpose : Runs SonarCloud rules and enforces the quality gate.
          Why here: Needs compiled classes and test coverage data from
Step 3.
Step 6  : AdvancedSecurity-CodeQL-Analyze@1
          Purpose : Finalises the CodeQL database and uploads findings to
GHAzDO.
          Why here: Needs the complete compilation the init step was
tracking.
```

This six-step security analysis sequence runs on every push to **`main`** and on every pull request targeting **`main`**. A developer who introduces a SQL injection vulnerability, a hard-coded credential, or a dependency with a known CVE will see a pipeline failure within three to four minutes of pushing their code, with a link to the specific line that caused the failure. This is the shift-left model in practice, where the build stage acts as the automated security reviewer that every commit must pass before it can proceed to deployment.

Configuring Quality Gate to Block Security Hotspots

The default SonarCloud quality gate fails on new bugs, new vulnerabilities, and new security hotspots with a rating of A. So here, we will tighten it by creating a custom quality gate named ***SpringBootAPI Security Gate*** that adds stricter thresholds for our project.

To do this, we navigate to SonarCloud portal, click ***Quality Gates***, and create a new gate with the following conditions.

```
Condition 1 : New Security Rating             is worse than A      → FAIL
Condition 2 : New Reliability Rating          is worse than B      → FAIL
Condition 3 : New Maintainability Rating      is worse than A      → FAIL
Condition 4 : New Coverage                    is less than 70%     → FAIL
Condition 5 : New Duplicated Lines (%)        is greater than 5%   → FAIL
Condition 6 : New Security Hotspots Reviewed is less than 100%    → FAIL
```

In the above, the Condition 6, requiring 100% of new security hotspots to be reviewed, is the most important addition. A security hotspot is a code pattern that requires human review to determine whether it is a genuine vulnerability. And its similar examples include calls to cryptographic functions, SQL query construction, and XML parsing operations. The SonarCloud flags these as hotspots rather than vulnerabilities because the same code pattern may be safe or unsafe depending on context.

With a requirement for 100% review of new hotspots before the quality gate passes, we will then ensure that no hotspot-producing code change merges to **`main`** without a developer explicitly marking it as ***Safe*** or ***Acknowledged vulnerability*** in the SonarCloud portal. This is going to be an effective manual security review embedded directly into the automated pipeline flow.

GHAzDO Autofix for Code Scanning Alerts

The GitHub Advanced Security's autofix feature uses GitHub Copilot's code understanding model to generate targeted code changes that resolve CodeQL alerts. When a code scanning alert is generated in the Advanced Security hub, we click ***Generate fix*** on the alert detail page. The Copilot analyses the vulnerable code path, produces a diff that addresses the specific vulnerability pattern CodeQL identified, and presents it as a suggested change that we can apply with a single click.

In the following, we will explore the workflow using a synthetic SQL injection example, in which we add the following deliberately vulnerable method to **`TutorialController.java`** temporarily to generate a CodeQL alert.

```
// VULNERABLE, added temporarily to demonstrate CodeQL autofix
// This method will generate a CWE-89 SQL Injection alert
@GetMapping("/tutorials/unsafe-search")
public ResponseEntity<List<Tutorial>> unsafeSearch(
    @RequestParam String keyword,
    EntityManager em) {
  String query = "SELECT t FROM Tutorial t WHERE t.title LIKE '%" +
keyword + "%'";
  List<Tutorial> results = em.createQuery(query,
Tutorial.class).getResultList();
  return ResponseEntity.ok(results);
}
```

This above code constructs a raw SQL query using string concatenation, which is the canonical SQL injection pattern. We commit this code to a feature branch, push it, and let the pipeline run. After the **`AdvancedSecurity-CodeQL-Analyze@1`** step completes, a ***SQL query built from user-controlled sources*** alert appears in the Advanced Security hub with ***Critical*** severity. We then click the alert row to open its detail page, read the CodeQL rule description that explains why string concatenation in a JPQL query is dangerous, and then click ***Generate fix***.

The Copilot then generates the following suggested replacement within seconds:

```
// FIXED, autofix replaces string concatenation with a parameterised query
@GetMapping("/tutorials/unsafe-search")
public ResponseEntity<List<Tutorial>> unsafeSearch(
```

```
        @RequestParam String keyword,
        EntityManager em) {
    String query = "SELECT t FROM Tutorial t WHERE t.title LIKE :keyword";
    List<Tutorial> results = em.createQuery(query, Tutorial.class)
                               .setParameter("keyword", "%" + keyword + "%")
                               .getResultList();
    return ResponseEntity.ok(results);
}
```

The above fix replaces the concatenated string with a named parameter **`:keyword`** and passes the user input through **`.setParameter()`**, which is the correct approach for preventing SQL injection in JPA. After this, we then apply the fix by clicking ***Apply fix***. The GHAzDO creates a new commit on the feature branch with the suggested change. We can then review the commit in VS Code, confirm it matches the expected pattern, and push the branch. The next pipeline run shows the CodeQL alert resolved, and we then remove this method entirely from the final production code since it was only added for demonstration purposes.

Remediating Bulk Vulnerabilities

The individual alert-and-fix workflow is appropriate for new vulnerabilities introduced by recent code changes. For organisations that enable GHAzDO on a repository for the first time and discover hundreds of existing alerts, the one-by-one approach is impractical.

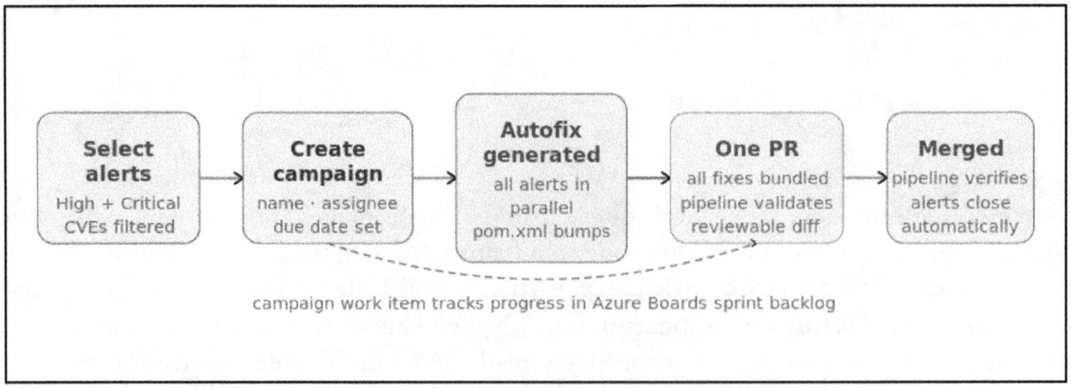

Fig 9.3: Security Campaign Lifecycle

The security campaigns address this by allowing security administrators to select up to 1,000 alerts at a time and trigger bulk autofix generation for all of them simultaneously.

Creating Security Campaign for Dependency Alerts

To do this, we navigate to ***Repos*** > ***Advanced Security*** > ***Dependencies*** tab. We filter the alert list to show only ***High*** and ***Critical*** severity alerts in ***Active*** state. For a mature codebase with several sprints of accumulated dependency debt, this list may contain dozens of entries. Among all of them, we select all visible alerts by ticking the header checkbox and click ***Create campaign***.

Next, on the campaign creation dialog, we fill in the following details.

```
Campaign name      : Sprint 2 Dependency Vulnerability Remediation
Description        : Remediate all High and Critical CVEs in direct and
transitive dependencies
Assignee           : Security Champion rotation
Due date           : End of current sprint
Alert types        : Dependency (all selected alerts)
```

After saving the campaign, the GHAzDO generates autofix suggestions for all selected dependency alerts in parallel. For dependency alerts, the autofix typically consists of a version bump in **`pom.xml`**, replacing the vulnerable version of a library with the minimum non-vulnerable version identified in the National Vulnerability Database entry for the CVE. The GHAzDO bundles all the suggested **`pom.xml`** changes into a single pull request against **`main`**, making the remediation reviewable and testable through the normal pipeline process.

So, we open the pull request, review the version changes, and confirm that the bumped versions are compatible with our Spring Boot parent POM version constraints. If any bump introduces a breaking API change, we address it in the same pull request before merging. The CI pipeline runs our full test suite against the updated dependencies, giving us confidence that the remediation does not break any existing functionality before it reaches production.

Integrating Microsoft Defender with Azure DevOps

The Microsoft Defender for Cloud monitors the security posture of Azure resources. It monitors the security posture of Azure resources, provides threat intelligence about active attacks, and connects application-layer security findings from GHAzDO with runtime infrastructure security data from the deployed environment. For DevSecOps practitioners, this connection is invaluable, since a code scanning alert that Defender for Cloud can correlate with an active exploitation attempt against the same resource in production receives an automatically elevated risk score that triggers immediate escalation.

Connecting Azure DevOps to Defender

To proceed, we at first, navigate to the Microsoft Defender for Cloud portal at ***https://portal.azure.com*** under ***Defender for Cloud*** > ***Environment settings***. We expand our Azure subscription tree to find the **`SpringBootRG`** resource group and click on it. We then navigate to ***Integrations*** > ***DevOps security***. We will now click ***Add*** and authenticate to our Azure DevOps organisation **`GitforGits`**. The Defender for Cloud immediately begins reading repository metadata, security posture data, and pipeline configurations from our organisation.

After the connection is established, the Defender for Cloud's ***DevOps Security*** page shows a security posture score for each connected repository. The score aggregates findings across three categories of secret exposure risk (are there exposed secrets in the repository history?), code security posture (what is the CodeQL and dependency scan finding count and severity?), and infrastructure security posture (do the Bicep and Terraform files follow security best practices?). For our **`SpringBootAPI`** repository, the score reflects all the controls we have configured across this book.

Enabling Infrastructure as Code Security Scanning

The Defender for Cloud includes an IaC security scanner that analyses Bicep, Terraform, and Kubernetes manifest files for misconfigurations. And, its findings include missing encryption settings, overly permissive network access rules, absent resource locking, and public IP assignments where private endpoints would be more appropriate.

We then enable IaC scanner for repository by adding **`MicrosoftSecurityDevOps@1`** task to the **`BuildJob`** in our pipeline. This task runs the Defender for Cloud analysis engine against all IaC files in the repository and posts findings to both the Defender for Cloud portal and the Advanced Security alerts hub in Azure DevOps.

```
    - task: MicrosoftSecurityDevOps@1
      displayName: 'Run Defender for Cloud IaC security scanner'
      inputs:
        categories: 'IaC'
        languages: 'terraform,bicep'
```

Next, we then add this task after **`AdvancedSecurity-CodeQL-Analyze@1`** step and before **`CopyFiles@2`**. The **`MicrosoftSecurityDevOps@1`** task installs the Microsoft Security DevOps scanning tools on the agent, analyses the **`infra/terraform/main.tf`** and **`infra/appservice.bicep`** files we created in Chapters 4 and 7, and returns any misconfigurations as SARIF-format findings. And here, the common findings for Terraform configuration includes the absence of **`network_profile.outbound_ip_address`** restrictions on the AKS cluster or the absence of Azure Key Vault integration for storing the SQL Server admin password instead of passing it as a parameter.

```
git add azure-pipelines.yml
git commit -m "Add Defender for Cloud IaC security scanner to BuildJob"
git push azure main
```

After the pipeline runs, we then navigate to ***Defender for Cloud*** > ***Recommendations***. Now here, any IaC misconfigurations found in our templates, will appear here with remediation guidance. We also see them in the Advanced Security alerts hub under a new ***IaC*** tab, where we then create Azure Boards work items for each Critical and High finding, assign them to the Security Champions group, and include them in the next sprint's security remediation campaign.

The Defender for Cloud risk score for our repository improves incrementally as we resolve each finding and the pipeline confirms the fixed template passes the IaC scan.

Supply Chain Security and SBOM Generation

In a software supply chain attack, an attacker compromises a legitimate open-source library and distributes a malicious version to all its consumers, have become one of the most significant threat vectors in modern software delivery. Our private Azure Artifacts feeds, configured in Chapter 5, provides the first layer of supply chain defence by proxying public registries and caching package versions immutably. The second layer is a Software Bill of Materials (SBOM), where a machine-readable inventory of every library, tool, and component included in the final application artifact, with the version number and provenance of each.

Generating SBOM with CycloneDX Maven Plugin

The CycloneDX is an open standard for SBOMs with native Maven support. At this point, we add CycloneDX Maven plugin to **`pom.xml`** so that every **`mvn package`** run produces a machine-readable SBOM alongside the **`.jar`** file.

So here, we will open **`pom.xml`** and add the plugin definition inside **`<build><plugins>`** block:

```
<plugin>
  <groupId>org.cyclonedx</groupId>
  <artifactId>cyclonedx-maven-plugin</artifactId>
  <version>2.8.0</version>
  <executions>
    <execution>
      <phase>package</phase>
      <goals>
        <goal>makeAggregateBom</goal>
      </goals>
    </execution>
  </executions>
```

```
  <configuration>
    <projectType>library</projectType>
    <schemaVersion>1.5</schemaVersion>
    <includeBomSerialNumber>true</includeBomSerialNumber>
    <includeCompileScope>true</includeCompileScope>
    <includeTestScope>false</includeTestScope>
    <includeRuntimeScope>true</includeRuntimeScope>
    <outputFormat>json</outputFormat>
    <outputName>springboot-api-sbom</outputName>
  </configuration>
</plugin>
```

In thte above script, the **makeAggregateBom** goal runs during the **package** phase, which is part of the **clean install** lifecycle our **Maven@3** task already executes. After the build, the **target/** directory contains **springboot-api-sbom.json**, a JSON file in CycloneDX 1.5 format listing every runtime dependency of our application with its group ID, artifact ID, version, license, and a hash of the component for integrity verification.

So now, we will update the **CopyFiles@2** task in our pipeline to also copy the SBOM file to the staging directory alongside the **.jar**.

```
    - task: CopyFiles@2
      displayName: 'Copy JAR and SBOM to staging directory'
      inputs:
        sourceFolder: '$(System.DefaultWorkingDirectory)/target'
        contents: |
          *.jar
          *-sbom.json
        targetFolder: '$(Build.ArtifactStagingDirectory)'
```

Now, with the SBOM published as part of the pipeline artifact, every versioned release of our application is accompanied by a verifiable inventory of its components. The security teams can query the SBOM to answer questions such as ***Which versions of our application include the Log4Shell vulnerability?*** or ***Do we have any deployed applications that use the compromised version of package X?*** without needing to rebuild or re-analyse old artifacts. The SBOM is also the input to Defender for Cloud's continuous monitoring feature, which compares the SBOM's component list against newly published CVEs and alerts when a component that was clean at build time is later found to be vulnerable.

Storing SBOM in Azure Artifacts

Next, we will publish SBOM as versioned Universal Package in **SpringBootDependencies** feed alongside the **.jar** artifact. The Universal Packages in Azure Artifacts accept any file type and apply the same versioning, retention, and access control rules as typed packages. When we store the SBOM as a Universal Package, it means any downstream system, a compliance scanner, a security audit tool, or a Defender for Cloud integration, can retrieve the SBOM for any deployed version by querying the feed by version number.

```
    - task: UniversalPackages@0
      displayName: 'Publish SBOM to Azure Artifacts'
      inputs:
        command: 'publish'
        publishDirectory: '$(Build.ArtifactStagingDirectory)'
        feedsToUsePublish: 'internal'
        vstsFeedPublish: 'SpringBootAPI/SpringBootDependencies'
        vstsFeedPackagePublish: 'springboot-api-sbom'
        versionOption: 'custom'
        versionPublish: '$(Build.BuildId)'
        packagePublishDescription: 'CycloneDX SBOM for build
$(Build.BuildId)'
```

After this step runs, the **SpringBootDependencies** feed in the Artifacts hub contains a ***Universal*** package named **springboot-api-sbom** with one version per pipeline build. Each version contains the **springboot-api-sbom.json** file produced by that build's CycloneDX plugin execution. The combination of a versioned SBOM in a private feed and the deployment-aligned database backup from Chapter 7 means that every production release is accompanied by both the data it wrote and the components it used, providing the complete traceability that compliance frameworks such as SLSA, FedRAMP, and ISO 27001 require.

Security at Operate Stage

Once the application is deployed, our DevSecOps responsibilities do not end. The operate stage introduces new security concerns, like runtime vulnerabilities in the live container image, attempts to exploit the running application, configuration drift in the deployed infrastructure, and the emergence of new CVEs that affect components that were clean at the time of deployment. The controls in this section run continuously in the production environment rather than once per deployment.

Enabling Defender for Cloud Runtime Protection on AKS

When Microsoft Defender for Cloud is connected to our Azure subscription and the Defender for Containers plan is enabled, it automatically instruments every node in our AKS cluster with a DaemonSet that monitors container behaviour at the kernel level. This agent detects anomalous activity such as a container executing a shell command that it does not normally run, a process making unexpected network connections, or a file system operation that modifies a previously read-only area. With this ready, we enable the Defender for Containers plan by navigating to ***Defender for Cloud*** > ***Environment settings*** > our subscription > ***Defender plans*** and toggling ***Containers*** to ***On***.

The Defender for Cloud also performs continuous image vulnerability scanning against the **`springboot-acr`** registry. Every image pushed to ACR is automatically scanned against the same vulnerability databases used by the pipeline dependency scanner. If a new CVE is published after an image was pushed and that CVE affects a component in the image, Defender for Cloud generates a new alert without requiring a new pipeline run. This is the critical difference between point-in-time pipeline scanning and continuous runtime monitoring.

Reviewing Complete DevSecOps Security Chain

We now have security controls operating at every stage of our DevOps lifecycle. The following summary maps each control to the stage where it runs and the threat it addresses.

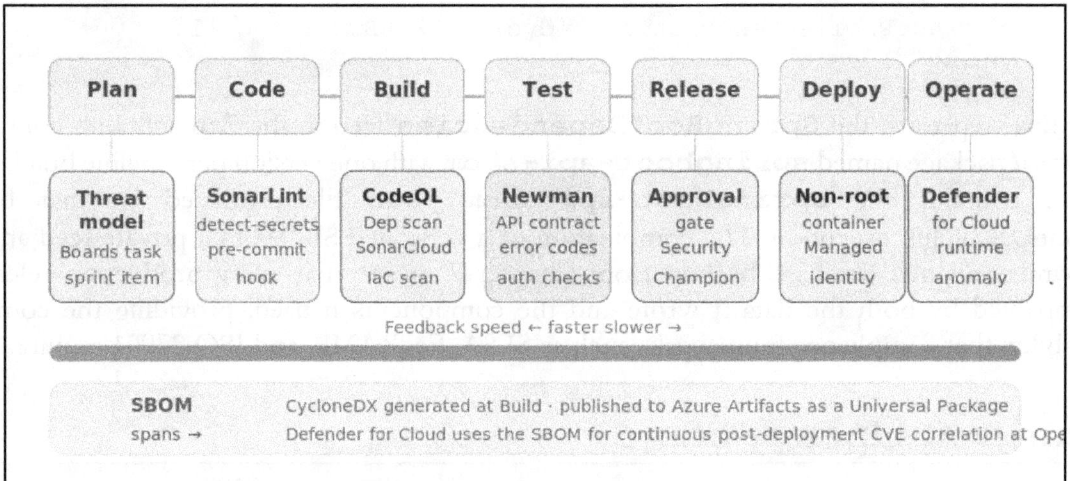

Fig 9.4: DevSecOps Lifecycle Map

Each row in this map represents a decision made deliberately at a specific stage to address a specific threat category. The pre-commit hook and SonarLint operate at the speed of the developer's keyboard. The build-stage scanners operate at the speed of the CI pipeline, three to five minutes per commit. The runtime controls operate continuously, 24 hours a day. Together they create a layered security posture where a threat that bypasses one control is likely to be caught by the next, and where no single point of failure can allow a vulnerability to travel undetected from a developer's IDE all the way to a production workload.

Summary

Throughout this chapter we assembled the DevSecOps layer that makes security an intrinsic property of our delivery system rather than an external gate. We began by establishing the three DevSecOps principles and then walked through every stage of the DevOps lifecycle and identified the security control that belongs to the respective stage. We then used security campaigns to generate bulk autofix pull requests for accumulated dependency vulnerabilities, reducing security debt systematically rather than reactively.

Later, we connected Microsoft Defender for Cloud to our Azure DevOps organisation and added the **`MicrosoftSecurityDevOps@1`** task to the pipeline to scan our Bicep and Terraform infrastructure files for misconfigurations. We generated a CycloneDX SBOM using the Maven plugin, published it as a Universal Package in Azure Artifacts alongside the application **`.jar`**. We enabled Defender for Containers on our AKS cluster for runtime anomaly detection and continuous image vulnerability scanning. And lastly, we saw a complete DevSecOps control map that aligns every security measure in our system to the lifecycle stage where it operates and the threat category it addresses.

CHAPTER 10

AI-ASSISTED DEVOPS WITH GITHUB COPILOT AND AZURE

Overview

Across the nine preceding chapters we built a complete, production-grade Azure DevOps delivery system. Every pipeline stage, every security control, every infrastructure template, and every quality gate was authored by hand, using tools and knowledge a skilled DevOps practitioner brings to the task. This final chapter introduces a new layer that transforms how those same tasks are performed, like the AI-assisted DevOps powered by GitHub Copilot for Azure and the Azure DevOps MCP Server.

The shift toward AI-assisted DevOps is not a replacement of the knowledge and practices we have built throughout this book. It is an acceleration of them. A practitioner who does not understand YAML pipeline structure, Bicep resource declarations, Terraform provider configuration, Kubernetes manifests, or the security controls in Chapter 9 cannot effectively direct an AI agent to produce correct, secure, and maintainable output in those domains. AI amplifies expertise; it does not substitute for it. With that principle established, we now explore what changes when we bring GitHub Copilot for Azure and Agent Mode into the centre of our DevOps workflow.

We proceed to start by understanding the AI tooling landscape, such as what GitHub Copilot for Azure is, how its Ask and Agent modes differ, and where each mode is most effective in a DevOps context. We then work through five hands-on scenarios that cover the complete span of our delivery system, such as using Copilot to author and correct YAML pipeline definitions, using Agent Mode to orchestrate multi-step infrastructure provisioning tasks, connecting the Azure DevOps MCP Server so that Copilot can read and act on our live work items, pipelines, and test plans, using Copilot to accelerate Bicep and Azure Developer CLI workflows, and applying Copilot to the security workflows from Chapter 9 to accelerate vulnerability remediation. We close this chapter by addressing governance, privacy, and the responsible use of AI in a DevOps context, where AI-generated infrastructure changes can have real cost and security consequences.

Agentic DevOps Overview

The term ***agentic DevOps*** describes the model where an AI agent does not merely suggest the next word in a code completion or answer a question about an Azure service, but instead decomposes a complex, multi-step DevOps task into a sequence of sub-tasks, executes each sub-task using the appropriate tool, observes the result, and adapts its plan if the outcome was unexpected. This is fundamentally different from the code completion model that most developers first encountered with GitHub Copilot in 2022.

Key Components of Agentic DevOps

In the code completion model, the developer writes `az aks create` and Copilot suggests the remaining flags based on the surrounding context. The developer remains in full control and Copilot's contribution is a time-saving suggestion. In the agentic model, the developer types a natural-language instruction such as ***Provision an AKS cluster with two nodes in eastus and attach our existing ACR to it***, and Copilot Agent Mode generates the corresponding Bicep or Terraform code, runs the deployment, monitors the output, detects any errors, proposes corrections, and verifies success, all within a single conversational session in VS Code. The developer's role shifts from typing commands to reviewing proposed actions and approving or redirecting them.

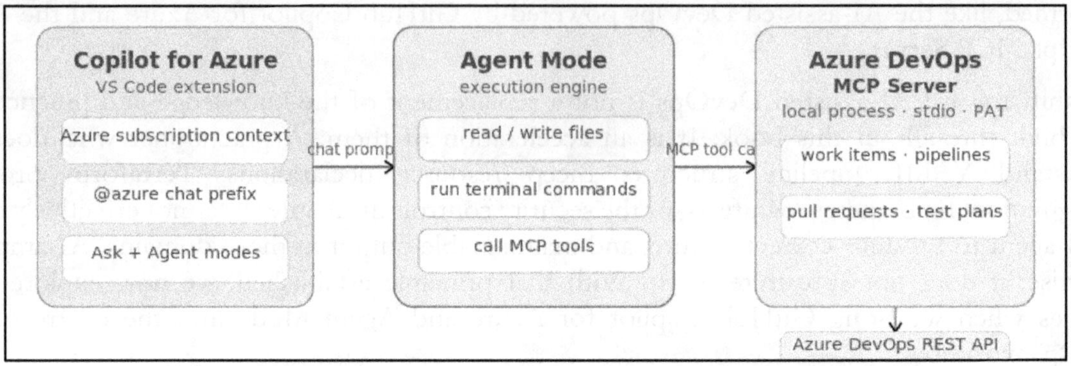

Fig 10.1: Three Technical Components of Agentic DevOps

The Azure's implementation of agentic DevOps rests on three technical components that became generally available in mid-2025:

1. The first is ***GitHub Copilot for Azure***, a VS Code extension that connects Copilot to the developer's real Azure subscription context, making AI responses specific to the actual resources, configurations, and policies in our environment rather than generic documentation answers.
2. The second is ***Agent Mode***, the execution engine within GitHub Copilot that can invoke tools, run terminal commands, read and write files, and chain multiple operations together autonomously within a human-in-the-loop approval model. And,
3. The third is the ***Azure DevOps MCP Server***, a local server that implements the Model Context Protocol and exposes Azure DevOps data, work items, pull requests, builds, test plans, pipeline definitions, as structured context that Copilot can read and act on inside VS Code.

Ask Mode vs. Agent Mode

As a tool, the GitHub Copilot for Azure operates in two distinct interaction modes that serve different purposes in a DevOps workflow. The first ever practical skill in AI-assisted DevOps going to be, is to use each mode.

The ***Ask mode*** is conversational and informational. We can use it to get answers about our Azure environment, to understand what a resource is doing, to look up the correct Bicep syntax for a resource type we have not used before, or to get an explanation of a pipeline failure. The Ask mode is activated by typing **`@azure`** in the Copilot Chat panel followed by a question. The

Copilot reads our subscription metadata, the open files in VS Code, and the current repository state to produce a contextualised answer. The Ask mode never executes commands or modifies files without explicit instruction.

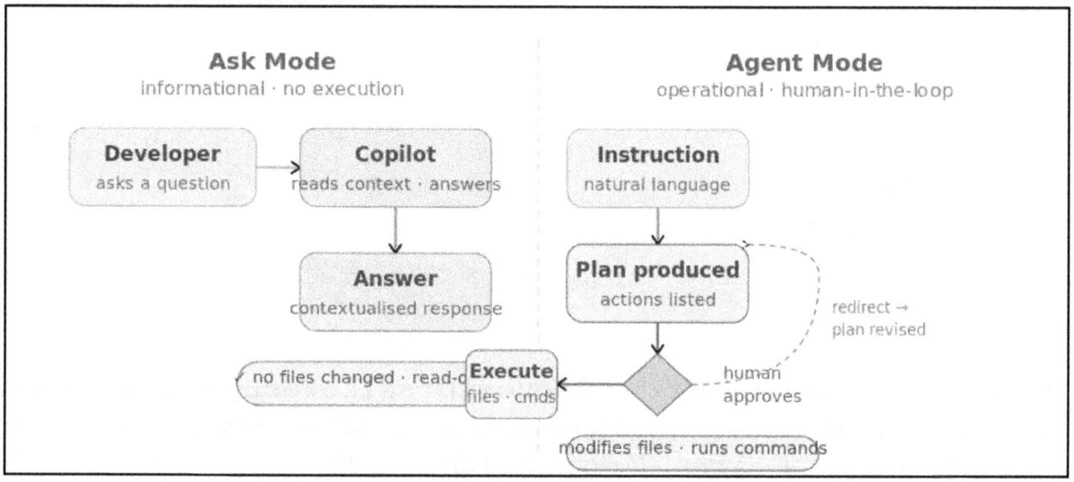

Fig 10.2: Ask Mode versus Agent Mode

The ***Agent mode*** is operational and autonomous. We can use it to perform actions, like provision infrastructure, deploy applications, run diagnostic commands, generate configuration files, and execute multi-step workflows. The Agent Mode is activated by clicking the ***Agent*** toggle in the Copilot Chat panel. In Agent Mode, Copilot presents a plan of the actions it intends to take and waits for our approval before executing each step. We can redirect, reject, or modify the plan at any point. The Agent Mode never executes a destructive or irreversible action without an explicit human confirmation in the conversation.

GitHub Copilot for Azure

We explored GitHub Copilot in the beginning of the chapter 1 when we installed it as part of our VS Code configuration. At that point we used only the **`@azure What resources do I have?`** query as a brief preview. Now, in this chapter, we work with the extension in depth across the full range of its capabilities. The extension requires an active GitHub Copilot subscription, and it uses the **`springboot-azure`** service connection's identity to read our Azure subscription context when answering questions about our resources.

Ask Mode for Pipeline Troubleshooting

One of the highest-value Ask Mode use case in daily DevOps work is pipeline failure diagnosis. When a pipeline run fails, the log output can be several hundred lines of Maven, Docker, Terraform, or Kubernetes output, and identifying the root cause within that volume of text is time-consuming. We can paste the failing log section directly into the Copilot Chat panel and ask Copilot to explain what went wrong and how to fix it.

So here, we will open the Copilot Chat panel and type the following in the failing stage log from a hypothetical Terraform apply failure.

```
@azure This Terraform apply failed. What is the cause and how do I fix it?
<paste failing log>
Error: creating/updating AKS Cluster: performing Create:
  PUT https://management.azure.com/.../managedClusters/springboot-aks
  Code="RequestDisallowedByPolicy"
  Message="Resource 'springboot-aks' was disallowed by policy.
  Policy: 'Require Kubernetes version 1.29 or higher'"
</paste failing log>
```

After this, the Copilot reads the error code **`RequestDisallowedByPolicy`**, recognises it as an Azure Policy enforcement error, and produces a contextualised response. Here, rather than a generic explanation of Azure Policy, it tells us the exact change needed in **`infra/terraform/variables.tf`**:\, like to update the **`kubernetes_version`** variable default from **`1.28`** to **`1.30`** or whichever version satisfies the policy, and it shows us the updated **`variables.tf`** block. The copilot also notes that the policy is applied at the organisation or subscription level and provides the Azure CLI command to list all policies in effect on our subscription so we can verify there are no other constraints we have not yet encountered.

Following is the expected response:

```
Copilot for Azure response:
The failure is caused by an Azure Policy that requires AKS clusters to run
Kubernetes version 1.29 or higher. Your current configuration specifies
version 1.28.
To fix this, update infra/terraform/variables.tf:
  variable "aks_cluster_version" {
    type    = string
    default = "1.30"   ← change from 1.28 to 1.30 or higher
  }
To list all policies on your subscription:
  az policy assignment list --scope /subscriptions/<id> -o table
```

This interaction illustrates why Ask Mode is most valuable for troubleshooting, where the AI combines knowledge of Azure error codes, Azure Policy mechanics, and our specific Terraform configuration to produce an answer that a documentation search alone could not provide in under a minute. We then apply the suggested change, push the fix, and the pipeline succeeds on the next run.

Ask Mode to Explore Resource Health and Cost

With Ask Mode, we can query the live resource state from our Azure subscription directly, without navigating the Azure Portal. For example, we can ask the following queries in the Copilot Chat panel to get a current snapshot of our production environment before a deployment.

```
@azure What is the current health status of all resources in SpringBootRG?

@azure Are there any certificates expiring in the next 30 days in my subscription?

@azure What is the estimated monthly cost of the SpringBootRG resource group based on the last billing period?
```

Here, the Copilot reads the resource metadata from our subscription using the Azure Resource Graph API and returns structured answers. The health status query returns a table of all resources in **SpringBootRG** with their current availability state. The certificate expiry query scans all App Service custom domain certificates and Key Vault certificates for approaching expiry dates. The cost query reads the Azure Cost Management API and returns the actual spend breakdown by service type for the previous billing period. All three queries run against live Azure data and complete in seconds. And, gives us an informed picture of our production environment before we make a change to it.

Using Copilot Agent Mode to Orchestrate Multi-Step DevOps Tasks

With Agent Mode, the GitHub Copilot for Azure moves from a helpful assistant to a productive colleague that can execute complex, multi-step DevOps workflows on our behalf.

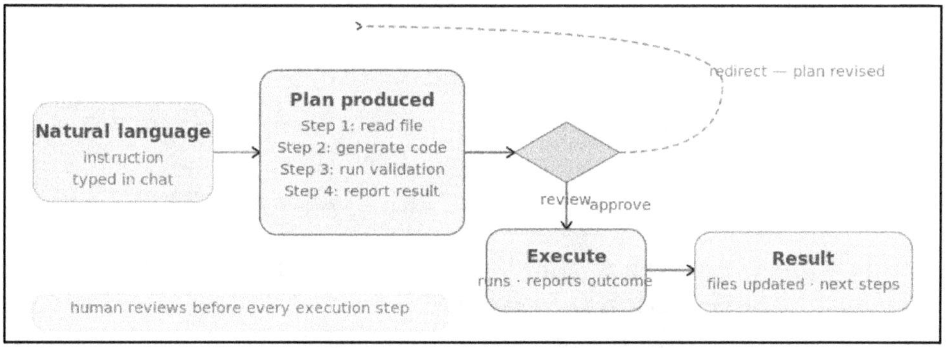

Fig 10.3: Agent Mode Plan-Approve-Execute Cycle

In this topic, we will practice through two Agent Mode workflows that cover infrastructure provisioning and pipeline authoring. These are those two tasks that consume the most engineer time in a typical DevOps sprint.

Provisioning Infrastructure from Natural Language Description

Here, at first, we click the ***Agent*** toggle in the Copilot Chat panel to activate Agent Mode. And then, we type the following instruction, describing what we want without specifying the implementation technology.

```
Provision a new Azure Container App in SpringBootRG in the eastus region.
It should use the springboot-containerapp-env environment we already have.
Pull the springboot-api:latest image from springbootacr.
Set min replicas to 1 and max replicas to 5.
Expose it externally on port 8080.
Use a system-assigned managed identity for ACR access.
Add it to infra/appservice.bicep alongside the existing Container App resource.
```

In response, the Agent Mode processes this instruction and presents a plan before executing anything. The plan describes each action it will take and the files it will modify.

```
Copilot Agent Mode, Proposed plan:
Step 1: Read infra/appservice.bicep to understand existing resource structure.
Step 2: Identify the existing Container Apps environment name and ACR reference.
Step 3: Generate a new azurerm Container App resource block for payments-api.
Step 4: Append the resource to infra/appservice.bicep with the specified parameters.
Step 5: Run az bicep build infra/appservice.bicep to validate syntax.
Step 6: Report completion and suggested next steps (re-run ProvisionInfra stage).
Confirm to proceed? [Approve] [Modify plan] [Cancel]
```

At this point, we click ***Approve***. The Agent Mode then opens **`infra/appservice.bicep`**, reads the existing **`springBootContainerApp`** resource block we wrote in Chapter 7, and generates a new resource block for the additional Container App with all parameters set exactly as we specified. It also appends the block to the file, saves it, and runs **`az bicep build infra/appservice.bicep`** from the integrated terminal to validate the syntax. The validation passes and Agent Mode reports completion with a suggested next step, like commit the file change and push to **main** to trigger the **ProvisionInfra** pipeline stage.

This whole workflow would have taken an experienced engineer several minutes of documentation lookup, Bicep syntax writing, and validation. With Agent Mode, it takes under a minute of reviewing and approving a plan. The key difference from a simple code snippet generation is that Agent Mode read the existing file first, understood the existing resource structure, and generated code that is consistent with that structure rather than producing a standalone template that would require manual integration.

Correcting a Failing Pipeline YAML

We can also use the Agent Mode to diagnose and correct YAML pipeline errors. For example, when a pipeline fails due to a YAML syntax or configuration error, we can activate Agent Mode and type the following.

```
The pipeline run for the BuildImage stage just failed with a YAML parsing error.

The error says 'mapping key already defined at line 47'.

Open azure-pipelines.yml, identify the duplicate key at line 47 and its surrounding context, explain what the conflict is, and fix it.
```

Here, the Agent Mode opens **azure-pipelines.yml**, navigates to line 47, reads the surrounding context, identifies that the **env** key appears twice inside the same step block, a common mistake when merging contributions from two developers, and proposes a fix that merges both **env** blocks into a single block with all environment variable entries combined. It shows the diff before applying it and waits for our approval. After we approve, it saves the file and suggests running **yamllint azure-pipelines.yml** from the terminal to confirm the fix is syntactically clean.

The entire diagnosis and repair cycle completes in under 30 seconds.

Connecting Copilot via Azure DevOps MCP Server

The Azure DevOps MCP Server is a self-hosted local server that implements the Model Context Protocol, a standard interface for giving AI models structured access to external data sources and tools. When the MCP Server is running on our machine, GitHub Copilot inside VS Code can read and act on our Azure DevOps data, work items, pull requests, builds, test plans, wiki pages, and pipeline definitions, as structured context within the same conversation window where we write code. This is the capability that transforms Copilot from a code-generation assistant into a genuine DevOps workflow partner.

Installing and Configuring Azure DevOps MCP Server

To start by, at first, we clone the Azure DevOps MCP Server repository from GitHub and install its dependencies. The server is a Node.js application that runs locally and communicates with the Azure DevOps REST API on behalf of Copilot.

```
git clone https://github.com/microsoft/azure-devops-mcp
cd azure-devops-mcp
npm install
```

Next, we will now configure the server by creating a **.env** file in the **azure-devops-mcp** directory. The server needs our Azure DevOps organisation URL and a Personal Access Token with the permissions listed below. So here, we use a dedicated PAT for the MCP Server rather than reusing the one created in Chapter 5 for Maven, following the principle of least privilege with separate tokens for separate purposes.

```
ADO_ORG_URL=https://dev.azure.com/GitforGits
ADO_PAT=<personal-access-token>
ADO_DEFAULT_PROJECT=SpringBootAPI
# Required PAT scopes:
# Work Items: Read & Write
# Build: Read
# Test Management: Read
# Code: Read
# Release: Read
```

With this ready, we then start the MCP Server from the terminal.

```
npm start
```

```
Azure DevOps MCP Server v1.4.0 started
Listening on stdio transport
Connected to: https://dev.azure.com/GitforGits
Default project: SpringBootAPI
Available tools: list-work-items, get-work-item, update-work-item,
                 list-pipelines, get-pipeline-run, list-pull-requests,
                 get-test-plan, create-work-item, link-work-item
```

After this, we can proceed to configure VS Code to use the running MCP Server by opening the Copilot Chat settings panel with **Ctrl + Shift + P**, typing **Copilot: Configure**

`MCP Servers`, and adding the Azure DevOps MCP Server entry. We can point it at the running server process using the stdio transport configuration. After VS Code connects to the server, a small ***Azure DevOps*** icon appears in the Copilot Chat toolbar, confirming the integration is active and Copilot can now access our project data.

Querying Work Items and Pipeline State from Chat Panel

With the MCP Server connected, we can ask Copilot questions about our live Azure DevOps project state using natural language.

```
Query 1:

Show me all work items assigned to me in the current sprint that are still
in Active state.

Query 2:

What was the last failing pipeline run on main? Which stage failed and
what was the error?

Query 3:

Are there any pull requests in the SpringBootAPI repository that have been
open for more than 3 days without an approval?
```

For Query 1, the Copilot calls the **`list-work-items`** tool on the MCP Server with the assigned-to and sprint filters and returns a formatted list of work items with their IDs, titles, story points, and state. For Query 2, the Copilot calls **`list-pipelines`** to identify the main branch pipeline and then calls **`get-pipeline-run`** for the most recent failed run, returning the stage name, the failing step, and the first error line from the log. And for Query 3, the Copilot calls **`list-pull-requests`** with a date filter and returns any open pull requests older than three days with their author, reviewer status, and a link to the PR in the Azure DevOps portal.

Using MCP Server to Create and Update Work Items

The MCP Server is not read-only. We can instruct Copilot to create new work items and update existing ones directly from the chat panel, without opening the Azure DevOps portal. This capability is most valuable during code review sessions when we discover a bug or a design issue that should be tracked but we do not want to lose our coding context by switching applications.

```
Create a Bug work item in the SpringBootAPI project with the following
details:

  Title      : PUT /api/tutorials/{id} silently nullifies title when field
is absent

  Priority   : 2

  Severity   : 2 - High

  Iteration : SpringBootAPI\Sprint 2
```

```
  Tags          : api-validation, regression
Link it to work item 42 (Tutorial CRUD API endpoints user story) with a
Child relationship.
```

The Copilot calls the **create-work-item** tool with the specified fields, then calls **link-work-item** to establish the Child relationship with work item 42. It returns the new work item ID and a direct link to it in the portal. The entire interaction takes about ten seconds and we never leave VS Code. This is the same bug we discovered during exploratory testing in Chapter 6.

AI-Assisted Infrastructure Authoring with Bicep and Azure Developer CLI

Among the most time-intensive DevOps tasks, are writing infrastructure code and configuring new application environments. Both are areas where GitHub Copilot for Azure delivers particularly high value because they require deep knowledge of Azure resource types, API versions, property schemas, and the interactions between resources, knowledge that Copilot has across the full breadth of the Azure platform and can apply immediately to our specific context.

Generating Bicep Resources with Copilot Inline Suggestions

With the Bicep VS Code extension and GitHub Copilot both active, we can get a combined experience where Copilot's inline suggestions are aware of the Bicep schema constraints enforced by the extension's language server. So here, we will open **infra/appservice.bicep** and add a comment describing the resource we want to add.

```
// Add an Azure Key Vault for storing the SQL admin password and app
secrets.
// Enable soft delete, set retention to 90 days, and use RBAC for access
control.
// Grant the production App Service's managed identity a Key Vault Secrets
User role.
```

After we type this comment and press **Enter**, the Copilot generates the full **Microsoft.KeyVault/vaults** resource block inline, including the soft delete configuration, the RBAC authorisation mode, the retention days property, and the **azurerm_role_assignment**-equivalent Bicep **roleAssignment** resource that grants the App Service identity the **Key Vault Secrets User** role at the vault scope. The generated code references the **productionApp.identity.principalId** from the existing resource in the file rather than using a placeholder value, because Copilot read the file before generating the suggestion and understood the existing resource names and identities.

Using Azure Developer CLI with Copilot Agent Mode

The Azure Developer CLI (**azd**) is the higher-level provisioning tool we installed in Chapter 1 alongside the Azure CLI. It operates on complete application environments described by a structured **azure.yaml** manifest file and can provision infrastructure, build and push container images, and deploy applications with a single **azd up** command.

The Copilot Agent Mode can generate and manage the **azure.yaml** manifest and orchestrate the full **azd** workflow.

```
Generate an azure.yaml manifest for our Spring Boot REST API project.

The application should be packaged as a Docker container using the
Dockerfile in the repository root. It should deploy to the springboot-
containerapp Container App in SpringBootRG. The infra/ directory contains
the Bicep templates. Include hooks for pre-deploy database migration using
Flyway.
```

Here, the Agent Mode reads the repository structure, the **Dockerfile**, the **infra/appservice.bicep** file, and the **src/main/resources/db/migration/** directory we created in Chapter 7 before generating the manifest. The resulting **azure.yaml** file correctly references the Docker build context, the Container App target, the Bicep infrastructure directory, and the Flyway pre-deploy hook command.

```yaml
name: springboot-api
metadata:
  template: springboot-api@0.0.1
services:
  api:
    project: .
    language: java
    host: containerapp
    docker:
      path: ./Dockerfile
      context: .
infra:
  provider: bicep
  path: infra
hooks:
  predeploy:
    shell: sh
```

```
    run: |
      flyway \
        -url="$SPRING_DATASOURCE_URL" \
        -user="$SQL_ADMIN_LOGIN" \
        -password="$SQL_ADMIN_PASSWORD" \
        -locations="filesystem:src/main/resources/db/migration" \
        migrate
```

With this manifest in place, the complete environment provisioning, container build, database migration, and Container App deployment cycle can be invoked with a single **azd up** command. The Copilot also explains that **azd pipeline config** can wire this manifest into an Azure Pipelines YAML file automatically, generating the pipeline stages for infrastructure provisioning, image building, and deployment without manual YAML authoring. For teams onboarding a new microservice, this workflow compresses the pipeline setup time from hours to minutes.

Accelerating DevSecOps Workflows with Copilot

The security workflows we configured in Chapter 9 benefit substantially from AI assistance. The writing of secure code patterns, generating IaC configurations that satisfy security policies, and triaging vulnerability findings, all require domain knowledge that Copilot can supplement effectively. In this topic, we will explore three AI-assisted security workflows that connect directly to the DevSecOps controls from Chapter 9.

Using Copilot to Write Secure Code Patterns

To start with, when we write a new API endpoint in **TutorialController.java**, the Copilot's inline suggestions are aware of the SonarLint rules active in our workspace because the SonarLint VS Code extension shares rule metadata with the Copilot Language Server. This means that when we start typing a method that would violate a security rule, Copilot's suggestion already incorporates the secure pattern rather than the naive, vulnerable one.

So here, we can demonstrate this by starting to write a new endpoint that accepts a file upload. Here, a naive implementation would write the uploaded file to a path derived from the filename supplied by the client, which is a path traversal vulnerability (CWE-22). The Copilot's suggestion, aware of both the Spring Security context in our project and the SonarLint rule **S2083** (Path Traversal), generates a file write that sanitises the filename using **Path.getFileName()**, validates it against an allowlist of accepted extensions, and writes to a configured upload directory rather than a path derived from user input. The secure pattern appears in the first suggestion rather than after a security review cycle.

Using Copilot to Triage CodeQL Alerts

When the pipeline generates a new CodeQL alert, the finding in the Advanced Security hub shows the vulnerable code path and the CWE classification but not always the business context of why the pattern is dangerous in our specific application. Here, we can simply paste the alert description and the flagged code into Copilot Chat and ask for a plain-English explanation tailored to our codebase.

```
@azure Explain this CodeQL alert in the context of our Spring Boot REST
API:

Alert: CWE-918 Server-Side Request Forgery

Rule : java/ssrf

File : TutorialController.java, line 89

Code : URL url = new URL(request.getParameter('imageUrl'));

       HttpURLConnection conn = (HttpURLConnection) url.openConnection();

Is this a true positive or a false positive for our application?

If true positive, what is the fix?
```

The Copilot then explains that the alert is a true positive, like the endpoint constructs a URL from a user-supplied parameter and opens a connection to it, which allows an attacker to make the server fetch any URL including internal Azure metadata endpoints, internal Kubernetes service addresses, or any external resource. It then generates the corrected implementation that validates the URL scheme to **`https`** only, checks the hostname against an allowlist of permitted external domains, and uses the **`RestTemplate`** bean configured with a connection timeout rather than opening a raw **`HttpURLConnection`**. The explanation includes the specific attack scenario for our Azure-hosted application (fetching ***http://169.254.169.254/metadata/instance***, the Azure IMDS endpoint) and why it is particularly dangerous in our environment, giving the developer the context to understand the severity rather than treating it as a routine static analysis finding.

AI-Assisted IaC Security Review

In addition, before we run the **`MicrosoftSecurityDevOps@1`** IaC scanner in the pipeline, we can use Copilot Agent Mode to perform a preliminary review of our Bicep and Terraform files and flag potential security misconfigurations. And, such a pre-commit review catches issues faster than the pipeline scanner, because the feedback arrives in the editor rather than in a pipeline run that takes several minutes to complete.

```
Review infra/terraform/main.tf and infra/appservice.bicep for security
misconfigurations.

Specifically check for:

  1. Any resources with public network access that should be restricted to
private
```

```
  2. Any storage accounts or databases without encryption at rest enabled
  3. Any network security groups with overly permissive inbound rules
  4. Any secrets or connection strings that should be in Key Vault instead
Report each finding with the file path, line number, and a suggested fix.
```

Here, the Agent Mode reads both files in full and returns a structured list of findings. For our Terraform configuration it flags that the AKS cluster's **`network_profile`** block does not restrict outbound traffic, recommending an **`outbound_type`** of **`userDefinedRouting`** for production clusters. For our Bicep configuration it flags that the Azure SQL Server's **`publicNetworkAccess`** property is not explicitly set to **`Disabled`**, meaning it defaults to publicly accessible. It provides the corrected property declaration for each finding. We apply both fixes before committing the infrastructure files, eliminating two findings that would otherwise fail the Defender for Cloud IaC scan in the pipeline.

Summary

Throughout this chapter, we introduced AI layer that completes this book's picture of a modern Azure DevOps delivery system. We began by explaining the distinction between agentic DevOps and traditional code completion, establishing that AI acceleration is most effective when applied by practitioners who already understand the underlying systems. We then worked through the full capability spectrum of GitHub Copilot for Azure, like Ask Mode for instant, contextualised answers about our live Azure environment and pipeline failures, and Agent Mode for autonomous, human-approved execution of multi-step infrastructure and pipeline tasks.

We then installed and configured the Azure DevOps MCP Server, connecting GitHub Copilot directly to our **`SpringBootAPI`** project. We demonstrated Ask Mode pipeline failure diagnosis, live resource health and cost queries, and Agent Mode plan-and-approve workflows for infrastructure provisioning and YAML error correction.

The book is complete for now. We began in Chapter 1 with an empty Azure DevOps organisation and a cloned Spring Boot repository. Over the set of ten chapters, we built an organisation structure, a multi-stage CI/CD pipeline with security scanning and quality gates, a private package registry, a structured test plan with manual and automated execution, a container-based deployment to AKS and Azure Container Apps backed by Infrastructure as Code, a database migration workflow, a disaster recovery configuration, a team collaboration model with DORA metrics measurement, a DevSecOps control layer woven through every stage of the lifecycle, and now an AI-assisted DevOps capability that accelerates every one of those practices. Each component was built on the same application, the same repository, and the same pipeline, growing progressively until the whole became a coherent, professional-grade delivery system ready for production.

Index

A

B

C

D

E

F

G

I

J

K

L

M

N

P

Q

R

S

T

U

V

W

Epilogue

You've got to the end of the book, but not the end of the journey. If you've worked through every chapter, you've got something more valuable than a certificate or badge. You've got a living, working system, and it's up to you to keep making it better.

The first thing I want to encourage you to do is keep shipping. Add a new stage to your pipeline to expand it. Add a performance test suite after Newman. So, what we need to do is introduce a step in our chaos engineering process that deliberately breaks a canary deployment, and then verifies the rollback. Every addition will teach you something you can't get from the pages of any book. The second thing is to invest in your DORA metrics. There are four key numbers that show if your engineering culture is doing well. These are deployment frequency, lead time for changes, change failure rate, and recovery time. Just make sure you keep track of them honestly, then share them with your team so they can help you improve next time.

Looking ahead, the Azure platform is evolving in directions that will reward everything you've learned here. Azure Container Apps is becoming the go-to choice for event-driven and AI workloads. Azure AI Foundry is becoming the go-to place for deploying and versioning foundation models, just like how Azure Artifacts handles packages right now. The Azure DevOps MCP Server is just the start of a bigger DevOps story, with AI agents that actively keep an eye on pipeline health, write up infrastructure change requests from incident tickets, and come up with sprint planning recommendations using data from past performance.

In addition, the GitHub Advanced Security campaigns will grow into a full security posture management layer, connecting vulnerability intelligence from Defender for Cloud directly into the developer workflow. The time it takes for threat detection and remediation to happen will be reduced from weeks to hours. Even though things are changing all the time, the principles you've been working with here won't change. Make sure you automate any tasks that are repetitive. Just move security left. Just make sure you keep the people involved in the loop when it comes to decisions that actually have real consequences. Keep measuring. Try to make systems that can recover automatically if they fail. These aren't just Azure ideas. They're engineering values, and they'll serve you regardless of the tools that come along in the next decade.

Many thanks for spending time with me and this material. Keep building!!

Thank You